# THE PROMISE
# OF THE FATHER

# THE PROMISE OF THE FATHER

## Jesus and God in the New Testament

## Marianne Meye Thompson

Westminster John Knox Press
Louisville, Kentucky

Scripture quotations from the New Revised Standard Version of the Bible are copyright © 1989 by the Division of Christian Education of the National Council of the Churches of Christ in the U.S.A. and are used by permission.

*Book design by Sharon Adams*
*Cover design by PAZ Design Group*

*First edition*
Published by Westminster John Knox Press
Louisville, Kentucky

This book is printed on acid-free paper that meets the American National Standards Institute Z39.48 standard. ∞

PRINTED IN THE UNITED STATES OF AMERICA

00 01 02 03 04 05 06 07 08 09 — 10 9 8 7 6 5 4 3 2 1

Library of Congress Cataloging-in-Publication Data is on file at the Library of Congress, Washington, D.C.

ISBN 0-664-22197-1

*To my faculty colleagues*

# Contents

# Acknowledgments

I want to thank all those who have helped in one way or another to bring this manuscript to its completion. I am grateful to Richard Mouw and John Thompson for reading parts of the manuscript and offering helpful comments and suggestions for its improvement, as well as for conversations along the way that stimulated my thinking and helped clarify various issues. My editor at Westminster John Knox, Carey Newman, was unflagging in his attentiveness and enthusiastic in his support as he helped to shepherd this project along toward its completion. Dan Braden was exemplary in his patience and perseverance throughout the entire editorial process. Diane G. Chen offered cheerful and diligent research assistance at every stage of the project.

I would like also to offer a special word of thanks for the kind hospitality of the Associated Mennonite Biblical Seminary in Elkhart, Indiana, and for their invitation to deliver a series of lectures which formed the backbone of this project. The gracious and thoughtful responses to each of the lectures have unquestionably improved the quality of this book.

The book was begun while I was on sabbatical leave, and I am grateful to the trustees of Fuller Theological Seminary for their generous sabbatical policy and support of its faculty in this and so many other ways. Two additional grants from the Pew Evangelical Scholars Program in 1992–93 and from the Henry R. Luce Foundation in 1995–96 afforded me time to do research that laid the groundwork for this volume. I am grateful for their support.

Chapter 5, "Heirs of God, Heirs with Christ," appeared in a slightly different form as " 'Mercy Upon All:' God as Father in the Epistle to the Romans," in *Romans and the People of God* (ed. Sven Soderlund and N. T. Wright; Grand Rapids: Eerdmans, 1999), 203–16. It is reprinted here with permission of the publisher.

A shortened form of chapter 6, "The Living Father," appears in *Semeia* 85: *"God the Father" in the Gospel of John.*

To my family, John, Allison, and Annelise, I am more grateful than I can adequately express in words, for the steady companionship, love, encouragement, and support which they offer on a daily basis. Without the interruptions which children's pursuits and needs also pose on a daily basis, many things would no doubt be completed more expediently—but that would be a poor trade indeed.

This book is dedicated to my faculty colleagues, past and present, at Fuller Theological Seminary, who over the years have been teachers, friends, and fellow workers in the service of the church of Jesus Christ. About a decade ago a number of us labored together on a seminary task force to study some of the concerns with which this book deals, and I am grateful for the stimulus and input of those discussions, as well as for the continued models of faithful discipleship which my colleagues hold up before me. In their friendship and collegiality, I have experienced now and again a foretaste of what it means to live together as the family of God, of which I have tried to write about in this book.

Marianne Meye Thompson

Advent, 1999

# Introduction

# God as Father

## The Contemporary Debate

"I believe in God the Father Almighty." So begins the Apostles' Creed, probably the most widely used of the creeds of the church.[1] The opening confession of the Nicene Creed, "We believe in one God, the Father Almighty," is nearly identical. From its earliest days, when the church cast its beliefs into the form of such creeds, at their head stood the confession of God as "the Father Almighty." The second article of the creed—"and in Jesus Christ his only Son"—linked Jesus, the Lord of the church, to God through the paired titles of Father/Son. These have not been the only designations used by Christians throughout the ages in theology, confession, baptism, prayer, liturgy, and hymns, but they have been foundational to the church's formulation of its faith. While many insist that the church's creeds mean what they say—that God is the Father Almighty, and Jesus is his only Son—others, most notably representatives of the diverse feminist movement, find the simple designation of God as Father and Jesus as Son so problem laden that they have challenged these classical Christian formulations. It is the contemporary challenge to the theological viability and propriety of speaking and thinking of God as Father that forms the context for the present project.

The biblical terrain here is highly contested. Advocates of consistent and nearly exclusive use of Father (as well as other male language and imagery) for God claim the Bible as precedent and norm for their

---

[1]For an analysis of the confession of God as "the Father Almighty" as reflective of the earlier Old Roman Symbol, see J. N. D. Kelly, *Early Christian Creeds* (3d ed.; New York: Longman, 1972), 131–39.

1

practices of speech and thought. Indeed, because the language of Father for God does appear in the scripture, those who defend and advocate its use have sometimes naively and simplistically assumed that the Bible is "on their side." But those who challenge the practice of addressing God exclusively or at all as Father also appeal to the Bible, pointing to the variety of terms for God which are equally biblical and arguing that the current understanding of God as Father is actually a far cry from the scriptural understanding of the same term. Both sides also make appeal to Jesus' use of Father for God. On the one hand, many assert that Jesus' usage demands the continuation of the practice and allows for no other. On the other hand, others argue that in Jesus' day the designation of God as Father so subverted traditional patriarchal norms that to continue today to use male terms exclusively actually subverts the intent and content of Jesus' own concept of God as Father.

As has often been pointed out in recent decades, one finds many images for God in scripture, including rock, shepherd, whistler, barber, king, mother, husband, as well as father. To take the full measure of the scriptural witness, one would also need to explore this range of imagery. But the purpose of this book is more limited and focused. Rather than survey all the imagery for God used in the Bible, the point of this study is to look again at the biblical imagery for God as Father. Because such imagery is found more frequently in the New Testament, it follows that the witness of the New Testament must be treated more fully. And even that field of inquiry can be narrowed further. For, as we shall see, it is particularly in the Gospels—and there mainly in the speech of Jesus— that one encounters the imagery of God as Father. Moreover, inasmuch as Jesus' address to God as Father has been taken as the starting point for a wide variety of studies and as a warrant for a variety of claims regarding the continued validity and importance of that address, it will not be surprising if our investigation begins with Jesus as well. A necessary part of this investigation will be a consideration of the highly influential arguments of Joachim Jeremias regarding the significance of Jesus' address to God as *abba,* an Aramaic term for father. We may then look back to the Old Testament, around to the context of Jesus' own day, and forward to the Gospels and the letters of Paul. In brief, then, the central subject of this book is the significance of Jesus' address to and imagery for God as Father and the way in which various authors of the New Testament argued that the story of Jesus' life, death, and resurrection made sense of that address.

## Challenge and Response:
## The Contemporary Debate about God Language

### *The feminist challenge*

To speak of "the feminist challenge" as though it were a single and unified entity would be to misrepresent the current situation as well as the complexity of the theological challenge. "Feminism" is neither a cohesive movement nor a single thing. Not all who identify themselves as "feminists" adopt identical stances toward the normativity of the scripture or "male" imagery for God—and certainly not all feminists describe themselves as persons of faith.[2] Three general stances toward the Christian tradition can be distinguished. For ease of discussion, we may label these three stances as *reformist, revolutionary,* and *rejectionist.* Some feminists adopt a stance of *reforming* the tradition, seeking to conserve what is best in it rather than to slavishly imitate or even repristinate it. These feminists hope for reform and flexibility in the church's language for God, arguing that the exclusive use of male imagery does not do justice to the biblical picture of God, yields but limited access to understanding God, and hinders relating to God. Because of the conviction that Father actually refers to a God who is confessed to be without gender, some feminists—and others—have therefore sought imagery for God "that is not exclusively male."[3] Hence, their prescription is not to discard Father language but to include a variety of other images as well; "mother" is but one addition to the terminology that may enrich the way in which human beings experience, think about,

---

[2]For discussion of the varieties of feminist approaches to the biblical text, see Carolyn Osiek, "The Feminist and the Bible: Hermeneutical Alternatives," in *Feminist Perspectives on Biblical Scholarship* (ed. Adela Y. Collins; Chico, Calif.: Scholars Press, 1985), 93–106; Katherine Doob Sakenfeld, "Feminist Uses of Biblical Materials," in *Feminist Interpretation of the Bible* (ed. Letty M. Russell; Philadelphia: Westminster, 1985), 55–64; Mary Ann Tolbert, "Defining the Problem: The Bible and Feminist Hermeneutics," in *Semeia* 28 (1983): 113–26; and idem, "Protestant Feminists and the Bible: On the Horns of a Dilemma," in *The Pleasure of Her Text: Feminist Readings of Biblical and Historical Texts* (ed. Alice Bach; Philadelphia: Trinity Press International, 1990), 5–23.

[3]Johanna W. H. van Wijk-Bos, *Reimagining God: The Case for Scriptural Diversity* (Louisville: Westminster John Knox, 1995), ix. While it is important to point out that "Father" language has never been construed by the theologians of the church as "male," nevertheless the fact remains that many people think of God precisely in this way.

and worship God, as well as the ways in which they relate to each other and think of themselves as human beings created in God's own image. For other feminists, however, no such compromise can be struck. The issues cannot be so easily resolved, and the answers needed are much more radical, amounting to a *revolutionary* stance toward tradition. The church's historic use of exclusively male language for God is so entangled with the entire patriarchal structure of church and society that both must be entirely remade. Rather than seeking reform within the present structures of the church or within traditional theological constructs, they offer a more radical agenda, which has implications not merely for language about God but also for the basic character of Christian faith and confession. So, for example, Rebecca Chopp writes, "The radical activity of feminist theology is . . . nothing short of a portend of a transformation of Christianity itself."[4] Such transformation is required because of Christianity's oppressive hierarchical structures which male language for God wittingly or unwittingly perpetuates. As Karen Bloomquist writes:

> A crucial theological agenda in the conversion from patriarchy is the transformation of God-language and imagery. Exclusively male imagery and language for God continues to legitimize patriarchy and the paradigm of male "control over" that undergirds the violence-laden situation we find ourselves in today. It is not that male God-language is in itself generative of violence, but that it comes to function that way within the central power-over dictates of patriarchy. . . . Changing God-language and imagery is not an elitist exercise but a key step in the conversion from patriarchy.[5]

Johanna van Wijk-Bos writes, in a similar vein,

> Parental and espousal images of God are rooted in the experience of patriarchal social relations. Today, these relations are

---

[4]Rebecca Chopp, *The Power to Speak: Feminism, Language, God* (New York: Crossroad, 1989), 18.

[5]Karen L. Bloomquist, "Sexual Violence: Patriarchy's Offense and Defense," in *Christianity, Patriarchy, and Abuse: A Feminist Critique* (ed. Joanne Carlson Brown and Carole R. Bohn; New York: Pilgrim, 1989), 67. See also Janet Martin Soskice, "Can a Feminist call God 'Father'?" in *Speaking the Christian God: The Holy Trinity and the Challenge of Feminism* (ed. Alvin F. Kimel, Jr.; Grand Rapids: Eerdmans; Leominster: Gracewing, 1992), 86.

revealed in all their violent and abusive potential. The problem with these images is not that they lack a connection to contemporary experience but that this experience is shot through with negativity.[6]

In other words, the problem is not abusive patriarchy; the problem is patriarchy *per se*. Patriarchy implies the superior role of men, and both the premise of male superiority as well as the mere supposition of hierarchy—of the superiority or dominance of any one being, person, or class of persons over another—cannot stand against the feminist theological critique. Hierarchy does not provide a serviceable vision for the relationship of God to the world, of persons to each other, or of God and human beings to all other beings. Thus Rosemary Radford Ruether eschews all designations for God, such as Lord, Master, or King, that presuppose some sort of hierarchical rule or authority. Instead, she defines God, whom she calls "God/ess" as "the Primal Matrix," the "great womb within which all things, gods and humans, sky and earth, human and nonhuman beings are generated."[7]

More radically still, some feminists fall into the camp of explicitly *rejecting* the traditions of Christian faith. Asserting that the Christian texts and faith are inevitably and intolerably patriarchal, they have abandoned Christianity altogether. Their objection has perhaps come to be most dramatically and pithily summarized in Mary Daly's oft-quoted dictum, "If God is male, then the male is God."[8] If indeed the Christian texts and traditions are thoroughly patriarchal and androcentric, the question arises whether one can be feminist and Christian. Many argue that the two commitments (that is, Christianity and feminism) cannot be maintained simultaneously. Daphne Hampson, for instance, writes that "feminism represents the death-knell of Christianity as a viable religious option."[9] Her objections are manifold and

---

[6]van Wijk-Bos, *Reimagining God,* 43.

[7]Rosemary Radford Ruether, *Sexism and God-Talk: Toward a Feminist Theology* (Boston: Beacon, 1983), 48–49. Similarly, Patricia Wilson-Kastner writes, "One of the most fundamental insights of feminism is that the various divisions of hierarchy—alienation of humanity from the animate and inanimate world about it, dualism of body and spirit—all need to be healed and overcome in us" (*Faith, Feminism and the Christ* [Philadelphia: Fortress, 1983], 114).

[8]Mary Daly, *Beyond God the Father: Toward a Philosophy of Women's Liberation* (Boston: Beacon, 1973), 19.

[9]Daphne Hampson, *Theology and Feminism* (Oxford: Basil Blackwell, 1990), 1.

are only partly taken up in her complaint against male conceptualization of God. She asks,

> Is it not the case that a religion in which the Godhead is represented as male, or central to which is a male human being, necessarily acts as an ideology which is biased against half of humanity? Is it not the case that such religion is by its very nature harmful to the cause of human equality?[10]

Hampson thus concludes that Christianity is indeed so thoroughly and detrimentally patriarchal at its core that feminists cannot make peace with it.[11]

But equally offensive to them is the Christian claim for the central and unique role of Jesus. "Christians believe in particularity," Hampson writes.

> They must say of Jesus of Nazareth that there was a revelation of God through him in a way in which this is not true of you or me. God is bound up with peculiar events, a particular people, above all with the person Jesus of Nazareth. Therefore reference must needs always be made to this history and to this person.[12]

In short, it is not just an isolated reference here or there to God as Father that is objectionable and has to go; equally to be jettisoned is the inescapable need to always make reference to "this history" and "this person." Thus Christianity's patriarchalism cannot be separated from its particularity, and these come together not only in its conception of God as Father but also in the designation of God as the Father of the central figure of its faith, Jesus of Nazareth.

Clearly not only human language for God but our very conceptions of God are implicated in this discussion. Indeed, for some feminists part of the agenda in dropping terms such as Father is to rid Christian faith of its transcendent and hierarchical God in favor of a more immanent

---

[10]Hampson, *Theology and Feminism,* 53.

[11]Similarly, Naomi Goldenberg writes, "Jesus Christ cannot symbolize the liberation of women. A culture that maintains a masculine image for its highest divinity cannot allow its women to experience themselves as the equals of its men. In order to develop a theology of women's liberation, feminists have to leave Christ and Bible behind them. . . . Feminist theology must cease depending on the metaphor of Jesus *him*self" (*Changing of the Gods: Feminism and the End of Traditional Religions* [Boston: Beacon, 1979], 22, 25.

[12]Hampson, *Theology and Feminism,* 8.

deity or in favor of a god "in whom all creation lives, moves, and has its being." When charged with robbing God of genuine "otherness," many feminists appear to be decidedly unrepentant.[13] That is, while critics of feminist ideology often charge that "mother" and "female" language for God conduce to pantheism or panentheism, many feminists do not recoil at the sting of the attack, because the reformulation of conceptions about God and God's relationship to the world lies at the heart of much of the feminist agenda. In other words, the problem lies as much with the confession of God as Almighty as it does with God as Father. The question remains whether by eliminating the traditional language with which Christianity speaks about and to God, one also effectively eradicates the Christian faith *as Christian* faith.

### Theological responses to feminism

The theological responses to the feminist challenge are no less varied than the challenge itself, ranging as it does from reformist, through revolutionary, to rejectionist positions. But not all those who defend traditional language adduce the same warrants for continuing to call God Father and for thinking of God in those terms. Not all are without sympathy for the feminist position; not all "traditionalists" are antifeminist. By "traditionalist" we simply mean those who, for one reason or another, argue for the necessity of the traditional designations for God, sometimes in spite of and sometimes because of their patriarchal overtones.

The similarly varied theological responses to the diverse feminist challenge comprise the second, equally important, context for this project. These responses have ranged across the theological and methodological spectrum. There has been extensive analysis of the nature of language and, more particularly, of the nature of simile, metaphor, and analogy.[14] The most typical way in which the traditionalist case is advanced is to distinguish, first, between simile, metaphor, and analogy; to argue, second, that

---

[13]For criticisms that feminist theology tends toward panentheism and fails to render a transcendent God, see, for example, the articles by Elizabeth Achtemeier, "Exchanging God for 'No Gods': A Discussion of Female Language for God," and Colin Gunton, "Proteus and Procrustes: A Study in the Dialectic of Language in Disagreement with Sallie McFague," both in *Speaking the Christian God.*

[14]On this point see especially Margo G. Houts, "Language, Gender, and God: How Traditionalists and Feminists Play the Inclusive Language Game" (Ph.D. diss., Fuller Theological Seminary, 1993).

Father is a metaphor while Mother is a simile; and then, third, to attribute determinative and final significance to metaphor. As part of this discussion, scholars who defend the continued use of Father have argued that Father is a name for God and that it is, specifically, the "revealed" or "proper" name of God, thereby granting it unique and definitive status among all possible designations for God.[15] Similarly, traditionalist scholars have rejected substitutes for the Trinitarian formula, Father, Son and Holy Spirit, such as Creator, Redeemer, Sustainer (or Sanctifier), or Mother, Lover, Friend, as theologically inadequate and liturgically offensive.

For traditionalist interpreters of Christian faith, not only is the understanding of God that lies at the heart of Christian faith sharply challenged by the elimination of Father language, but Jesus' own authority is called into question as well. The canonical Gospels uniformly depict Jesus as calling on God as Father, and therefore to delete that designation from Christian vocabulary amounts to a denial of the validity of Jesus' practice and his command to pray by addressing God as Father. One theologian puts it this way:

> First of all, we have to do with revelation in time, through historical particularity. We have to do with a Jew in first-century Palestine who called God his Father and who has invited us to pray on his warrant (in his name) to God as Father. . . . There is no exhaustively necessary reason we can cite to show why Jesus should have used this language. The fact is simply that he did . . . and so must we.[16]

In other words, whereas Daphne Hampson invoked Christianity's particularity as one of its inevitable and also damning traits, others have appealed precisely to this characteristic as necessarily definitive of Christian confession. For example, Robert Jenson writes,

---

[15]See, for example, the essay of Alvin F. Kimel, Jr., who writes in defense of the Trinitarian formula, "The triune God has named himself, and he likes his name" ("The God Who Likes His Name: Holy Trinity, Feminism, and the Language of Faith," in *Speaking the Christian God,* 188.) A number of the other essays in this volume make the same point.

[16]Gerhard O. Forde, "Naming the One Who Is above Us," in *Speaking the Christian God: The Holy Trinity and the Challenge of Feminism* (ed. Alvin F. Kimel, Jr.; Grand Rapids: Eerdmans; Leominster: Gracewing, 1992), 118. See also Robert W. Jenson, "The Father, He . . ." in *Speaking the Christian God,* 103–4.

That Jesus called on God with "father" rather than with "mother" is a fact about the historic person Jesus that we can no more change than we can decree that he was not Jewish, or a wandering rabbi, or unpopular with the Sanhedrin. Since the church's address of God is authorized only as repetition of Jesus' address, this fact about him is determinative for the church.[17]

Examples of such argumentation could easily be multiplied. It is clearly the case that a central argument against the feminist challenge to language for God as Father is Jesus' own practice of addressing God as Father, as well as his command that his disciples are to pray, "Our Father."

The normativity of Jesus' address to God as Father for shaping contemporary practices leads ineluctably to a second argument for maintaining the traditional language, namely, that such address to God is the language of the Bible. Some advocates of the traditional language of Father for God and of the Trinitarian formula are willing to leave it at that: we are simply to repeat the language of the Bible. In his defense of "biblical patterns" of speech for God, John Cooper's recent work claims that one must *imitate* the patterns of speech found in the Bible, so much so that these patterns become virtually more important than any content embodied in them. Thus, for example, Cooper argues that inasmuch as Father is a biblical term for God, but the belief that God is without gender is not explicitly found in the Bible, it is better to use Father and run the theological and personal risks of misunderstanding the term than to be guided by the (even genuinely sound) theological insight that God is without gender.[18] Cooper writes,

If Scripture is the source and norm for the God-language of the Christian faith, that language will not be gender-inclusive. However, if Christian language must be gender-inclusive, then the doctrine of divine genderlessness is in fact operating at a more basic and determinative level than Scripture.[19]

He thus concludes, "The only reasonable conclusion is that the intended practice of Scripture as a whole is to speak of God as a masculine

---

[17]Jenson, "The Father, He . . . ," 104.

[18]John W. Cooper, *Our Father in Heaven: Christian Faith and Inclusive Language for God* (Grand Rapids: Baker, 1999), especially ch. 7.

[19]Cooper, *Our Father,* 188.

person."[20] This is the pattern which should have primacy for those who make any sort of claim to heed the authority of scripture.

Certainly not all advocates of traditional language share the same insistence on adopting the patterns of speech of the Bible, although many find it crucial to maintain the language lest the bonds to scripture and to Jesus be severed. Obviously Jesus' use of Father and the authority of the witness of scripture are closely if not inseparably linked, for it is only through the Bible that we have access to Jesus' mode of address to God and his commands to his disciples to pray to God as "our Father." Although numerous theological arguments for preserving the traditional language and formulations have also been advanced, these would carry far less weight should the argument from either the precedent of Jesus or of scripture fall by the way.

But those who have responded to the feminist challenge have not simply rested their case on precedent, whether set by Jesus or scripture. For some, the theological significance of the term Father is far-reaching indeed. For example, Wolfhart Pannenberg writes, "On the lips of Jesus 'Father' became a proper name for God. It embraces every feature in the understanding of God which comes to light in the message of Jesus."[21] That Father is a proper name for God which embraces *every* feature of Jesus' understanding of God is indeed a sweeping claim. Yet it has been affirmed by others. T. F. Torrance writes:

> When we turn to the Scriptures of the New Testament, we find a radical deepening of the Old Testament doctrine of God, for 'Father' is now revealed to be more than an epithet—it is the personal name of God in which the form and content of his self-revelation as Father through Jesus Christ his Son are inseparable. "Father" is now the name of God that we are to hallow, as our Lord Jesus taught us: "Our *Father* who art in heaven, *hallowed* be your *name*."[22]

Another scholar ventures this opinion:

> The name "Father" is the one best calculated to manifest the novelty of the God of Jesus, as compared not only with the

---

[20]Cooper, *Our Father,* 114.

[21]Wolfhart Pannenberg, *Systematic Theology* (vol. 1; Grand Rapids: Eerdmans, 1991), 262.

[22]Thomas F. Torrance, "The Christian Apprehension of God the Father," in *Speaking the Christian God,* 131.

God of the Greeks but with the God of the Jews. Compared with the God of Israel the God of Jesus represents a revolution in so far as God is the God of grace before being the God of the law.[23]

Similar claims often surface in more popular Christian literature. In an influential and widely read book, *Knowing God,* J. I. Packer summarizes as follows:

> Everything that Christ taught, everything that makes the New Testament new, and better than the Old, everything that is distinctively Christian as opposed to merely Jewish, is summed up in the knowledge of the Fatherhood of God. "Father" is the Christian name of God.[24]

John Cooper advances a similar argument:

> [Feminine images] for God are greater in number and directness in the Old Testament than in the New Testament. In other words, as the Bible progressively reveals God as Father, Son, and Holy Spirit and Jesus as the Messiah, the Son of God, the feminine imagery for God does not increase but recedes into the background.[25]

The triune name thus has "definitive revelatory status."[26] In one way or another, then, these arguments appeal to the relationship of the New to the Old Testament, to "progressive revelation" or to the definitive revelation of God in Christ, or to Father as the definitive name for God, suggesting that all of these arguments point to the unique and irreplaceable status of Father. In short, Jesus' use of Father in the Gospels of Christian scripture becomes the basis for all subsequent argumentation for holding on to the traditional language.

---

[23]Claude Geffre, "Father as the Proper Name of God," in *God as Father?* (ed. Johannes-Baptist Metz and Edward Schillebeeckx; Concilium 143: Dogma; Edinburgh: T. & T. Clark; New York: Seabury, 1981), 44.

[24]J. I. Packer, *Knowing God* (Downers Grove: InterVarsity, 1973), 182–83. Similarly, Cooper (*Our Father,* 105) calls Father "The Distinctive New Testament Title-Name."

[25]Cooper, *Our Father,* 90. Cooper also argues that even if the Hebrew *ruah* is feminine, in the LXX and the New Testament the word *pneuma* is neuter, somehow implying a diminution in feminine imagery for God as we progress toward the New Testament!

[26]Ibid., 110.

For post-Christian feminists, those who reject the traditions of Christian faith, the insistence that God can be spoken of only in the language of Jesus as found in the Bible has opened the doors to leave the church and the Christian faith. Jesus and the Bible are not the solution; they are the problem. The mere use of Father for God actually underscores and enforces Christianity's inherent androcentrism, patriarchalism, and hierarchicalism. By contrast, some feminists who have chosen to stay within the church have argued that Jesus' own understanding of God's "fatherhood" alleviates the patriarchalism inherent in the term. Inherent within Jesus' use of father and hence also within the scripture one finds the corrective to patriarchy and hierarchy. On this view, Jesus redefined the character of God and discipleship in terms of service and self-giving love. Although Jesus undercut the oppressive and negative force of the "father" image, the church has not done so well. Elisabeth Schüssler Fiorenza, for example, takes as central Jesus' statement, "Call no one father for you have one father (and you are all siblings)." Commenting on her own reconstruction of this saying of Jesus, Schüssler Fiorenza writes:

> The new kinship of the discipleship of equals does not admit of "fathers," thereby rejecting the patriarchal power and esteem invested in them. . . . The "father" God is invoked here, however, not to justify patriarchal structures and relationships in the community of disciples but precisely to reject all such claims, powers, and structures. . . . The address "father" used by Jesus and his disciples has caused many Christian feminists great scandal because the church has not obeyed the command of Jesus "to call no one father," for you have "one father," and because it has resulted in legitimizing ecclesial and societal patriarchy with the "father" name of God, thereby using the name of God in vain.[27]

Similarly, Brian Wren argues that "Jesus knew and named God as Abba/father in such a way that the patriarchal order itself was called into question. . . . The name no longer has the power, *in our context,* to subvert patriarchal norms; indeed it is angrily invoked in defense of them."[28] For these critics of contemporary use of male language for

---

[27]Elisabeth Schüssler Fiorenza, *In Memory of Her: A Feminist Theological Reconstruction of Christian Origins* (New York: Crossroad, 1983), 150–51.

[28]Brian Wren, *What Language Shall I Borrow? God-Talk in Worship: A Male Response to Feminist Theology* (New York: Crossroad, 1991), 186–87.

God, one must ask whether the church today most faithfully honors the intention and content of Jesus' address to God as Father by adopting an alternate form of address, since Father today no longer means what Father did when Jesus used it. But the question then becomes, what does Father mean in Jesus' usage in the Gospels? The explication of the content of Jesus' address to God as Father has attracted enormous attention in the world of biblical scholarship. But here, too, there is division rather than unity, for not all biblical scholars agree what Jesus did mean with this form of address.

### The Bible and Biblical Scholarship in the Contemporary Debate

As already suggested, a number of theologians have argued that Jesus' address to God as Father marked a significant advance over views of God held by Jesus' contemporaries. It is precisely in Jesus' address to God as *abba* that this superior conception of God is to be located. But if we leave the rhetoric of superiority aside for a minute, the issue that calls for judicious discussion is whether Jesus did in fact hold decidedly new convictions about the God of Israel, or whether his understanding for the most part falls in with the views of his contemporaries. On this question, as already hinted, we find a diversity of opinions.

On the one hand, some scholars stress the continuity between Jesus' convictions about God and those of the Jewish matrix from which he came. One finds conclusions such as the following: "Jesus brought no new concept of God, but he demonstrated in action the full extent of God's redemptive will for the world which was from the beginning."[29] Along these lines, N. T. Wright interprets the parable of the prodigal son, often deemed to represent most clearly Jesus' distinctive vision of a loving and forgiving God in contrast to the begrudging attitude of the Pharisees, as follows:

> For Israel's god to act in this way is not an innovation; it is consistent with his character as revealed throughout Israel's long and chequered history. This is who he is, who he will be.[30]

---

[29]Brevard S. Childs, *Biblical Theology of the Old and New Testaments* (Minneapolis: Fortress, 1992), 358.

[30]N. T. Wright, *Jesus and the Victory of God* (Christian Origins and the Question of God, vol. 2; Minneapolis: Fortress, 1996), 130.

Wright in fact contends that Jesus shared fundamental beliefs with Jewish monotheism about God and God's relationship to Israel, and that Jesus' own convictions about his mission depended upon those beliefs. In particular, Jesus held that God had promised to deliver Israel, and upon this belief he based his own conviction that such deliverance was now being effected through his mission to Israel. Jesus would not have appeared as a teacher of new ideas, including new ideas about God, however much his later interpreters sought to argue to the contrary. Rather, his work and word were undergirded by shared and common assumptions about God. It was the appropriation of these beliefs to his own mission and vocation that distinguished Jesus.

On the other hand, some biblical scholars have advanced fairly radical claims for Jesus' use of Father for God on the basis of their historical investigations. For example, Wilhelm Bousset, Rudolf Bultmann's teacher, wrote:

> What is most completely original and truly creative in the preaching of Jesus comes out most strongly and purely when he proclaims God the heavenly Father. . . . The [Judaism of Jesus' time] had neither in name nor in fact the faith of the Father-God; it could not possibly rise to it.[31]

Bultmann repeated Bousset's views that Jesus had proclaimed the nearness of God as Father over against a view of God as a distant and remote sovereign.

> [In Judaism] God had retreated far off into the distance as the transcendent heavenly King, and His sway over the present could barely still be made out. For Jesus, God again became *a God at hand.* This contrast finds expression in the respective forms of address used in prayer. Compare the ornate, emotional, often liturgically beautiful, but often over-loaded forms of address in Jewish prayer with the stark simplicity of "Father"! . . . Unlike the prophets' preaching his preaching is directed not primarily to the people as a whole, but *to individuals.*[32]

---

[31]Wilhelm Bousset, *Jesu Predigt in ihrem Gegensatz zum Judentum: Ein religionsgeschichtlicher Vergleich* (Göttingen: Vandenhoeck und Ruprecht, 1892), 41, 43, cited and translated in G. F. Moore, "Christian Writers on Judaism," *HTR* 14 (1921): 242. I am indebted to the dissertation of W. E. Nunnally, Jr., ("The Fatherhood of God at Qumran," Hebrew Union College-Jewish Institute of Religion, 1992) for this and other references and helpful discussion.

[32]Rudolf Bultmann, *Theology of the New Testament* (2 vols.; ET New York: Charles Scribner's Sons, 1951, 1955) 1:23, 25.

Similarly, in his article on ἀββᾶ for the *Theological Dictionary of the New Testament,* Gerhard Kittel wrote,

> Jesus' term for God . . . shows how this Father-child relation-ship to God far surpasses any possibilities of intimacy assumed in Judaism, introducing indeed something which is wholly new.[33]

It is noteworthy how often Jesus' designation of God as Father, or the way in which he used the term, is seen as new and distinct, surpass-ing all previous characterizations of God, including those found even in the Bible that Jesus read. Time and again one reads discussions of what is "new," "novel," or "distinctive" in Jesus' mode of address to God and in his convictions about God. In an effort to demonstrate Jesus' author-ity, he must be made innovative. He cannot say what others said; he must speak with a different voice. One does not need to scratch very far below the surface to uncover the view that the New Testament God is a God of love and nearness, while the Old Testament God is a hidden and fearsome God, or that New Testament revelation must necessarily "sur-pass" what is found in the Old Testament. In a variation on this view, first-century Judaism is thought to have held that God was transcendent and inaccessible, whereas Jesus offered an immanent God with whom intimate relationship was possible. Even when these ideas are neither explicitly adopted nor rejected, the idea that Father implies a new *con-tent* to Jesus' or early Christian understanding of God remains firmly entrenched in biblical scholarship. It is also clear that appeal to the novelty of Jesus' convictions about God as Father goes a long way toward establishing the "definitive" status of that designation for God. Once again it becomes apparent that Jesus' own mode of address and reference to God as Father plays a pivotal role in current theological discussions.

## Exploring the Terrain Again

The present study seeks to make a contribution to the contemporary theological discussion by looking again at the biblical imagery for God as Father. From the previous survey it will have become clear to what extent Jesus' own use of Father figures in the discussion for both the-ologians and biblical scholars. Not all who make Jesus' mode of address

---

[33]Gerhard Kittel, "ἀββᾶ," *TDNT* 1:6.

definitive for the church today appeal to the *originality* of Jesus' address to God as Father for the basis of their claim. For some interpreters, the simple fact that Jesus used this form of address for God mandates the church's use of it. But the impression lingers that the argument can at least be helped along if Jesus' conception of God remains in some way distinctive and thus implicitly "better" than that of his contemporaries. Subsequently some far-reaching claims have been made for Jesus' address to God as Father, and some imposing theologies have been erected on this foundation, either in the name of honoring the central role of Jesus himself or the normative witness of scripture.

However, once the claim has been made that scripture warrants the continued exclusive use of Father (or Father, Son, and Holy Spirit), the reasons that are advanced seem to be little interested in the actual contours of the biblical witness. T. F. Torrance, for example, argues that since "there is no likeness between the eternal being of God and the being of creaturely things," then one may not derive knowledge of God from creaturely knowledge, or one runs the risk of simply projecting that knowledge onto God.[34] Hence, "we cannot think or speak of God except in the forms of thought and speech which he has elected to use in the unique mediation of his Word to humankind."[35] Gerhard Forde asserts that human attempts to name God lead to "abstractions that choke and kill us" and render only a God of wrath.[36] Roland Frye argues against feminist, inclusive language for God on the grounds that such language would disrupt and even destroy "the delicate and subtle distinctions that have allowed the presentation of three persons in a single monotheistic godhead."[37]

Too often the whole discussion about language for God proceeds as though the significance of the biblical imagery of God as Father were somehow self-evident, and the primary theological task is merely defense of such imagery. But it must not be presumed that the biblical picture of God as Father is self-evident, as though one could merely say "Father" and instantly evoke a common understanding of its significance. In fact it is doubtful that the understanding of God as Father provides any positive way of construing collective Christian identity for

---

[34]Torrance, "The Christian Apprehension of God the Father," 132–33.

[35]Ibid., 137.

[36]Forde, "Naming the One Who Is above Us," 114, 117.

[37]Roland M. Frye, "Language for God and Feminist Language: Problems and Principles," in *Speaking the Christian God*, 24.

most Christians today. Clearly Jesus of Nazareth lies at the heart of Christian faith. As the post-Christian feminist Daphne Hampson puts it in her criticism of traditional Christianity:

> They must say of Jesus of Nazareth that there was a revelation of God through him in a way in which this is not true of you or me. God is bound up with peculiar events, a particular people, above all with the person Jesus of Nazareth. Therefore reference must needs always be made to this history and to this person.[38]

Hampson is correct. Without reference to "this history and to this person," the Christian faith will cease to be Christian. But in what way is the designation of God as Father bound up with "this history and this person"? If the Christian faith will cease to be Christian should it lose its moorings to the history of Israel and of Jesus of Nazareth, will it also cease to be Christian if it loses or even loosens its understanding of God as the Father Almighty?

## *The plan of the present study*

In order to begin to answer such vexing questions, we will first examine the arguments that Jesus consistently addressed God as *abba*. Any discussion of Jesus' use of *abba* owes much to the labors of Joachim Jeremias. Hence, Jeremias's arguments and conclusions require close scrutiny, especially in light of the fact that they are often misread and misused in arguments about the significance of calling God Father. Moreover, in recent decades the previously "assured result" of New Testament studies—that Jesus used *abba* in direct address to God—has been disputed, and the publication of new material from Qumran has suggested that Jeremias's arguments require revision. In short, there are numerous good reasons to reassess Jeremias's work on *abba*.

In the second chapter we shall turn from the narrow focus on Jesus' use of *abba* to the larger question of the contexts of and sources for Jesus' use of the language and imagery of Father for God. Specifically, we will examine various texts from the Old Testament and Second Temple Judaism which together comprise the theological and historical matrices in which the New Testament was written. The point is not simply to reduce the Old Testament or Jewish texts to the ways in which

---

[38]Hampson, *Theology and Feminism,* 8.

they were "used" by Jesus or the earliest Christian authors. Their voices need to be heard on their own terms. But it is an inescapable fact that the Old Testament was scripture for Jesus and the church. Part of the task here, then, is to suggest the convictions and contexts that shaped their reading of these scriptures, particularly as these convictions and contexts bear on the understanding of God as Father.

From such an examination it will become clear that the designation of God as Father was neither Jesus' invention nor the creation of the early church. Rather, though somewhat limited in frequency, the designation of God as Father appears regularly in both the Old Testament and in Jewish texts. Of the characteristic descriptions of the activity or attributes of a father, and particularly of God as Father, three figure most prominently and importantly: (1) The father is the head of a clan or family, and hence the "ancestor" who gives life to and bequeaths an inheritance to his heirs. (2) The father is one who loves and cares for his children. (3) The father is a figure of authority, who is worthy of obedience and honor. This threefold understanding of God shapes Jesus' own use of Father for God and comes to expression repeatedly in the New Testament.

From this foundation, we will turn to assess the way in which Jesus' use of Father illumines his own aims and intentions. Anyone at all familiar with the last century of New Testament scholarship will immediately be aware of the theological and historical issues raised by the attempt to uncover Jesus' own aims and intentions. Both the validity and the possibility of pursuing "the Jesus of history" have been called into question. This effort must be deemed doubly problematic in speaking of Jesus' own convictions about God, inasmuch as these are often understood to be the product of his own "experience" of God. If it is difficult enough to get at the Jesus of history, how much more complicated the task to uncover the "experience" of Jesus! My contention is that Jesus' address to God as Father does not in the first instance bear witness to his own "experience" of God but, rather, to his convictions that God's renewal and restoration of Israel—a hope depicted in the prophets as the return of the exiles to their home and as the return of the children of Israel to God as Father (Isa. 64:8–9; Jer. 31:9)—were being effected through his mission. That Jesus spoke of God as Father was not a matter of private experience; it was a matter of public mission.

But precisely because it belongs in the historical context of Jesus' own mission, Father cannot simply be reified or treated as though its meaning were self-evident apart from that context. Hence the point of this chapter is not to pursue "the quest of the historical Jesus" for its own sake. Nor is it to offer some allegedly historical reconstruction in place of the Gospel's own witness to Jesus or to his address of God as Father. But there are insights about Jesus and his understanding of God as Father that can be gleaned from historical study, and these are neither to be disparaged nor to be treated as an unshakable foundation upon which all subsequent theology may build. Rather, in this instance, historical study may serve as a sort of ground-clearing exercise by which dubious conclusions, whatever they may be, can be shown to be just that.

After this historical investigation of the Old Testament, Judaism, and Jesus, we will then examine in turn the Synoptic Gospels; the letters of Paul, and especially those letters, Galatians and Romans, in which Paul mounts an argument that those who are in Christ call upon God as *abba;* and the Gospel of John, which accentuates God as Father as does no other document of the New Testament.

Finally, having surveyed these data from the New Testament, we will want to stand back and offer at least a tentative assessment of their significance. We may anticipate at least some of the conclusions of this study. First, the chief features of the portraits of God as Father in the Old and New Testaments are marked more by continuity than by discontinuity. Jesus and early Christians did not originate the conception of God as Father. And yet Jesus did appropriate the biblical imagery for himself and his community in order to articulate his vocation within Israel as the heir of the kingdom and Son of the Father through whose mission God was effecting the restoration of Israel. Second, although characteristics or functions of the father in ancient Israel and Judaism are used to speak of God as Father, these are never linked with any sort of ontological gender or "masculine" essence of God, and, conversely, God's "Fatherhood" never becomes a model for the conduct of human fathers or men. Instead, where God's identity as Father becomes a model at all, it serves as an example for the entire community of faith, to foster mercy, justice, and humility, as well as individual and corporate response and obedience to God. Third, while human beings are depicted as ideally calling upon and knowing God as Father, that confession is not in the first instance an expression of an interior experience of or attitudes toward God, but rather a confession of God's redemptive and faithful love toward his people. To speak of God as Father is to point first of all to the redemptive and life-giving work of God, and then only subsequently and secondarily to human experience of God's faithfulness. Finally, then, although in creeds and confessions God is preeminently and almost exclusively "the Father of our Lord Jesus Christ," that confession stands at the pinnacle of Christian confession of God as Father, rather than as the originating idea of such confession. Put differently, it is because God is first the Father of his people Israel that we speak of God as Father and as the Father of Israel's Messiah, Jesus of Nazareth. Through and in Jesus, Christians confess God as Father and so confess their place within the people created by God's redemptive love.

I want to make it clear at the outset that I have no wish or intent to excuse the abuses perpetrated by Christians in the name of the Father. For some it may be impossible to redeem, for the present and in so short a space, the understanding of God as Father at all. My question is not so much whether we should continue to address God as Father as how it was that Jesus thought of God as Father and how the story of Jesus' life, death, and resurrection makes sense of that address and so can make sense of contemporary address to God in this way. Only within the framework of the biblical narrative can our understanding of God as Father be simultaneously illuminated and demystified as one way of speaking of God's faithfulness and love as embodied particularly in Jesus Christ.

# 1

# Joachim Jeremias
# and the Debate about *Abba*

About twenty years ago, R. G. Hamerton-Kelly wrote:

> Although not without its critics, the thesis that the Abba experience of Jesus is the starting point of Christology, and the key to Jesus' eschatology, commands widespread support. . . . It has become one of the assured results of modern scholarship.[1]

Hamerton-Kelly labeled this thesis "first in importance among the several vital contributions [Joachim] Jeremias made to our modern understanding of Jesus and the gospel witness."[2] About a decade after Hamerton-Kelly rendered his verdict, Edgar Krentz reaffirmed it when he wrote, "It is a truism in New Testament studies today that Jesus called God by the Aramaic term *abba*." In support of his contention, Krentz simply footnoted the work of Joachim Jeremias, as if mere reference to Jeremias's work would suffice to corroborate the point. Krentz continued:

> *Abba* expressed closeness to God because it is an intimate familial term. Jesus lived in the conviction that the Father knew him, that he knew the Father, and that through him God as Father is close to the disciples and known by them as a God of mercy. . . . Jesus proclaimed the nearness of God to save.[3]

---

[1]Hamerton-Kelly, "God the Father in the Bible," 101.
[2]Ibid., 98.
[3]Edgar Krentz, "God in the New Testament," in *Our Naming of God* (ed. Carl E. Braaten; Minneapolis: Fortress, 1989), 88–89.

James D. G. Dunn draws much the same conclusion, noting the unusual agreement of scholarship at this point:

> Somewhat surprisingly, in scholarly circles there is a widespread agreement that Jesus probably did indeed see himself as God's son, or understood himself in relation to God as son. In terms of historical critical analysis the point is most securely based on the tradition of Jesus' prayer to God using the Aramaic form of address, "Abba" ("Father").[4]

Commenting on the significance of Jesus' address, Dunn notes elsewhere:

> "Abba" was a surprising word to use in addressing God. In its natural usage it was a family word and usually confined to the family circle. . . . It was a word resonant with family intimacy. . . . The point is that to address God in such a colloquial way, with such intimacy, is hardly known in the Judaism of Jesus' time. . . . What others thought too intimate in praying to God, Jesus used because of its intimacy.[5]

In his posthumously published *New Testament Theology,* G. B. Caird wrote in a similar vein:

> Another certain fact about Jesus is his use of the word "father," attested by the Aramaic word *abba* in the records. The prayer in Gethsemane (Mark 14:36) ("*Abba,* Father . . . ") is on all hands recognized as an authentic word of Jesus.[6]

Caird continued,

> The further back we go [in the tradition], the more we discover the intense conviction of Jesus that God is his Father and he is

---

[4]James D. G. Dunn, *The Partings of the Ways between Christianity and Judaism and their Significance for the Character of Christianity* (London: SCM Press; Philadelphia: Trinity Press International, 1991), 170; idem, *Jesus and the Spirit: A Study of the Religious and Charismatic Experience of Jesus and the First Christians as Reflected in the New Testament* (Philadelphia: Westminster, 1975, repr., Grand Rapids: Eerdmans, 1997), 21.

[5]James D. G. Dunn, *The Evidence for Jesus* (Philadelphia: Westminster, 1985), 48; Scot McKnight, *A New Vision for Israel: The Teachings of Jesus in National Context* (Grand Rapids: Eerdmans, 1999), 61.

[6]G. B. Caird, *New Testament Theology* (completed and edited by L. D. Hurst; Oxford: Clarendon, 1994), 398.

His son. This is supported by the word *abba,* an address used at times by children to their father, indicating an intimacy and directness not contained in the more formal *abinu* ["our father"]. Certainly other Jews believed in the fatherhood of God, but this was a creedal affirmation. . . . The synoptic passages speak of an intimacy of filial relationship . . . For Jesus the fatherhood of God has become a profoundly personal religious experience, long before it became a doctrine to be communicated to others.[7]

These scholars not only speak confidently of a consensus on the point of Jesus' use of *abba* but also show remarkable agreement with respect to the conclusions to be drawn from such usage. What is less obvious, unless one also has access to their footnotes, is that all these scholars also acknowledge their dependence upon the studies of Joachim Jeremias, who argued that "the complete novelty and uniqueness of *Abba* as an address to God in the prayers of Jesus shows that it expresses the heart of Jesus' relationship to God."[8] Jeremias's statement encapsulates the two prongs of his argument which have been subsequently adopted by others: first, as an address to God, *abba* is unique; second, as such, it uniquely discloses Jesus' own understanding of his relationship to God. Jeremias's conclusions exerted enormous influence on subsequent discussions of the use of Father for God, as well as on discussions of the mission and message of the historical Jesus.

## A Rift in the Consensus

Even the most "assured results of scholarship," however, will have their opponents. In 1992, about the time some scholars were speaking confidently of "widespread agreement" and "certain facts," Mary Rose D'Angelo countered, "*Abba* cannot be shown to have been unique to Jesus, characteristic of Jesus, or even to have been used by Jesus."[9] D'Angelo thus denied Jeremias's conclusion that *abba* was characteristic of Jesus' language for God, let alone that it was unique. But

---

[7]Caird, *New Testament Theology,* 400–401.

[8]Joachim Jeremias, *New Testament Theology: The Proclamation of Jesus* (New York: Charles Scribner's Sons, 1971), 67.

[9]Mary Rose D'Angelo, "*Abba* and 'Father': Imperial Theology and the Jesus Traditions," *JBL* 111 (1992): 616. For a contrary view, see John P. Meier, *A Marginal Jew: Rethinking the Historical Jesus* (vol. 2: Mentor, Message and Miracles; New York: Doubleday, 1994), 358–59; Dale C. Allison, *Jesus of Nazareth: Millenarian Prophet* (Minneapolis: Fortress, 1998), 47–50.

D'Angelo extended her negative judgment, contending that Father as an address to God "may also, but need not, have gone back to the practice of Jesus and his companions."[10] In light of the widespread consensus, one may find D'Angelo's wholesale rejection of Jesus' use of all Father language for God surprising. But D'Angelo was not the first to raise a dissenting voice against the reigning consensus. In a review of Hamerton-Kelly's work, Phyllis Trible had already alleged that the Gospel evidence for Jesus' use of *abba* was too slight to be convincing. Contrary to Hamerton-Kelly, she argued that Father was not central to Jesus' understanding of God.[11]

Two very different positions emerge in this debate. One side argues for the historical uniqueness of Jesus' address to God as *abba* and infers from that historical distinctiveness the unparalleled character of Jesus' experience. That experience undergirds his entire mission, providing the impetus not merely for patterns of speech but also for Jesus' sense of identity. On the opposite side are those who argue that the historical evidence for the distinctive character of Jesus' use of *abba* falls short of proof. The evidence found in the Gospels simply cannot substantiate the claim that Jesus used *abba,* nor would evidence from his historical context support the contention that Jesus' conception of God as Father was unique.

But it is not primarily with a historical assessment of Jesus' habits of speech that D'Angelo is concerned. Eventually she concludes,

> Neither Jesus nor the NT can be shown to have used the word "Father" in a way that constitutes a transhistorical revelation that is unique and will be irreparably lost if twentieth-century theology and practice choose other imagery for God.[12]

Here D'Angelo's larger agenda surfaces, for her interest clearly lies in denying transhistorical revelatory status to Father language for God. To do so, she must gain leverage against the dominant scholarly position that *abba* is unique in Jesus' historical context as address to God. D'Angelo thus mounts her attack on two primary fronts. First, she argues

---

[10]D'Angelo, "*Abba* and 'Father,' " 618.

[11]See Phyllis Trible's review of Hamerton-Kelly's earlier work, *God the Father: Theology and Patriarchy in the Teaching of Jesus* (Overture to Biblical Theology 4; Philadelphia: Fortress, 1979) in *ThTo* 37 (1980): 116–19.

[12]D'Angelo, "*Abba* and 'Father,' " 630.

against the historical uniqueness of Jesus' mode of address, canvassing Jewish literature of the time to demonstrate the continuity of the conception of God as Father in the New Testament with that of contemporary Judaism. But D'Angelo pushes even further, concluding that, given the paucity and nature of the evidence, it is more likely that Jesus did not use *abba* than that he did. Obviously, if Jesus never used *abba* at all, then any interpretation of Jesus' experience and understanding of God that has been attributed to him through the medium of that address will have to be abandoned. With it will fall the attendant claims to "transhistorical revelation."

The effort to gain theological traction by undercutting the historical foundation on which the theological edifice has been built shows the extent to which Joachim Jeremias's approach and conclusions continue to loom large in discussions of the use of Father for God. And, as we saw in the introduction, numerous theologians have based claims for the continued validity of addressing God as Father on Jesus' own use of that address, underscoring its significance by claiming novelty for it in its context, whether measured against contemporary Judaism or the Old Testament. Because of the influence Jeremias's work has had on subsequent scholarship, it merits at least a brief review here.

## A Review of Jeremias's Argument

While Jeremias's work has cast a long shadow, the irony is that his work is often misinterpreted and misused as a witness for a position that he himself did not advance, namely, that Jesus held and taught a unique and novel view of God as near, loving, and accessible, rather than distant and remote. Jeremias did not argue that Jesus' *view of God* was novel or unique but that Jesus' *mode of address* to God was novel and unique because *his experience of God* was distinctive. For Jeremias, in other words, the cash value of the historical evidence for the uniqueness of *abba* lay not in what it could tell us about Jesus' view of God so much as what it could tell us about Jesus' understanding of his own relationship to God and his mission. Hence, precisely because Jeremias is so often lionized for a conclusion that he did not in fact draw from his evidence, another look at his argument is in order.[13]

Jeremias's position can be set forth in his own words:

---

[13]I am indebted to Dr. Edward M. Cook for his help with technical aspects of the *abba* argument.

In the literature of Palestinian Judaism *no evidence has yet been found* of "my Father" being used by an individual as an address to God. . . . It is quite unusual that Jesus should have addressed God as "my Father"; it is even more so that he should have used the Aramaic form *Abba*. . . . We do not have a single example of God being addressed as *abba* in Judaism, but Jesus *always* addressed God in this way in his prayers.[14]

One should take careful note of the qualifications Jeremias attached to his assertions. He was specifically concerned with texts that met these three criteria: (1) They should stem from *Palestinian* Judaism, Jesus' milieu. (2) They must show an *individual,* rather than a collective body, speaking of God as Father, for this is what we find in the Gospels in Jesus' use of "my Father" and *abba.* (3) The texts needed to show an individual *addressing* God as Father, and not merely speaking about God as a father. Texts that did not meet these three criteria were dismissed. Jeremias contended that texts from Diaspora Judaism were influenced by the Greek example of calling God "Father" (e.g., Sir. 23:1, 4; *3 Macc.* 6:3, 8; Wis. 14:3). Rabbinic prayers to "our Father" manifested a corporate, rather than individual, understanding of God's Fatherhood, and hence did not help to explain Jesus' use of the term.[15] Father imagery *for* God, rather than personal address *to* God, was not a true parallel to Jesus' use of *abba* in prayer.[16] What was new in Jesus' prayer, therefore, was that as an individual he directly addressed God as Father.

Jeremias also noted that Jesus used the Aramaic *abba,* which he understood as the language of children for their fathers. Coupling this fact with the singularity of Jesus' individual address to God, Jeremias concluded:

---

[14]Jeremias, *The Prayers of Jesus* (ET Philadelphia: Fortress, 1967), 57, emphasis his; see also *New Testament Theology,* 65–66.

[15]As is true of the prayers of the Jewish liturgy, the *Ahabah Rabbah,* which begins, "Our Father, merciful Father" and the fourth and sixth benedictions of the Amidah ("Graciously favor us, our Father" and "Forgive us, our Father"). For discussion and examples, see Jeremias, *New Testament Theology,* 62–67.

[16]So, for example, the oft-cited rabbinic text in which children petition Honi for rain: "*Abba, abba,* give us rain!" He said to [God]: "Master of the world, grant it for the sake of these who are not yet able to distinguish between an *Abba* who has the power to give rain and an *abba* who has not" (*b. Ta'an.* 23b). Jeremias points out that while God is compared to an *abba,* he is nevertheless *addressed* as "Master of the world."

> The complete novelty and uniqueness of *Abba* as an address to
> God in the prayers of Jesus shows that it expresses the heart of
> Jesus' relationship to God. He spoke to God as a child to its
> father: confidently and securely, and yet at the same time rev-
> erently and obediently.[17]

It is important to add that Jeremias retracted an earlier view that *abba*
was the language of a tiny child, "baby-talk" or babble—a position that
he himself had once advanced.[18] As James Barr put it in a now famous
essay, *"Abba* Isn't 'Daddy.' "[19] In texts where *abba* occurs, it appears as
the address of an adult to one's father, as Jeremias himself acknowledged.[20] On the one hand, Jeremias writes, "It would have seemed
disrespectful, indeed unthinkable, to the sensibilities of Jesus' contemporaries to address God with this familiar word. Jesus dared to use *Abba*
as a form of address to God."[21] On the other hand, Jeremias also admits
that "even grown-up sons addressed their father as *abba*."[22] So when
Jesus addresses God as *abba*, "the word is by no means simply an
expression of Jesus' familiarity in his converse with God."[23] Unfortunately, the only parts of Jeremias's arguments that tend to be remembered are his stress on *abba* as a child's word that connoted
familiarity—two items that Jeremias himself took pains to qualify.

But in spite of Jeremias's concession at this point, the frequent
homiletical assertion that *abba* meant "daddy" surely comes from

---

[17]Jeremias, *Prayers of Jesus,* 62–63; *New Testament Theology,* 67, 68.

[18]Jeremias, *Prayers of Jesus,* 62; *New Testament Theology,* 67. Jeremias
speaks of "the mistaken assumption that Jesus adopted the language of a tiny
child" and admits "even I believed this earlier" (*New Testament Theology,* 67).

[19]James Barr, *"Abba* Isn't 'Daddy,' " *JTS* 39 (1988): 28–47. Barr (38–39)
acknowledges that Jeremias himself did not argue that Jesus called God
"Daddy."

[20]See Jeremias, *Prayers of Jesus,* 62; *New Testament Theology,* 66.

[21]Jeremias, *New Testament Theology,* 67. So also McKnight, *A New Vision
for Israel,* 61.

[22]Barr (*"Abba* Isn't 'Daddy,' " 35–39) points out that in Galatians 4 and
Romans 8, Paul renders *abba* with *ho patēr,* "father," rather than a diminutive,
such as *patridion* (πατρίδιον) or *pappas* (πάππας), which would be more
natural if *abba* had been so construed. Furthermore, since in Galatians 4 Paul
argues that those under the Spirit have become heirs, hence adults, and have out-
grown the need for the supervision appropriate to a child, to assign to them a
child's word would be curiously out of keeping with the tenor of his argument.

[23]Jeremias, *Prayers of Jesus,* 62.

Jeremias's comments that *abba* was a child's intimate address for one's father.[24] Obviously, any word for father could be a "child's word," depending on how one construes "child."[25] And if *abba* is already attested as an adult's word for one's father, then the view that *abba* is the language of very small children or infants needs to be qualified, if not abandoned. Jesus did not scandalize his contemporaries by the application of "baby talk" to God.[26] Indeed, Jeremias's main point was that Jesus' use of *abba* reveals his consciousness of his special relationship to God, which found expression in the reverent and obedient address to God as *abba,* and that such address expressed his conviction that the eschatological hour of salvation was near.

### Evaluating Jeremias's Position

What, then, are the strengths and weaknesses of Jeremias's arguments regarding Jesus' use of *abba?* It is true that when the Gospels show Jesus addressing God directly, he is always shown as speaking to God as Father, except for the so-called cry of dereliction from the cross—"My God, my God, why have you forsaken me?"—which is a quotation of the opening line of Psalm 22. Although Jesus uses many images for God, including landowner, farmer, master, king, and judge, he never addresses God by any of these terms, not even king, although this is not uncommon in rabbinic prayers. And he never teaches his disciples to use any other form of address. Jeremias was correct, then, to suggest that it would be direct address to God as Father that would prove most fruitful for understanding the significance of the term in the Gospels.

But it is somewhat sobering to be reminded that *abba* actually occurs only *one time,* and in only one Gospel, namely in the prayer of Jesus in Gethsemane as it is recorded in Mark (Mark 14:36). Although both Matthew and Luke report this prayer, each deletes the Aramaic term. In

---

[24]As N. T. Wright, *Jesus and the Victory of God,* 649 n.132 comments, "Jeremias is widely credited with urging that '*Abba* means Daddy'"; he may be responsible at one remove for this misunderstanding, but he never actually asserted it."

[25]Barr, "*Abba* Isn't 'Daddy,'" 34–35.

[26]The one Gospel that shows Jesus' adversaries at all distressed by his reference to God as Father—namely, John—does not even have the term *abba,* where Jesus' offense is his claim to exercise the Father's prerogative to work on the Sabbath (5:17–18).

other narratives of the Gospels, Jesus is recorded as praying to God as Father, but in none of these accounts does the Aramaic term *abba* actually occur. Thus to say, as do Jeremias and others, that Jesus *always addressed God as abba* can mislead if taken to imply that we have numerous examples to support the contention.[27] In fact, the assumption is more properly unverifiable, if for no other reason than that our canonical Gospels come to us in Greek, whereas Jesus almost certainly spoke regularly in Aramaic. In order to argue that Jesus *always* used *abba* in address to God one has to take the single use in Mark as determinative. It is in part the paucity of evidence that led both Trible and D'Angelo to conclude that "*Abba* cannot be shown to have been unique to Jesus, characteristic of Jesus, or even to have been used by Jesus." In a subsequent chapter we will return to the evidence that Jesus did use *abba* for God, but for the moment it will suffice to point out that Jeremias's contention that Jesus "always addressed God as *abba*" is a deduction drawn from the whole gospel tradition rather than merely a descriptive summary of the evidence in that tradition.

The more important issue is what Jeremias claimed for Jesus' use of *abba.* Jeremias rested much of his argument on the observation that in Palestinian Judaism there were no examples of individual address to God as Father, let alone as *abba.* Jesus proved an exception. Not only did he use an otherwise unattested form of address for God, but as an individual he addressed God with a term that connoted familial intimacy. From these two points, Jeremias drew the conclusion that Jesus' address to God indicated his consciousness of his special filial relationship to God.[28] Nearly all of this comprises an argument from silence. Address to God as *abba* is *unattested* in the literature of pre-Christian Palestinian Judaism. Moreover, address to *human fathers* as *abba,* from which the meaning of *abba* as applied to God has been deduced, is similarly unattested in the literature of pre-Christian Palestinian Judaism. Jesus' address to God as *abba* thus has no extant parallels, but neither does *abba* itself. Precisely from the lack of parallels to Jesus' use, Jeremias reasoned to the distinctive character of his use. Clearly Jeremias wished not only to establish the novelty of Jesus' mode of address but also to draw some conclusions about that novelty for Jesus' distinctive

---

[27]Gottlob Schrenk, "πατήρ," *TDNT* 5:985.

[28]For discussion and criticisms of Jeremias's methods and arguments, see also Allen Mawhinney, "God as Father: Two Popular Theories Reconsidered," *JETS* 31 (1988): 181–89.

self-understanding. His approach reflects the then dominant view that the quest for the historical Jesus should begin with that which distinguished Jesus from his sociocultural milieu.

But just here such an approach finds itself at an impasse. For if we have no evidence for the use of the term, how, then, can we draw any conclusions about what it would have meant for Jesus to use it? The term may have been a bold and colloquial way of addressing God, but this is an argument from silence. It is, of course, entirely possible that the term stands out and was remembered because it is Aramaic, rather than Hebrew, and in prayers Hebrew was favored as the appropriate language to address God.[29] In fact, there are texts from Qumran in which God is addressed as "my father," as we shall see in the next chapter, but the term is *abhi,* a Hebrew term meaning "my father." But even if Jesus' use of the vernacular in prayer were the decisive issue, it is still curious that no one is ever shown as objecting to Jesus' use of *abba* because of its startling connotations. In the Gospel of John, Jesus' adversaries do challenge his reference to God as Father (5:18), but in that Gospel *abba* does not appear at all. In the Synoptic tradition, Jesus is challenged on many points, but he is never even queried regarding his use of Father or *abba* for God. In short, the lack of first-century evidence, as well as the relative silence of the Gospels, for the use and meaning of *abba* ought to warn us against rash and dogmatic conclusions about its connotations.[30]

Perhaps the aspect of Jeremias's argument that is most often repeated, even when his basic assumptions about the uniqueness of *abba* are modified or qualified, is that Jesus' use of *abba* articulates his experience of God and that this experience of God provides the clue to his own self-consciousness or sense of identity.[31] But it is surely perilous to extrapo-

---

[29]John P. Meier, *A Marginal Jew: Rethinking the Historical Jesus* (vol. 1: The Roots of the Problem and the Person; New York: Doubleday, 1991), 266 comments that the "clear presence of an Aramaic substratum in many of Jesus' sayings stands in stark contrast to the relative absence of Hebrew words and constructions."

[30]See on this point the caution of Meier, *A Marginal Jew,* 1:174: "Since we are not terribly well informed about popular Jewish-Aramaic religious practices and vocabulary in early 1st century Galilee, modesty in advancing claims is advisable."

[31]McKnight, *A New Vision for Israel,* 61, writes, "Jesus did not come to teach about God; he came to experience God, to dwell in that experience with God, and out of that experience to point others to the kingdom." See also Caird, *New Testament Theology,* 401; Dunn, *Jesus and the Spirit,* 39; T. W. Manson, *The Teaching of Jesus: Studies of Its Form and Content* (Cambridge: Cambridge University Press, 1935; repr., 1959), 108.

late from the text that we have before us to Jesus' *experience of God* and then to Jesus' sense of sonship. In his recent study of religious experience in early Christianity, Luke Johnson suggests that there is a wide register of language in the New Testament that catalogs and refers to *experience* of transcendent power.[32] Nevertheless, Johnson also admits that the category of "human experience" is an extraordinarily difficult category with which to work.[33] As he notes, "Analysis of experience necessarily depends on some sort of report from the one experiencing. . . . Experience is inaccessible except through subjective consciousness and the communication of that consciousness."[34] The problem, of course, is that the Gospels recount nothing that purports to be a "report" from Jesus of his "experience" or "subjective consciousness." We do not know, because we have no evidence for it, that Jesus considered his understanding of God as Father an aspect of his inner experience or that he "experienced" God as Father. The Gospels do not portray Jesus as explaining whence he derived this designation for God.[35] It may have arisen from his personal or inner experience, but to posit personal experience as the origin of the designation and then to argue that Jesus' use of Father gives us direct access to his experience of God is simply a circular argument.[36]

Furthermore, to argue that Jesus' *abba* address renders some aspect of his experience begs the question: What would it mean to *experience* God as Father? What experiences would count in leading someone to call on God as Father? In order to arrive at this conclusion, one would need some sort of framework in which experience could be interpreted in order to speak of it as an experience of God as Father. For Jeremias, the experience was to be lodged to a large extent in Jesus' consciousness of himself as Son, his reverent obedience to God, and his conviction that

---

[32]Luke T. Johnson, *Religious Experience in Earliest Christianity* (Minneapolis: Fortress, 1998), 7.

[33]Ibid., 39–68.

[34]Ibid., 48.

[35]Paul attributes the believer's empowering to call upon God as Father to the Spirit; but that this can immediately be translated to an *experience* of God for Paul, or what that might mean, is less clear.

[36]This is what George Lindbeck calls the "experiential-expressive" theory of doctrine and religion. It characterizes various liberal theologies and, according to Lindbeck, has its origins in Schleiermacher's argument that the source of all religion is "the feeling of absolute dependence." See *The Nature of Doctrine: Religion and Theology in a Postliberal Age* (Philadelphia: Westminster, 1984), 16.

the eschatological hour of salvation was at hand. But even if Jesus did think that he stood in some special or particular relationship to God, there is no reason, self-evident in its context, that he should have couched this in terms of Father and Son. These very terms depend on some prior or other understanding of each term, of himself, and of God, in order to have been used in the first place. To put it this way means that we assume that the content of the terms, or the convictions embodied within them, will have had to make sense in Jesus' own first-century context within Judaism. One of those points which Jeremias regularly underscored was Jesus' reverent obedience to God. But whereas obedience recurs as a prominent theme in Jeremias's discussions of the significance of *abba,* it is typically downplayed by other scholars in their treatments in favor of a stress on the intimacy and accessibility of God as *abba.*

Jeremias needs to be given credit on another score. Jeremias did not argue that Jesus' address to God as *abba* embodied a radically new conception of God.[37] Rather, Jeremias argued that Jesus' conception of God as Father had much in common with the portrayal of God as Father in the Old Testament and Judaism. Jeremias more modestly suggested only that there were new elements in the way Jesus spoke of God's Fatherhood. Jeremias wrote that "the expressions of God's fatherly goodness are *eschatological events,*" and that Jesus gave his disciples, "the community of *the time of salvation,*" a share in his own relationship with God.[38] According to Jeremias, "In Jesus' eyes, being a child of God is not a gift of creation, but an eschatological gift of salvation."[39] It was not a new conception of God that prompted Jesus' use of Father. Instead, Jesus' conviction that God's eschatological salvation was now proffered through his own person and work led him, conscious of this distinctive role and of his unique relationship to God, to address God,

---

[37]Thus Willem A. Van Gemeren wrongly criticizes Jeremias for asserting "that Jesus' teaching on the Fatherhood of God is a completely new revelation" ("*Abba* in the Old Testament?" *JETS* 31 [1988]: 388). It would be more accurate to say that Jeremias has often been misinterpreted and misused as arguing for the uniqueness of Jesus' conception of God, rather than for his consciousness of his special relationship to God.

[38]Jeremias, *Prayers of Jesus,* 43, 63; emphasis added.

[39]Jeremias, *New Testament Theology,* 1:181. So also Richard Bauckham, "The Sonship of the Historical Jesus in Christology," *SJT* 31 (1978): 249.

personally and directly, as *abba*.[40] This important part of Jeremias's argument, which lodges Jesus' use of *abba* not merely in his filial consciousness but in his convictions that God's purposes of salvation were now being brought to a climactic moment, is too often overlooked. *Abba* has been extracted from Jesus' eschatological proclamation that "the kingdom of God is at hand" and turned into a code word to identify God as loving, accessible, and near. For Jeremias, Jesus asserted that God was to be known as Father *within* the particular context of his own ministry. What it means for Jesus to speak of God as Father cannot be separated from the narrative of his mission and life and is illumined both by the scriptures of the Old Testament and the context of Jesus' own day.

Particularly at this point, then, it is puzzling that Jeremias drew so little on the range of the various Old Testament passages in which God is spoken of as Father or addressed in those terms. For a number of the prophetic passages in which one finds address to God as Father either lament the broken relationship between God and Israel or express hope for the restoration of that relationship. Jeremiah, for example, frames the return of the weeping exiles to Jerusalem in terms of God's becoming "a father to Israel" (Jer. 31:9), thus linking Israel's restoration with God's "fathering." And Isaiah sets "our Father" and "our Redeemer" parallel to each other (Isa. 63:16), and appeals to the LORD who is "our Father" to forgo his anger and forgive Israel's sin (64:8–9). Like Jeremiah, Isaiah pictures Israel's rescue from punishment with the image of a father's forgiving love. Whether such hopes can properly be labeled "eschatological" depends to a large extent on one's definition of the term. But these two passages from the prophets point to a future hope, a hope for restoration, and do so by calling upon God's mercy and forgiveness as Father.

Had Jeremias drawn on these passages from the prophets, he would have strengthened his argument that Jesus' use of Father designated the nearness of eschatological salvation. Although Jeremias took pains to underscore the distinctiveness of Jesus' address, a greater appeal to themes from the Old Testament would actually have served to bolster Jeremias's argument concerning the significance of Jesus' own use of Father for God. And the same argument can be made concerning Jeremias's attempts to draw a line in the sand between Jesus' use of Father for God and similar

---

[40]T. W. Manson anticipated much of this discussion in his book *The Teaching of Jesus.* He argued that "the experience of God as Father dominates the whole ministry of Jesus" (102).

practices in contemporary Judaism. If Jeremias had been willing to erase or at least look beyond the edges of that line, he would have found support for his own view on the other side. In numerous Jewish texts in which an individual or the nation is depicted as calling on God as Father, the emphasis falls on God's provision and care, often specifically conceived of in terms of rescue, deliverance, or salvation. God is the Father of those faithful to the one who could be trusted as merciful.

Jeremias was correct in maintaining the essential continuity between Jesus' own view of God as Father with that of the Old Testament, and he rightly lodged the heart of Jesus' use of Father in his convictions regarding the nearness of the hour of salvation. Had he taken the additional step of linking these two assertions together and shown how it was precisely because of Jesus' own convictions regarding the approaching hour of salvation that he spoke to his disciples of God as Father, he might have forestalled the misuse of his work to argue for Jesus' unique and distinctive view of God as near and loving in contrast to the Jewish view of God as distant and remote.

Jeremias also correctly noted that any explanation of Jesus' use of *abba* must account for its appearance in *address* to God. Again, had Jeremias laid greater stress on continuity rather than discontinuity with the Old Testament and voices in Judaism of the day, he would have found the emphases there eminently amenable to his own interpretation of Jesus' proclamation of the nearness of the kingdom of God. Those who address God as Father do so in the hope and expectation of God's rescue and deliverance. They do not offer theological dogma about God; rather, they call on the one who has the power and desire to save them. Address to God as Father thus expresses confidence and trust.

We may agree with Jeremias that Jesus did not teach new doctrines about God. Rather, he announced the inbreaking of God's kingdom and taught his disciples to pray for it as they spoke to God as Father. In prayer, hope for salvation comes to expression in calling upon God as Father. Jesus' preference for *addressing* God as Father fits hand in glove with his conviction that God's promised salvation was now coming to realization. It was not his task to offer treatises regarding the nature of the kingdom but, rather, to proclaim it through word and deed, in reliance upon the one to whom the kingdom belonged and who could be trusted to give bread, not stone, to his children who asked for it (Matt. 7:9–11). In order, then, to grasp the significance of Jesus' discourse regarding God as Father, it is necessary to place it both within the context of scripture and within the context of first-century Judaism. It is to this task that we turn in the next chapter.

# 2

# God as Father
# in the Old Testament
# and Second Temple Judaism

Christian theologians have often accentuated the distinctiveness of the portrait of God as Father in the New Testament on the basis of an alleged discontinuity between the Old and New Testaments. T. F. Torrance spoke of the presentation of God as Father in the New Testament as a "radical deepening of the Old Testament doctrine of God," and J. I. Packer averred that "everything that makes the New Testament new, and better than the Old . . . is summed up in the knowledge of the Father-hood of God."[1] Similarly, biblical scholars have often sketched the differences between the view of God found in the teachings of Jesus and the New Testament and the Jewish context from which they sprang, ending in the observation of the novelty, uniqueness, or superiority of the presentation of God in the New Testament. So Wilhelm Bousset spoke of that which was "most completely original and truly creative" in Jesus' understanding of God, and Gerhard Kittel designated Jesus' view of God as something that was "wholly new."[2] Such contentions arguably depend on a preexisting framework that assumes what is Christian or revelatory must in some way be clearly distinguishable from its historical and theological context.

Old Testament scholars have also insisted that its use of father language for God is not drawn from the conception of God as a father in religions of its historical and cultural contexts. Francis Martin argues that the Israelite notion of God as Father could not have been borrowed from the patriarchal imagery for God of surrounding cultures, because

---

[1]For these quotations, see the Introduction to the present volume, 10–11.
[2]For these quotations, see the Introduction to the present volume, 14–15.

in those cultures the "father God" was "brutish, incompetent, ineffective, and generally inert."[3] Instead, according to Martin, "The source of Israel's belief in God as the Father of his people was their theological reflection on the mystery of God's choice of Israel, expressed in his action by which they were rescued from slavery and given a land." Ironically, other scholars have argued that Israel had to use male and father language for God instead of female metaphors, which were available from surrounding cultures, precisely because the female metaphors were inadequate and even dangerous for use in picturing Israel's unique and transcendent deity. So, for example, Elizabeth Achtemeier argues that inasmuch as it is women who give birth to offspring, female language for God opens the door to an identification of God with creation in ways that promote pantheism and the idolatrous confusion of the creature with the Creator.[4] Depicting God as Father preserves the distinction between Creator and creature in ways in which a depiction of God as Mother cannot.

T. F. Torrance seems willing to allow some use of cultural conceptions of fatherhood to be applied to God, but he distinguishes between the "characteristics" that are used to speak of God's activity from descriptions of God's "very nature," apparently referring to the ontological being of God. In this argument, the language of father is used for the characteristics of God in the Old Testament, but not for the nature of God:

> In the Scriptures of the Old Testament, the power and compassion of God towards his people are frequently described in colorful figurative language reflecting qualities characteristic of the parental authority and care of a human father or mother, but without conceptions of human fatherhood or motherhood being read back into the very nature of God.[5]

---

[3]Francis Martin, *The Feminist Question: Feminist Theology in the Light of Christian Tradition* (Grand Rapids: Eerdmans, 1994), 271. Martin caricatures the surrounding cultures with this description. For a discussion of cultures surrounding Israel and their views of God as father, see the texts and discussion of Rex Mason, *Old Testament Pictures of God* (Regent's Study Guides; Oxford: Regent's Park College; Macon: Smyth and Helwys, 1993), 52–56.

[4]Achtemeier, "Exchanging Gods for 'No Gods': A Discussion of Female Language for God," in *Speaking the Christian God.*

[5]Torrance, "Christian Apprehension of God," 130.

Karl Barth also sought to sever the bonds between conceptions of human fatherhood and God's Fatherhood, or at least to insist that any relationship between those conceptions must give priority to God's Fatherhood. That is to say, it is the understanding of God as Father that sheds light on what it means to be a father, and not the other way around: "We do not call God Father because we know what that is; on the contrary, because we know God's Fatherhood we afterwards understand what human fatherhood truly is."[6] Barth also contended that the doctrine of the Fatherhood of God derives from the fact that God is the Father of the Son, Jesus Christ. "God is unknown as our Father . . . to the degree that He is not made known by Jesus."[7] While Barth acknowledged that the idea of God's Fatherhood is "not entirely unknown" in religious vocabulary, he nevertheless seemed more intent on denying that comprehension of God as Father is in some way illumined by or arises from "the familiar human name of father."[8] Barth's point seems to be that Father is not simply an appellation for God that human beings found appropriate for some reason or other, but that God is the Father of the Son for all eternity. While Barth's argument that the doctrine of the Fatherhood of God rests on the confession that God is the Father of Jesus Christ certainly explains Trinitarian formulations, it does not help to account historically for the designation of God as Father in the Old Testament. By reading the Bible in canonical order, one might come to quite another conclusion regarding the significance of calling God Father—and without subtracting anything from the centrality of Jesus Christ or the significance of the revelation of God as Father in and through him.

One of the worries that comes to expression in the writings of Torrance, Barth, and others is the fear that theology will be reduced to anthropology. If human experience and conceptions are projected onto

---

[6]Karl Barth, *The Faith of the Church: A Commentary on the Apostles' Creed according to Calvin's Catechism* (New York: Meridian Books, 1958), 14. Elsewhere Barth writes, "We must not measure by natural human fatherhood what it means that God is our Father (Isa. 63:16). It is from God's fatherhood that our natural human fatherhood acquires any meaning and dignity it has" (*Church Dogmatics* [ed. Thomas F. Torrance; trans. Geoffrey W. Bromiley; 4 vols.; Edinburgh: T. & T. Clark, 1936–1969], I/1:389; cf. 392–93).

[7]Barth, *Church Dogmatics,* I/1:390. So also Alvin Kimel contends that only the Son can introduce us to his Father ("The God Who Likes His Name: Holy Trinity, Feminism, and the Language of Faith" in *Speaking the Christian God,* 199).

[8]Barth, *Church Dogmatics,* I/1:391.

God, then theology becomes little more than anthropology, and God becomes the one made in our image, rather than the other way around. Other scholars have not, however, been convinced that these are the only options. In his book on *The Language and Imagery of the Bible,* G.B. Caird advances a mediating position:

> Man begins with the familiar situations of home and community and derives from them metaphors to illuminate the activity of God; but the application of these terms to God establishes ideal and absolute standards which can be used as instruments for the remaking of man in God's likeness.[9]

Such a way of framing the problem is much more helpful theologically and historically. When we turn to the Old Testament itself, we find that particular aspects of the father's role or behavior were used to illumine the character and activity of God. In speaking of God as Father, various texts in the Old Testament do not simply use "colorful figurative language" to reflect "qualities characteristic of the parental authority and care of a human father or mother, but without conceptions of human fatherhood or motherhood being read back into the very nature of God."[10] Rather, the distinction between God's "qualities" and God's "very nature" simply does not exist. In speaking of God's mercy, compassion, and love, and the way in which God as Father is turned toward Israel for Israel's salvation and wholeness, we are speaking of the "very nature of God." Moreover, as we shall see in subsequent chapters, even when the New Testament speaks of God as the Father of Jesus Christ, we have not somehow crossed into the territory of speaking of the very nature of God by leaving behind an understanding of God's qualities or characteristics. The very elements of God's Fatherhood in the Old Testament, illumined as they are by the role of the father in Israelite society, provide the substantive framework for understanding the assertions of the New Testament that God is the Father of the Lord Jesus Christ.

However, even granting these concessions, one cannot simply start with "fathers" as a category in general and begin to draw deductions about the character of God. Not all the traits or characteristics of a father apply directly to God as Father. Nor can one start with God and transfer all God's attributes to even ideal fathers. The Old Testament pas-

---

[9]G. B. Caird, *The Language and Imagery of the Bible* (Philadelphia: Westminster, 1980), 178.

[10]Torrance, "Christian Apprehension of God," 130.

sages that do use the image of Father for God can be shown to reflect a view of the human father that comes to light in the biblical texts elsewhere. The following three assumptions about a father in Israelite society shed light on the references in the Old Testament to God as Father. (1) Above all, the father is the source or origin of a family or clan, who as the founding father provides an inheritance to his children. (2) A father protects and provides for his children. (3) Obedience and honor are due to the father, and, hence, when children disobey or go astray, they are corrected or disciplined.

These three aspects of fatherhood recur in various configurations in Old Testament passages where God is pictured as Father. However, the appearance of any one of them in a particular context may imply that God is being represented as a father, even when God is not explicitly described as a father. Of these three characteristics, the first—that the father provides an inheritance to his offspring—would most easily and naturally suggest that a father is in view. Other figures are to be honored; the fifth commandment specifically states, "Honor your father and mother." Proverbs 31 presents the ideal woman as a mother who provides for her family. But in Israelite culture it is the father who provides an inheritance to his offspring. Hence, this particular conception, more than either of the others, indicates a role unique to the father.

Just as one does not need to have all three of these aspects of fatherhood in view to conclude that in a particular passage God is being depicted as Father, one does not necessarily need to have the word "father" present to argue that the image of God as Father lies behind a particular passage, if that passage includes images or descriptions of activities that peculiarly belong to human fathers in that historical context. For example, passages that speak of God's "begetting" of Israel, or that portray Israel as the first-born or beloved son of God, can be taken as implicitly suggestive of God's Fatherhood, because of the way in which these images are otherwise used in the Old Testament with reference to human fathers. However, passages in which the actual term "father" does appear often tend to serve as the most helpful avenues into the depiction of God as Father in the Old Testament.

Still, it is unwise to exaggerate the number of passages that present God as Father. The relative infrequency of the term "Father" for God does contrast sharply with the regular use of the term in the New Testament. But the scarcity of the term as over against the New Testament does not signal radical discontinuity with the presentation of God in the Old Testament. The pattern of usage in the New Testament is obviously more important than the frequency of usage, and, as we shall see, there are important lines of continuity between the Old and New Testaments in the use of Father for God. And, as we shall see in subsequent chapters, the three notes sounded above—that God provides an inheritance, cares for his children, and merits honor and obedience—are central to the New Testament portrayal of God as Father as well. Moreover, these lines of continuity can be traced through various texts of Second Temple Judaism. For although biblical scholars and theologians alike have sought to emphasize the differences between Jesus' view of God and his Jewish context, important lines of continuity run not only from the Old Testament to the New Testament but also from the Old Testament through Second Temple Judaism, to Jesus and the New Testament. Again, to a large extent these common elements lie along the trajectory plotted by the three points already enumerated. The purpose of this chapter is to begin to trace those lines by first looking carefully at some of the Old Testament passages in which God is presented as Father and then to look at the image of God as Father in Second Temple Judaism. If we are inclined to look for continuity rather than discontinuity, we will discover much that is illuminating and useful for understanding the designation of God as Father in the New Testament.

### God as Father in the Old Testament

The Israelites were not the first or only people to picture their God as a father. Extant texts from ancient Babylon and Egypt picture God as a father because he is the creator of all the earth, the father of the king and, in henotheistic religion, the father of all other gods. As Rex Mason comments, "It is not hard to imagine how such an evidently widespread concept of God could have developed. A father was thought of as the procreator, not just of his own immediate children born of his wife or wives, but of the whole family, clan or nation which traces its origins back to him."[11] The human father's chief and primary role is as the ancestor of a clan or family; this role is what makes him a father. As the ancestor of a family or clan, the father begins the line that his children perpetuate.

This aspect of fatherhood characterizes God as Father in the Old Testament as well, albeit in a different way. No passage in the Old Testament pictures God as the physical father of any people or individual. Yet as Jon Levenson notes, kinship language in ancient Israel can express relationship other than the purely biological. Hence to label "father" and

---

[11]Mason, *Old Testament Pictures of God,* 55.

"son" language as purely "metaphorical" can be somewhat misleading.[12] There is a sense in which the predication that God is "father" of Israel is a literal statement. God is the Father of Israel as its founder, the ancestor of the "clan" of the Israelite nation insofar as he brought it into being (Jer. 31:9; Deut. 32:4–6; cf. Deut. 32:18).[13] The Deuteronomist, for example, speaks of God as "the Rock that begot you" (32:18 RSV).[14] While the specific term "Father" is not used, the imagery of "begetting" does fit with other instances of the Bible's use of "father" for God, specifically in applying God's act of "begetting" to God's acts of redemption. However, because it is a mixed metaphor, it prevents a construal in terms of a physical act, inasmuch as a rock does not procreate.

While some passages of the Old Testament speak of God's "begetting" in connection with the creation of all peoples (cf. Isa. 45:9–13), in general the "fatherhood of God" refers neither to God as universal creator nor to some attribute or quality of God. It refers specifically to God's purposes and blessings for Israel (Isa. 63:16; 64:8; Jer. 3:19; 31:9). This is where Israelite faith takes a turn from its neighbors. While it speaks of the one God, creator of all that is, as Father, it limits that Fatherhood particularly to the people of Israel. Although it does not specifically name God as "Father," Hosea contains one of the most cited passages portraying God's paternal love:

> When Israel was a child, I loved him,
> and out of Egypt I called my son. . . .
> [I]t was I who taught
> Ephraim to walk,
> I took them up in my arms;
> but they did not know that I healed them.
> (Hos. 11:1, 3)

Similar is the description of God's instruction to Moses in the book of Exodus, in which God commands Moses to "let my son go," rather than the more familiar "let my people go."

---

[12]Jon Levenson, *The Death and Resurrection of the Beloved Son: The Transformation of Child Sacrifice in Judaism and Christianity* (New Haven: Yale University Press, 1993), 40.

[13]Mason, *Old Testament Pictures of God,* 52; Jeremias, *The Prayers of Jesus,* 13.

[14]The text also speaks of the "God who gave you birth," imagery that pictures the woman's role rather than the father's role. Because it is set in parallelism to "the Rock that begot you," it also refers to the creation, through acts of deliverance, of the people of God.

> [Y]ou shall say to Pharaoh,
> "Thus says the LORD: 'Israel is my firstborn son. . . .
> Let my son go that he may worship me.'"
>                                         (Exod. 4:22–23)

These passages portray God as a deliverer of Israel, the "firstborn" or beloved son or child. Other passages make explicit the link between God as Father and God as Redeemer.

> Look down from heaven and see,
> from your holy and glorious habitation.
> Where are your zeal and your might?
> The yearning of your heart and your compassion?
> They are withheld from me.
> For you are our father,
> though Abraham does not know us
> and Israel does not acknowledge us;
> you, O LORD, are our father;
> our Redeemer from of old is your name.
>                                         (Isa. 63:15–16)

Similar, too, is Jeremiah's highly charged description of the "return" of the exiles, both to their land and to their God:

> With weeping they shall come,
> and with consolations I will lead them back,
> I will let them walk by brooks of water,
> in a straight path in which they shall not stumble;
> for I have become a father to Israel,
> and Ephraim is my firstborn.
>                                         (Jer. 31:9)

It is the relocation of the terminology of "begetting" (and "birth") to the sphere of redemption that renders impossible any understanding of God's act of "begetting" in physical terms, or even in connection primarily with the act of creation. Furthermore, the imagery serves to place the emphasis on God's initiative in the calling of Israel.[15] Even as a child plays no role in her own conception, or birth, neither does Israel figure in its own calling, a point that is further underscored by setting the image of God as Father in parallelism with the image of God as a potter:

---

[15]Mason, *Old Testament Pictures of God,* 56.

> Yet, O Lord, you are our Father;
> we are the clay, and you are our potter;
> we are all the work of your hand.
> Do not be exceedingly angry, O Lord,
> and do not remember iniquity forever.
> Now consider, we are all your people.
>
> (Isa. 64:8–9)

The act of calling a people is the prerogative of God. However, as this passage also illustrates, that act of calling is pictured as an act of love and grace. Indeed, it becomes the basis for the present appeal to God to forgive the sins of the people.[16]

In its presentation of God as Father, then, the Old Testament regularly interprets the act of "begetting" in terms of redemption or calling out a people, rather than as an act of creation. To be sure, a people is "created" or constituted by God's act of calling or begetting, but God's Fatherhood is not construed in terms of bestowing physical life. Hence of the three aspects of fatherhood that are instructive for thinking of God as Father in the Old Testament, we find that the first—that a father is one who is the "ancestor" or head of a family line—plays an important role. But it is interpreted by locating the act of "begetting" in redemption rather than creation, by limiting the "begetting" to a particular people, Israel. Thus a construal of God as Father already carries with it from the Old Testament into the New Testament the *particularity* of God's Fatherhood. The view that the Bible teaches the universal Fatherhood of God would find no foothold here.

This, then, is part of that first aspect of God's Fatherhood as outlined above. But it has an inseparable corollary. For to think of God as the head of a clan or family also implies that God bequeaths an inheritance to his offspring. Not only does the God who is Father call a people together, but the relationship does not end there. For just as a human father provides an inheritance to his firstborn son (Zech. 12:10; Mic. 6:7; Gen. 49:3; Exod. 13:15), so God provides Israel, God's "firstborn," with an inheritance (Jer. 3:19; 31:9; Isa. 61:7–10; 63:16; Zech. 9:12).

---

[16]Paul Ricoeur takes this forward-looking emphasis as determinative for construing the significance of God as Father in the prophets. The prophets looked toward a future kingdom of God, in which the Father was a figure of "futurity and hope" ("Fatherhood: From Phantasm to Symbol," in *The Conflict of Interpretations: Essays in Hermeneutics* [ed. Don Ihde; Evanston: Northwestern University Press, 1974]).

The inheritance is passed down from father to son—to *one* son—as an exclusive birthright. Some of the most poignant and memorable narratives of the Old Testament pivot around the births of heirs and the rights of inheritance that those heirs possess. One such account is the central narrative of God's promise of an heir to Abraham (Gen. 12:1–3; 15:1–6), the births of Ishmael (Genesis 16) and Isaac (Genesis 21), and the conflict between their mothers, expressed particularly in Sarah's hostility to Ishmael's right to inherit (Gen. 21:10). Isaac's own sons, Jacob and Esau, are caught in the same conflicts. Jacob first dupes Esau of his birthright (Gen. 25:29–34) and then cheats his older brother of his rightful paternal blessing (Genesis 27). Similarly, Israel is portrayed as the firstborn son who has the rights of inheritance. That Israel is God's heir may indicate the joy and pride that a parent has in a child, and so when applied to Israel, call to mind God's particular love for Israel. In this sense, the begetting or creation of a people is closely linked with its status as the heirs of an inheritance, for it is only those who are "begotten" of God who are also the heirs of the Father. Inasmuch as "begetting" is tied to redemption or deliverance, rather than creation, the act of redemption and of the giving of an inheritance belong more closely together when speaking of God as Father than when speaking of human fathers and their offspring.

The exact nature of the inheritance, however, may vary. Most typically, the inheritance that is in view is the land of Canaan (e.g., Exod. 32:13; 34:9–10; Lev. 20:24; Num. 16:14; 26:53–56; Deut. 1:38; 4:21; 4:38; 12:10; 16:20; 25:19–26:1; Josh. 11:23; 13:6–8; 1 Kgs. 8:36; Ps. 105:11; Lam. 5:2–3). As God's "firstborn," Israel inherits the land. However, sometimes Israel is itself spoken of as God's inheritance (Deut. 26:9; 1 Sam. 10:1; 1 Kgs. 8:53, 2 Kgs. 21:14; Isa. 19:25; Jer. 10:16; Mic. 7:18; Zech. 2:12), showing the distinctive relationship between Israel and God in contrast to the other nations of the earth and underscoring the prerogatives that God grants to Israel. At other times God is spoken of as Israel's portion or inheritance (Ezek. 44:28), especially with reference to the Levites or priests. The tribe of Levi has no share in the land, for their inheritance is the Lord (Num. 18:20–24; Deut. 10:9; 12:12). Thus although the image of the inheritance varies, the distinctive relationship between God and Israel, as portrayed through the giving and receiving of that inheritance, remains constant.

Because of his love, a father protects, disciplines, and provides for those who are his children. This is the second of the three aspects of God's Fatherhood listed earlier. God is the "father of orphans and protector of widows" (Ps. 68:5; 27:10), who "gathers me up if father and

mother forsake me" (Ps. 27:10). This God has compassion "as a father
has compassion for his children" (Ps. 103:13). This aspect of God's
Fatherhood, coupled with the imagery of God's "begetting" of Israel,
also provides the basis for hope for the future.[17] As Father, God not only
has "begotten" Israel but also has compassion upon his sometimes wayward firstborn. Both in Jeremiah and in the last part of Isaiah, the exiles
call upon God as Father in distress and hope for deliverance and return
to the land (Jer. 31:9; Isa. 63:16). Interestingly, at Isaiah 63:16 and 64:8,
the Targum translates "father" as "he whose mercies upon us are more
than a father's upon sons," thus not only avoiding the anthropomorphic
implication of God actually "begetting" offspring but also highlighting
one of the characteristic activities of God captured in the epithet Father.
As Father to Israel, God is merciful, compassionate, and abounding in
steadfast love. The evidence for God's mercy toward Israel can be found
in the redemption from Egypt, the provision in the wilderness, and the
giving of the law (*Tg. Isa.* 63:16–18). At Isaiah 64:8 the Targum translates "you are our potter" as "you are our creator," which might seem at
first glance to suggest a universal application of God's Fatherhood. Yet
the context indicates that it is God's actions with respect to Israel,
including the desolation of Jerusalem, that lead to the appeal for God to
be merciful again.[18]

But although love, compassion, and pity are attributed to the ideal
father, the final effect is not a sentimentalized portrait of that father.
"Father" finds its place in a relationship in which "father" and "children"
are not equals; this is not a democratic relationship of peers. Fathers
require obedience and honor, and a father was also accorded the task of
discipline and correcting his children (Prov. 1:8; 4:1; 6:20; 15:5;
30:17).[19] The command to "honor one's father and mother" (Exod. 20:12)
has a parallel in the command to honor God, as the following passage
from Malachi aptly shows: "A son honors his father, and servants their
master. If then I am a father, where is the honor due me? And if I am a
master, where is the respect due me? says the LORD of hosts" (Mal. 1:6).

The passage from Malachi further shows that fathers are also viewed

---

[17]Mason, *Old Testament Pictures of God,* 65–66.

[18]Whatever the date of the *Isaiah Targum* or traditions in it may be, its stress
on the mercy of God as Father, as demonstrated in the redemption from Egypt,
is not an innovation but a reflection of ideas elsewhere in the Old Testament, as
well as in other Jewish literature.

[19]On this point see Anthony A. Myrick, " 'Father' Imagery in 2 Corinthians
1–9 and Jewish Paternal Tradition," *TynBul* 47 (1996): 163–71.

as those who instruct and discipline the wayward. The graciousness and kindness of the father in no way eliminate his status and authority as one to whom obedience and faithfulness are owed.[20] This, then, is the third aspect of God's Fatherhood delineated earlier. In a number of passages where God is described as the Father of Israel, the image underscores both God's call to obedience and, often, Israel's lack of it (Hos. 11:1, 3, 4; Jer. 31:9, 18, 20; cf. Prov. 3:11–12). So Jeremiah upbraids the people for casually addressing God as Father and assuming him to be "the friend of my youth," while having "done all the evil that you could" (3:4–5).

> Have you not just now called to me,
> "My Father, you are the friend of my youth—"

Again in Jeremiah 3:19, the prophet laments in the name of God,

> I thought
> how I would set you among my children,
> and give you a pleasant land,
>     the most beautiful heritage of all the nations.
> And I thought you would call me, My Father,
>     and would not turn from following me.[21]

In Deuteronomy, we read this reproof:

> Do you thus repay the LORD,
> O foolish and senseless people?
> Is not he your father, who created you,
> who made you and established you?
>                                                      (32:6)

A similar theme can be found in Hosea. Although Hosea does not explicitly speak of God as Father, nevertheless the prophet does speak of Israel as God's child who, in spite of all God's compassion, love, and mercy, refused to obey God (Hos. 11:1–8). The themes of God's love, and Israel's disobedience, along with the reference to Israel as God's

---

[20]Mason, *Old Testament Pictures of God,* 68; Jeremias, *Prayers of Jesus,* 11–12, states that the two aspects of God's fatherhood stressed in the Old Testament are God's tenderness and "absolute authority."

[21]At both Jeremiah 3:4 and 19, the Targum substitutes "my Lord" for "my Father." Robert Hayward, the editor of the Targum, comments, "The two titles are close: cf. 'Father of the World' and 'Lord of all the Worlds.' "

son, indicate that God is portrayed here as a father who with determination and love seeks his erring child.

Even as Israel owes its Father obedience, they are in turn obligated to deal faithfully with others who name the same Father. In Malachi 2:10, the queries "Have we not all one father? Has not one God created us?" serve as the basis for an appeal to faithfulness among members of the covenant community: "Why then are we faithless to one another, profaning the covenant of our ancestors?" Thus while Father language indicates authority, the primary realm in which this is to be construed is not that of the relationship of the individual to God, nor is the relationship between Father and children to be understood primarily hierarchically. God's Fatherhood relates primarily to the corporate entity of Israel, and that framework implies the obligation of the children to each other.

One final aspect of God's Fatherhood in the Old Testament deserves mention. The covenant of God with Israel is sometimes focused in the promises to the king. The relationship between God and the king is often depicted as the relationship of father and son. So, for example, God's promise to David, delivered through Nathan the prophet, is that God will establish the kingdom of David's son: "I will be a father to him, and he shall be a son to me. When he commits iniquity, I will punish him with a rod such as mortals use, with blows inflicted by human beings" (2 Sam. 7:12–16). Perhaps the most succinct expression of this father-son relationship of God and the king is found in Psalm 2:

> "I have set my king on Zion, my holy hill."
> I will tell of the decree of the LORD:
> He said to me, "You are my son;
>    today I have begotten you.
> Ask of me, and I will make the nations your heritage,
>    and the ends of the earth your possession."
>                                                   (2:6–8)

While God is not here explicitly referred to as Father, he does address the king as "my son" and refers to his "begetting" the king, as well as to his willingness to give him all the nations as his inheritance. This application of "son" to the king shifts the focus from God as the Father of all Israel to God as the Father of one individual. However, insofar as the king also serves as the head and representative of a people, the corporate element of God's Fatherhood is not necessarily eliminated. Such texts are, however, something of an anomaly when set against the rest of the Old Testament passages.

In sum, in the Old Testament the designation of God as Father pertains primarily to the relationship between God and Israel. Israel is God's firstborn child and, as such, is also God's heir, who receives from God the promised inheritance, portion, or share of God's blessings specifically intended for Israel. God provides, cares for, and sometimes also disciplines Israel in its disobedience. As Father, God merits honor and obedience. Obviously individuals are implicated in these statements, but the various promises and injunctions focus on the relationship of the people to God, what God has done for them, and on their obligations to each other within the community. The one notable exception to the idea that God is the Father of the people, but not of individuals, is the relationship of God and the king, but even here the king functions as a representative of the people. As we turn to the literature of Judaism, we will find, not unexpectedly, that it is these biblical themes which are adopted and sometimes modified in portraying God as Father.

## God as Father in Second Temple Judaism

In the literature of Second Temple Judaism there are texts that both characterize and invoke God as Father.[22] This simple fact is important to note, given the apparently common assumption that the New Testament view of God as Father was somehow novel, presenting God in a way hitherto unimagined. Jeremias's arguments about Jesus' address to God as Father inadvertently contributed to this picture, inasmuch as he dismissed virtually all the texts cited below as irrelevant to his point. And, indeed, as we shall see, many of these texts do not fit the criteria set forth by Jeremias, and so they played little or no role, except negatively, in his discussion of Father in the prayers of Jesus. In the abbreviated survey of some of the literature of Second Temple Judaism offered below, we will see that in a variety of texts God was referred to or addressed as Father and that such usage tended to be grounded in the

---

[22]Texts that speak of God as the Father of an individual or portray an individual addressing God as Father include Wis. 2:16; 14:3; Sir. 23:1, 4; 51:10; *3 Macc.* 6:3, 8; *Jub.* 19:29; 4Q460 5 I, 5; 4Q382 55 II, 1–9; 4Q379 6 I, 1–7; *Jos. Asen.* 12:8–15. Texts that speak of God as the Father of the nation include 1 Chr. 29:10 (LXX); Tob. 13:4; Wis. 11:10; 1QH IX, 35; *Ant.* 2.6.8; *3 Macc.* 2:21; 5:7; 7:6; *Jub.* 1:25, 28; *Apocr. Ezek.* fragment 2.

[23]Dieter Zeller, "God as Father in the Proclamation and in the Prayer of Jesus," in *Standing Before God: Studies on Prayer in Scriptures and in Tradition with Essays in Honor of John M. Oesterreicher* (ed. Asher Finkel and Lawrence Frizzell; New York: KTAV, 1981), 119.

special election of Israel by God.[23] Moreover, the notes of authority and mercy continue to be sounded as well. As Father, God's authority is to be acknowledged in obedience; God's mercy may be depended upon in times of distress or need. Clearly these texts thus show themselves beholden to the picture of God as Father in the Old Testament.

The book of Tobit contains this description of God as Father:

> Blessed be God who lives forever,
>> because his kingdom lasts throughout all ages.
> For he afflicts, and he shows mercy. . . .
> Acknowledge him before the nations, O children of Israel;
>> for he has scattered you among them.
>> He has shown you his greatness even there.
> Exalt him in the presence of every living being,
>> because he is our Lord and he is our God;
>> *he is our Father and he is God forever.*
> He will afflict you for your iniquities,
>> but he will again show mercy on all of you.
>
> (13:1–5)

This passage places "Lord" and "Father" in parallel, underscoring the authority of the Father. Other functions or actions traditionally associated with God as the Father of Israel are here as well: God disciplines, but God also shows mercy.

We may also refer to *3 Maccabees,* for there, when the Jews were prepared to be trampled by elephants, they called upon "the Almighty LORD and Ruler of all power, their merciful God and Father" (6:2–3). Because God is "almighty" and "ruler of all power," he is able to deliver; because he is Father, his mercy may be sought. In this same document, God is spoken of as the one who "oversees all things, the first Father of all, holy among the holy ones" (*3 Macc.* 2:21; cf. 6:8, 28; 7:6). God is "first Father," implying that he is the source or origin "of all," and he "oversees all," implying his universal sovereignty. The emphasis on "all" and on God as "first Father" gives some clue to the polemical edge of these claims. The emphasis on the universal scope of God's Fatherhood and sovereignty are features of Jewish monotheistic polemic. Inasmuch as Zeus is routinely referred to as "father of gods and mortals," the reference to Israel's God as the "first Father of all" scores a point for the uniqueness of Israel's God. In the depiction of the Creator as Father, we do encounter something of a difference from texts of the Old Testament, which do not forge such a link. The difference lies not in an understanding of God's activity or person, for clearly the

Old Testament portrays God as Creator as well, but in the use of Father to refer to the creative activity of God. Even so, in referring to God's relationship to Israel, *3 Maccabees* does refer to "*their* merciful God and Father," subtly alluding to the particular relationship that exists between God and Israel.

*Jubilees* also speaks of God as a Father to Israel. God's Fatherhood is primarily manifested in God's authority to command and the Israelites' willingness to obey, a state of affairs that will be realized only when God creates a new spirit for the Israelites: "And they will do my commandments. And I shall be a father to them, and they will be sons to me. And they will all be called 'sons of the living God.' . . . I am their father in uprightness and righteousness. And I shall love them" *(Jub.* 1:23–25).[24] Later in the same book, Abraham offers this prayer for his son, Jacob: "May the Lord God be for you and for the people a father always and may you be a first-born son" (19:29), indirectly alluding to the promise of God to Israel, here pictured as God's "firstborn."

Until recently, the sole text quoted from Qumran as providing evidence that God was thought of or addressed as Father in that community was 1QH IX, 35–36, "Thou art a Father to all the sons of thy truth," a text that again manifests the corporate understanding of God's Fatherhood. But in more recently published scrolls there are additional references to God as Father, and these references include direct, personal address to God in prayer (Hebrew *abhi*). There is, for example, a prayer attributed to Joseph, "My father and my God, do not abandon me in the hands of the gentiles, do me justice, so that the poor and afflicted do not die."[25] At least two texts contain address to God as "my father," although the language of address is still Hebrew. In light of these texts, Jeremias's argument regarding the uniqueness of Jesus' individual address to God as Father would have to be modified somewhat, although Jesus' use of the *Aramaic* term *abba* is still without parallel.

Another document that contains several references to God as Father

---

[24]In *Pss. Sol.* 17:26–32, the Messiah brings together for God a holy people who are all "children of God."

[25]See Eileen Schuller, "*4Q372* 1: A Text about Joseph," *RQ* 14/55 (1990): 343–70; and Schuller, "The Psalm of 4Q372 1 Within the Context of Second Temple Prayer," *CBQ* 54 (1992): 67–79; and the discussion in Nunnally, "The Fatherhood of God at Qumran."

is the *Testament of Job,* in which the references are to be found above all in prayers (33:3, 9; 40:2–3; possibly 47:11; 50:3).[26] Similarly, in the book of Sirach, we find personal and individual invocations to God as Father in prayers for assistance and mercy (Sir. 23:1, 4).[27] In these prayers, the individual petitioner addresses God as "Lord, Father and Ruler of my life" and "Lord, Father and God of my life" and so lodges all three designations for God in the personal sphere. God is conceived of as Lord, Father, and God of "my life."[28] The use of Father for God, particularly in Sirach, stands alongside the frequent affirmation of God as "Maker" of the individual (47:8; see also 10:12; 32:13; 33:13.) Although God is thus identified as the Maker of the individual, Sirach's vision clearly encompasses God's creation of the world, as well as his providential superintendence of its workings. God is creator (15:14; 17:1; 18:1; 24:8, and passim), who filled the earth with good things, including life and health (16:30; 34:20; 39:25); there is no other God (36:5) than the Lord who is God of the ages (36:22), who lives forever (18:1). But what we do not have in Sirach is a corresponding universalizing sense of God as Father. Although terms such as Lord, God, and Maker apply to God both in the universal and individual sense, father appears to be used only in relationship to individuals. However, that statement must be qualified in light of the command, found elsewhere in Sirach, "Be a father to orphans, and be like a husband to their mother; you shall then be like a son of the Most High, and he will love you more than does your mother." These texts conceive of God as the Father of Israel, or perhaps more specifically, as the Father of all righteous Israelites.[29] In this regard, the text from Wisdom 2:13–20 may be noted, where the unrighteous person "boasts that God is his father" (2:16), whereas the truly righteous child of God will be delivered by God.

But in Josephus and Philo we do find another tendency, namely, the

---

[26]Bruce Chilton notes that the locution appears to be conventional ("God as 'Father' in the Targumim, in Non-Canonical Literatures of Early Judaism and Primitive Christianity, and in Matthew," in *Judaic Approaches to the Gospels* [International Studies in Formative Christianity and Judaism 2; Atlanta: Scholars Press, 1994], 57–60).

[27]As R. P. Spittler notes, " 'Father' is used of God . . . as the Father of individuals at least since Ecclus. 23:4 (cf. 23:1)" ("Testament of Job," *OTP* 1:855, n. 33g).

[28]Jeremias ruled this text out of consideration because of his reconstruction of the Hebrew as "God of my father" rather than "God, my father" (*New Testament Theology,* 1:64).

[29]Henry J. Wicks, *The Doctrine of God in the Jewish Apocryphal and Apocalyptic Literature* (New York: KTAV, 1971), 344.

tendency to designate God as Father of all human beings. Josephus designates God as Father in order to portray him as the source or creator of all living things. Although Josephus does refer to God as the Father of Israel (*Ant.* 5.93, "Lord and Father of the Hebrew race"), he more typically has in view the universal application of the title, as for example in referring to God as "father and source of the universe, as creator of things human and divine" (*Ant.* 7.380; 4.262). God is "the Father of all" (*Ant.*1.230; 2.152), the "universal Father who beholds all things" (*Ant.* 1.20). In such epithets, Josephus echoes the Homeric characterization of Zeus as "Father of gods and human beings" (e.g., *Iliad,* 15.47), rather than the more typical Old Testament designation of God as the Father of Israel or the Father of the righteous.

The use of Father to designate God's role as the "source of the universe" and creator of all things is found also in Philo.[30] God is the sole uncreated—hence eternal—being, and so necessarily the source of the life of the world (*Her.* 42.206). God is Creator and Maker of all (*Spec.* 1.30; *Somn.* 1.76; *Mut.* 29; *Decal.* 61); the "cause of all things" (*Somn.* 1.67);[31] as well as Father;[32] and Parent (*Spec.* 2.197). Because God created all that is, God is therefore the Father of all human beings: "Created things, in so far as they are created, are brothers, since they have all one Father, the Maker of the universe."[33] God's Fatherhood therefore pertains to the creation of the world, rather than to the salvation of specific persons, whether that salvation be construed corporately, as the people of Israel, or individually, in terms of specific righteous individuals.[34] But precisely in these emphases, Philo stands out from rather

---

[30]In the Sybilline Oracles, God is several times referred to as one who begets; hence, "the great Begetter" (3:295); "the one who has begotten all" (3:550); "the immortal begetter" (3:604).

[31]See *Decal.* 52: "The transcendent source of all that exists is God."

[32]The Father: *Spec.* 2.197; *Opif.* 74, 76; *Mut.* 29; "Father of all things, for he begat them," *Cher.* 49; "Father and Maker," *Opif.* 77; "Father and Maker of all," *Decal.* 51.

[33]Philo, *Decal.,* 64–65.

[34]In rabbinic literature, God is the Father both of the nation and of righteous individuals. God loves and educates, cares for and protects them. There is an emphasis on God's mercy. In a noteworthy parallel to Luke 6:36, the *Jerusalem Targum I* on Lev. 22:28 reads, "My people, children of Israel, as our Father is merciful in heaven, so you shall be merciful on earth." Israelites call to their Father in times of peril for assistance, for rain, or for forgiveness. There is also an emphasis on obedience to the will of the Father in heaven (*Tg. Onq.* Deut. 32:6; *Tg. Yer. I* Deut. 32:6; *Song Rab.* 2:16 §1; *m. 'Abot* 3:14; *Num. Rab.* 17 on Num. 15:2; *Mek. Exod.* 14:19; *Exod. Rab.* 46.4–5 on Exod. 34:1; *m. Sotah* 9:15; *Tg. Yer. I* Exod. 1:19). For discussions of these and other passages, see Zeller, "God as Father," and D'Angelo, "*Abba* and 'Father.'"

than reflects the more typical emphases of either the Old Testament or Jewish thought of the day.

## Summary Remarks

There are two distinct ways of construing the Fatherhood of God in these texts of Second Temple Judaism. On the one hand, Josephus and Philo link together the ideas of God as creator and as Father, thus allowing and assuming the universal scope of God's Fatherhood. God is Father of all because God is creator of all.[35] A second group of texts characterize God as Father in relationship to the faithful, specifically in terms of God's care, mercy, love, discipline, and the obedience that is owed in turn. Some of these texts do indicate that individuals understood the Fatherhood of God in a personal way, rather than a "corporate" way. Although the evidence may not be overwhelming, it is, as Richard Bauckham once put it, "a little more impressive, when assembled, than Jeremias seems to admit."[36] In other words, there is evidence in Second Temple Judaism that God was thought of and addressed as the Father of the faithful, whether the faithful be construed as Israel or as the righteous individual within Israel.

Thus texts that envision God's Fatherhood in terms of creation have in view the universal scope of God's life-giving activity, whereas texts that refer God's Fatherhood to redemption also have a particular focus, namely, the people of Israel or those who belonged to Israel. But whether God is understood to be Father of all, or the Father of the faithful, it is the conviction that God is the origin and source of existence that provides the rationale for thinking of God as Father. Where God is appealed to as the Father of all the living, it is because God is the origin of their existence, the source of their life. Where God is appealed to as the Father of Israel, it is because God has called them into being, created or established them as a people. By extension, this understanding applies when God is taken to be the Father of the faithful within Israel.

But whichever view is adopted, all authors agree that because God is Father, God is owed obedience and honor. Indeed, for Philo and Josephus, God's Fatherhood becomes the ground to call all people to obedience and worship. Several other themes run throughout many of these texts. God as Father is understood to be not only the source of life but

---

[35]In the New Testament, several texts reflect the view that as "Father" God is the source of all that is (1 Cor. 8:6; Eph. 2:18; 3:14–19; 4:6; 5:20, 6:23).

[36]Bauckham, "Historical Jesus in Christology," 247.

also the one who bestows an inheritance upon those who are his children. In the collective "our Father," as well as in the sectarian appropriation of "fatherhood," the idea of a peculiar and exclusive relationship between a father and his heir may also be applied to the community. As Father, God is understood to exercise mercy and discipline toward his children, whom he also cares for and delivers. Typically, then, God is addressed as Father in petitions when people are in peril or need.

Thus the identifying characteristics of fatherhood, which shape the imagery of God as Father in Jewish literature, are derived from the world of kinship, family, and inheritance. To reiterate briefly, the father is, first, the source or origin of a family or clan and provides an inheritance to his children. Whereas in the Old Testament the inheritance is most often the land itself, in later Jewish sources the inheritance varies. For example, in Sirach the law is the inheritance that God grants to Israel (so also *1 En.* 99:14). Elsewhere, one inherits eternal life (*Pss. Sol.* 14:10, *1 En.* 40:9; cf. *2 En.* 50:2; *2 Bar.* 44.13), a usage that finds resonance in New Testament texts and in the question, "What must I do to inherit eternal life?" (Mark 10:17; Luke 10:25; 18:18). Second, a father protects and provides for his children. Third, a father is a figure of authority to whom obedience and honor are properly rendered. And because obedience and honor are due to the father, when children disobey or go astray they are corrected or disciplined.

These characteristics of a human father are used to depict God's relationship to Israel in the Old Testament, or to the remnant within Israel. And while these characteristics mirror the function and roles of human fathers within Israel, they are not used to provide human fathers an explicit model after which to pattern their own fathering. Nor is male gender in some way "ontologized" into the being of God, as if that which were "male" or "masculine" in and of itself served to render the biblical God more faithfully. When God is characterized with "male" or "masculine" imagery, these attributes are not derived from characteristics inherent in the male gender but, rather, from a specific set of functions which were appropriate to fathers in that Israelite culture.

The same features of God's Fatherhood are also found in the New Testament, and in the following chapters we turn to examine its witness. Because of the important role that Jesus' own use of the language of father has played in biblical and theological scholarship, we will begin first with the witness of the Gospels. The Gospels depict Jesus' speaking of a new family gathered about him, a family that honors the Father and does his will. Jesus promises that the heavenly Father will provide for his children as a father provides bread for his children. And Jesus speaks of the kingdom as an inheritance that God gives to them. This tapestry is woven with threads that come from the pages of the Old Testament, and reappear in Jewish literature contemporary with Jesus. We turn, then, to the Gospels, in order to examine more closely their witness to Jesus' appropriation of the biblical imagery of God as Father.

# 3

# Jesus and the Father

At the heart of much of the current theological debate regarding the significance of calling God Father lies Jesus' own use of the term. If part of our aim is to discover Jesus' own practices of speaking to and about God, and the convictions that come to expression in those practices, we may find the goal not so easy to attain. For each of the Gospels reflects a different pattern in its depiction of God as Father. John, for example, uses the imagery of Father/Son over 120 times, suggesting that it was central to Jesus' public and private discourse. But in Mark God is referred to as Father only four times. Could one conclude from such a record that Jesus made the term central to his ministry? Could one even infer much at all about Jesus' use of the term? Similarly, Matthew has numerous sayings in which Jesus uses the possessive form, "my Father," while John prefers the absolute "the Father" or "the Father who sent me." Can we with confidence draw conclusions about Jesus' preferred form of reference to God, let alone what can be inferred from it, especially since we are already dealing with traditions in their Greek form? While Joachim Jeremias made much of the fact that Jesus regularly *addressed* God with the familiar Aramaic *abba,* only one Gospel, Mark, actually uses *abba,* and then only one time. While Matthew, Luke, and John all contain more instances of direct address to God as "Father" or "my Father," none of them records the Aramaic *abba.* In short, no two Gospels provide exactly the same picture of Jesus' address or reference to God as Father.

The mixed nature of the evidence from the Gospels throws into sharp relief two primary questions: (1) What is the evidence that Jesus called God Father, and that the form of address that Jesus used was the Aramaic *abba*? (2) Assuming for the moment that Jesus did indeed call upon God as Father, then what is the significance of the Fatherhood of God for Jesus? The agenda for this chapter is set by these two questions.

The significance attributed to Jesus' use of the term ranges along a spectrum. On the one end there lies the view that Jesus' address to God as Father was decidedly new, even countercultural, in its day. Jesus applied to God a familial designation that betokened his unprecedented familiarity and intimacy with God. Somewhat differently, Elisabeth Schüssler Fiorenza and others have held that Jesus' view of God as Father was countercultural in that it undercut the very structures of patriarchy and hierarchy that it seems to embody. Moving along the spectrum a bit, we find the view that Jesus did not introduce a new designation for, or understanding of, God in calling him Father, but that he made this designation central to his mission and teaching.[1] Clearly what these views share is the assumption that Jesus did indeed call God Father; and most also hold that the term that he probably used for God was *abba*. On the other end of the spectrum, however, we find a bald denial that Jesus used the designation Father for God at all. One might speak of the significance that the term Father had for the early church and its witness to Jesus, but the discussion would stop there.[2] Hence the twin questions regarding Jesus' use of the term Father and the significance of the term are closely related to each other, and it is these two interrelated questions that we shall pursue here.

At the outset of this chapter, however, a note of explanation is in order. These questions, as framed above, lead us into the territory typically occupied by "the quest for the historical Jesus," the attempt to derive a portrait from the Gospels of Jesus "as he really was." Anyone familiar with the course of New Testament studies in the last two centuries will be aware that this "quest for the historical Jesus" has yielded little agreement about the appropriate methods for undertaking it or about the resultant reconstruction of Jesus. My point in this chapter is not to "get behind the Gospels" in order to put a reconstruction of Jesus' ministry in their place nor, more specifically, to suggest that we can find what Jesus "really meant" when he called God Father,

---

[1]Scot McKnight, *A New Vision for Israel*, 55, asserts, "There is nothing in Jesus' use of *abba* that was not also known in Judaism . . . What he meant by *abba* is what it meant in Judaism. The centrality he gave it, however, reserved for it a special significance among his followers."

[2]Most notably, Mary Rose D'Angelo, "*Abba* and 'Father': Imperial Theology and the Jesus Traditions," *JBL* 111 (1992): 611–30.

assuming for the moment that he did indeed do so. Rather, in light of the Old Testament and Jewish texts that speak of God as Father, as well as our knowledge of first-century Judaism more broadly speaking, we may suggest how Jesus' address to God as Father fits within the context of his ministry as it is portrayed in the Gospels. Such an investigation can at least prohibit us from reaching hasty conclusions about the substance and significance of Jesus' designation of God as Father. So while the twin questions about Jesus' own use of Father and its significance set the agenda for the chapter, they do so as much to show where our answers must remain suggestive, and where we must admit what we do not know.

### Did Jesus Speak of God as Father?

The first question posed above, whether Jesus spoke of God as Father or as *abba,* arises in part from the mixed evidence of the Gospels. The nature of the evidence has led some to challenge the contention that Jesus used Father at all. So, for example, in her discussion of the Gospels, Mary Rose D'Angelo contends that they cannot support the conclusions that Jeremias and others have drawn from them.

> *Abba* cannot be attributed to Jesus with any certainty. It was certainly of significance in the early Greek-speaking Christian communities of Paul and Mark, where it expressed empowerment through the spirit. It may have originated or been of special importance in the Syrian communities, where Paul began his career and which many scholars see as the venue of Mark. . . . "Father" as an address to God cannot be shown to originate with Jesus, to be particularly important to his teaching, or even to have been used by him.[3]

D'Angelo also concludes, in contrast to Jeremias, that "if Jesus indeed used the title 'father' for God, he did so *with* rather than against the stream of Jewish piety."[4] She then goes on to discuss the increasing frequency of Father language for God in early Christianity:

> It is clearly the case that "father" increased in importance in early Christianity. It is placed on the lips of Jesus in Matthew

---

[3]D'Angelo, "*Abba* and 'Father,'" 630.
[4]Ibid., 613.

and Luke, significantly more frequently than in Mark and Q. There can be little doubt that development of Christology was the most significant factor in the importance of "father" in Christian theology.[5]

What emerges from D'Angelo's study is a sketch of the development of the Christian tradition that places the increase in the language of Father for God alongside the development of christological speculation. Because Jesus is increasingly spoken of as the Son of God, God is naturally spoken of as Father. However, the roots of this development cannot be traced back to the practice of Jesus himself.

D'Angelo's conclusion stands diametrically opposed to the research of Jeremias and those who argued that Jesus' use of the Aramaic *abba* for God gave rise to the church's subsequent practice. The question remains, then, whether it is possible to adjudicate between these two views and on what basis one might do so. In order to assess such competing conclusions, New Testament scholars developed the so-called criteria of authenticity to determine the probability that a particular element of the gospel tradition can be traced to Jesus himself. Quite a number of these criteria have been proposed at one time or another, and they have rightly come up for criticism and review for a variety of reasons. The point here is not to open the particular issue of the validity of the criteria again but simply to note that by these criteria a good case can be made for the authenticity of Jesus' use of Father for God.

### The criterion of multiple attestation

The so-called criterion of multiple attestation holds that an element of the Gospels that is spread across multiple sources has greater claims to authenticity. Father is used for God in multiple sources (Mark, Q, M, and L). Of the four references to God as Father in Mark, two (11:25; 13:32) reappear in the same form or in a variant in Matthew, and the other two (8:38; 14:36) reappear in both Matthew and Luke. This material includes a reference to the Son of Man coming in the glory of his Father (8:38); a command to forgive others as God forgives (11:25); reference to the knowledge that the Father, but not the Son, has (13:32); and the prayer in the Garden of Gethsemane (14:36). From Q there is not only the (contested) saying regarding the mutual knowledge of Father and Son (Matt. 11:25–27; Luke 10:21–22) but also the query about a father's provision for his children (Matt. 7:9–11; Luke 11:11–13), and the promise that the

---

[5]D'Angelo, "*Abba* and 'Father,'" 622.

heavenly Father will provide for his children as he does for the grass and the birds (Matt. 6:25–34; Luke 12:22–31). Luke, or Luke's source, contributes several sayings linking the Father and the kingdom (e.g., 12:32; 22:29–30) and the Father and the Spirit (11:13; 24:49). And of course there is also the parable of the prodigal son, justifying Jesus' table fellowship with outcasts and sinners, and Jesus' prayers from the cross. Matthew's distinctive material includes a parable about two sons asked to work in the vineyard by their father (21:28–32), a command to call no one but God "Father" (23:8–10), and the parable of the last judgment, in which those "blessed by my Father" are invited by Jesus to "inherit the kingdom" (25:31–46). The material is not only drawn from multiple sources but also appears in multiple forms of the gospel tradition, including parable, prayer, apocalyptic sayings, and ethical exhortation.[6]

Statistical analysis alone, however, does not establish the case. What makes the case for Jesus' use of Father more compelling is that in those various sources and forms, the designation Father for God is associated regularly with a limited number of motifs. Those motifs include (1) the promise of God's provision for his children, (2) the concomitant call for those who are God's children to demonstrate impartial love and generous forgiveness of others, (3) the particular role of the Son in bringing or mediating the kingdom, and (4) petition to God as Father especially, but not only, in times of need.

The limited scope of Father language merits attention for two important reasons. First, the consistent and limited use of Father language suggests that Father has not simply been inserted arbitrarily into any and all contexts in the Gospels but is, instead, associated with a limited number of themes. Second, precisely in the link between those particular themes and the Fatherhood of God, the Gospels stand in continuity with the portrait of God as Father in both the Old Testament and various sources of Second Temple Judaism. For in those sources, God is the Father who bequeaths an inheritance to his children, provides for and cares for them, and expects obedience in return. In the Gospels, the inheritance that the Father provides is the kingdom, rather than the land or the law. Jesus promises that God will provide for those who seek the kingdom. Therefore, he also addresses God as Father, teaching his disciples to do the same. And he calls upon them to do the will of God, particularly in imitation of God's impartial and generous love and forgiveness. This second point—that the Fatherhood of God in the Gospels

---

[6]Except in John, "father" plays little or no role in the miracle tradition.

has definite links with certain themes found in the Old Testament and Jewish sources—leads us to a discussion of a second "criterion of authenticity," the so-called criterion of dissimilarity.

### The criterion of dissimilarity

The most notorious of the criteria of authenticity is certainly the "criterion of dissimilarity." Through application of this criterion to the Jesus tradition, scholars expected to determine which elements of the tradition were historical by isolating those elements which were novel or distinctive with respect either to first-century Judaism or the early church. In other words, elements of the tradition that had no precedent in first-century Judaism and that could not be shown to have made a significant impact on the developing traditions of the early church could with greater confidence be attributed to Jesus himself. The problems with this peculiar criterion have often been pointed out. For one thing, although the criterion was deemed to be rigorously historical, it actually makes nonsense of historical study altogether. Few historians, outside of New Testament specialists, treat their subjects by assuming that they hover above their historical, social, and cultural contexts, or that what is "historical" is precisely that which can be explained neither by historical context nor have given rise to subsequent historical developments. The criterion of dissimilarity ignores just these points in holding that what is genuinely historical is also that which is novel. Thus the criterion already assumes what it sets out to establish.

Even though the criterion has rightly fallen on hard times, the basic assumption that what was novel in Jesus' teaching provided the most direct access to his own sense of mission and purpose has played an important role in investigation of Jesus' understanding of God as Father. Many scholars have stressed the distinctive nature of Jesus' understanding of God as Father with respect to the Old Testament or Jewish conceptions. Jeremias placed a premium on the value of Jesus' use of *abba*, because as a form of address to God it was otherwise unattested in first-century Judaism.

By contrast, D'Angelo contends that Jesus' use of the term *abba* reflects that he was swimming *with* rather than *against* the streams of Jewish piety of his day.[7] She is not alone in this conclusion. Recently Scot McKnight put it this way: "There is nothing in Jesus' use of *abba* that was not also known in Judaism."[8] This conclusion reflects a trend

---

[7]D'Angelo, *"Abba* and 'Father,'* " 613. It should be remembered, however, that D'Angelo deems it unlikely that Jesus actually used the term.

[8]McKnight, *A New Vision for Israel,* 55.

toward situating Jesus more firmly within his own historical context, rather than in somehow trying to account for his mission by removing him from that context. This trend, which may even be said to be something of an emerging consensus in studies of Jesus today, places Jesus squarely within his first-century context in two ways.

First, it assumes that the primary historical context for understanding Jesus is first-century Palestinian Judaism. Jesus' actions, words, and the responses to him must make sense from within this context. This does not mean that Jesus did not adapt, modify, or create new symbols, challenge important tenets of first-century Jewish convictions, or offer new interpretations of the religious traditions of Judaism, including appropriate ways of speaking to and about God. But the traditions are those of first-century Judaism, and those who wish to argue for "newness" or "novelty" need first to understand Jesus' context and place him in his proper setting. This is just what Jeremias sought to do in arguing for the novelty of *abba*. In his attempts he was considerably more judicious than others who projected an enormous gulf between first-century Judaism and Jesus' own understanding of the God of Israel.

Second, while Jesus' actions and words should be interpreted from within their context in first-century Judaism, they must also be interpreted so as to explain credibly the rise of the early church. This is not to claim that theological developments did not occur within the early Christian community. Even so, one should expect to find discernible lines of continuity from Jesus to the church. Indeed, it is strange to have gotten to a place in New Testament studies where such continuity is assumed to be the exception, rather than the norm. But in E.P. Sanders's memorable application to the Gospels of a proverbial saying, where there is smoke there is fire.[9] Perhaps as much may be gained, then, by looking at the "smoke," the evidence for the use of Father outside the Gospels, as there is by staring at the fire, hoping to find yet one more spark to be fanned into flame.

The question of the development of the tradition needs careful attention in the current discussion about Jesus' use of Father as well as the use of Father for God in the New Testament. Earlier in the chapter we cited the conclusion of Mary Rose D'Angelo that the application of Father to God became increasingly important in early Christianity,

---

[9]E. P. Sanders, *Jesus and Judaism* (Philadelphia: Fortress, 1985), 3.

being placed on the lips of Jesus in Matthew and Luke significantly more frequently than in Mark and Q. She writes, "There can be little doubt that development of Christology was the most significant factor in the importance of 'father' in Christian theology."[10] In other words, the development of christological thought goes hand in hand with an increased attribution to God of the role or title of Father. The "higher" the christology, the more one finds God called upon as Father. This is arguably the case in the Gospel of John. But it is not necessarily borne out by the rest of the New Testament.

### The theological development of the tradition

Upon close examination, the lines of theological development do not run so smoothly or directly as one might expect. Interestingly, while Matthew and Luke do show an increase in the *frequency* of the use of Father for God, especially vis-à-vis Mark, the distinctive material in Matthew and Luke is not uniformly more christological, in the sense of always serving the articulation of a "higher" Christology. In fact, the evidence is curiously mixed. Matthew and Luke, but not Mark, contain quite a lot of material with a decidedly *communal* and *ethical,* rather than a more narrowly christological, focus, which elaborates the significance of God's Fatherhood for the community of disciples. God is Father of the community gathered around Jesus; and this relationship creates and shapes the commitment that those in the community owe to each other. By contrast, the Gospel of John—which clearly contains the greatest frequency of Father for God, and purportedly manifests the "highest" Christology as well—limits the Father–Son relationship almost exclusively to Jesus. It is as if Matthew and Luke develop the implications of God's Fatherhood for the community, whereas John presses the significance of God's Fatherhood in relationship to the Son.

But the span of time between the Gospels does not account adequately for the differences in the tradition. Granting that Mark was used by both Matthew and Luke some 10 to 15 years after it was written, that length of time is scarcely adequate to account for the striking difference between Mark's material, with but scant evidence that Jesus spoke of God as Father, and Matthew and Luke's evidence that

---

[10]D'Angelo, "*Abba* and 'Father,'" 622.

Jesus did so regularly—and did so particularly with his disciples in view. Moreover, because Mark postdates the Pauline correspondence, where Father and Son appear regularly for God and Jesus, the later date of Mark raises a large question mark against the theory that christological speculation and designation of God as Father belong together. At least if Paul's designations of God and Jesus as Father and Son were known to Mark, he felt under no obligation to incorporate them regularly into his account of the life of Jesus. Similarly, John's decided preference for limiting Son to Jesus and virtually eliminating all elements of the tradition that point to God as the Father of the community that gathered around Jesus might be labeled a "development"; but it is not a development that flows directly out of the sorts of traditions enshrined in Matthew and Luke. In fact, it is closest to Mark in its presentation of God as Father and Jesus as Son. It seems unlikely that "early" and "late" considerations alone will help answer questions regarding Jesus' use of *abba* or Father for God.[11] It seems, rather, that from the beginning there were different emphases with respect to God's Fatherhood in the traditions about Jesus and that these have been used and developed in varied ways.

Luke-Acts and Paul provide indirect evidence that Father or "my Father" was characteristic of Jesus' address to God. In the Gospel of Luke, as already noted, Jesus both addresses God as Father and teaches his disciples to pray to the Father. But after the first two chapters of Acts, in which the Father fulfills the promise to send the Spirit (1:5, 8; 2:33), God is not again referred to, either in prayer or in any other way, as Father. That God is Father is never the subject of the apostles' public proclamation or teaching in Acts. The situation is nearly the same as with Jesus' use of "Son of Man." "Son of Man" appears in the Gospels only on the lips of Jesus (with one exception, John 12:34), but it virtually disappears from the rest of the New Testament (cf. Acts 7:56; Heb. 2:6; Rev. 1:13; 14:14). Similarly, while Jesus speaks of God as "my Father," no one else in the Gospels does so, nor does Jesus commend this particular form of address to others. They pray "Father" or "our Father," but no individual speaks of God

---

[11]D'Angelo seems to assume that because Mark and Q are the earlier written sources, they also enshrine the oldest traditions, or that Matthew and Luke will always reflect greater "development." But this does not necessarily follow. For discussion, see Dale C. Allison, *Jesus of Nazareth*, 19–20.

as "my Father."[12] Outside the Gospels, "my Father" appears only in the words of Jesus (Rev. 2:27; 3:5, 21). Believers call upon God as "Father" or "our Father," but the form of address is never explicitly individualized.

Moreover, as we shall see, the use of "our Father" in Paul is relatively limited—not in terms of frequency, but in terms of its scope or application—occurring primarily in confessional or liturgical formula, blessings, and prayers. "Our Father" and "the Father" do not simply usurp the place of all other designations for God, or of the more common *theos* (θεός; God). Outside the Synoptic Gospels, the New Testament does not bear witness to the proliferation of Father imagery for God but, rather, to a disciplined appropriation of the terminology in keeping with the main motifs also found in the Gospels. Inasmuch as the Gospels postdate the majority of the Pauline letters, as well as a number of other documents in the New Testament, it could be that the Gospels reflect usage already developed in the early Christian church; that is, that they merely reflect what is already in Paul. But a more plausible hypothesis, in light of the restricted use of Father in Paul and its virtual disappearance in Acts and other New Testament books, is that the usage was deemed characteristic of Jesus and thus was taken over in continuity with Jesus' own usage. Hence, the persistent use of "our Father" and the absence of "my Father" from the rest of the New Testament may suggest that both could be traced back to Jesus, with "our Father" as a form of address commended to his followers, and "my Father" limited to Jesus himself. In either case, the preferred form of address includes a personal, possessive pronoun, indicating that "Father" is primarily a relational term.

## The contexts of Jesus' use of Father

These data argue against the theory of a proliferation of the term Father as an arbitrary substitute for God or a number of other epithets and titles for God. Rather, Father is particularly apposite for the relationship of Jesus to God, in speaking of God's giving or granting the kingdom to his children, for the language of prayer, and as a warrant for

---

[12]The one possible exception is found in the parable of the prodigal son, where in thinking over his situation the son says, "I will get up and go to my father." Yet when the son imagines what he should say, he begins, "Father, I have sinned," thus speaking to his father as Jesus admonished his disciples to address God (Luke 15:18, 21; 11:2).

the community's conduct toward each other. In other words, Father appears in the Gospels relative to its context, and not simply as the new designation of God. Not surprisingly, then, there are also parables of the kingdom in which the primary image is of a farmer, sower, landowner, master, moneylender, a baker woman, shepherd, and so on. Again, these designations for God are used when a particular image suits the context. If the parable concerns growth or harvest, then the main character may be a sower or farmer. If a saying has to do with forgiveness of debts, then perhaps a moneylender or master plays the key role, and so on. Father is not the fountain from which spring up all other terms for God but a form of address or image that is used in conjunction with certain conduct in specific contexts. Those contexts include direct address to God as Father in prayer and in exhortations to trust in God and to treat each other mercifully. These contexts underscore both the relational nuance inherent in the term as well as the originating role of the Father with respect to that community. Parents are the source of the family's existence, and the father is the originator of a line and the one who possesses the name and inheritance to bequeath to his descendants. Address to God as Father thus acknowledges the fundamental and inescapable duality of the relationship both to God and to brothers and sisters in the family.

We may speak not only of the contexts appropriate to the use of Father but also of the historical milieu of such address. In Jesus' socio-historical milieu, numerous circumlocutions were used in place of the proper name of God. Interestingly, then, first-century Judaism also had its own discussion about the proper means of addressing and "naming" God. The name of God, derived from God's self-revelation to Moses in the burning bush (Exod. 3:14), which was not to be pronounced except by the High Priest on the Day of Atonement, came to be read as *Adonai* or *ha-shem* ("the name"), because it was deemed too holy to utter. Similarly, when Jesus speaks of doing something "in the name of" God, or prays that God's name "be hallowed," he both refers to the holy name of God and follows first-century Jewish custom by using a well-attested substitute for that name. Such practices contribute in part to the impression that first-century Jews thought of God as aloof and distant, who could be spoken of only with circumlocutions ("the Place," "the Name," "Heaven," "the Blessed"). Even the phrase "kingdom of God" or "kingdom of heaven" is an indirect way of speaking of God, with particular respect to God's sovereignty. However, even when numerous substitutes or circumlocutions are used in place of the name of God, and used more frequently and as direct address, they are not regarded as usurping the holy name of God. God is addressed in countless other ways, but never directly by his own holy name.

Jesus provides for his disciples a way of addressing God that is personal and relational but that does not violate the sanctity of the holy name of God. Father is a circumlocution for the proper name of God that speaks of God not in terms of an attribute—such as holiness, sovereignty, or power ("the Holy One," "King," or "the Almighty")—but in terms of a relationship that can be described in terms characteristic of a father. Jesus' use of Father thus also places him squarely within the practices of first-century Judaism which addressed and spoke of God in ways appropriate to his character ("all merciful one"), attributes ("all wise God"), or power ("all powerful one"). Jesus uses the term Father because of his convictions that God's relationship to Israel could be described with the imagery of particular texts of the Old Testament that portrayed God as a loving and forgiving Father.

Of course this argument assumes that Jesus did use Father for God and that he instructed his disciples to do so as well. These conclusions seem difficult to doubt. For in spite of their differences, the Gospels manifest a high degree of consistency in their different depictions of God as the Father of Jesus and of his disciples. The Gospels uniformly witness that Father is the term that Jesus used to address God and that he instructed his disciples to pray in this manner as well. Jesus may have used other forms of direct address for God, but they are not attested in the Gospels. He promised his followers God's provision and a share of the kingdom that God would give, and he commanded them to manifest the same mercy to others that the Father had shown to them. In short, they were to live as children of the heavenly Father. Whether or not the case can be regarded as proved, the evidence tips the balance in favor of Jesus' use of Father for God. We shall take up at greater length the significance of the Fatherhood of God for Jesus below. But first we may ask whether the evidence also tips the balance in favor of the conclusion that Jesus used the Aramaic *abba* for God.

### Did Jesus use Abba?

According to Joachim Jeremias, *abba* was Jesus' preferred and exclusive mode of address to God. In light of such a broad claim, it may be somewhat surprising that he is actually shown addressing God as *abba* only one time, in Mark's account of the prayer in the Garden of Gethsemane. The most suggestive piece of evidence for Jesus' use of *abba* may well lie in the appearance of the term not in the Gospels but in the Pauline epistles (Gal. 4:6; Rom. 8:15). These letters actually provide our earliest attestations of the Aramaic term *abba* in the vocative case, whether for God or a human father.[13] What is particularly arresting about the appearance of *abba* in these Pauline letters is the use of an Aramaic word in Greek epistles written to predominantly Gentile churches. The retention of the Aramaic in Mark and Paul needs to be explained. It cannot, of course, be ruled out that the language goes back only as far as the Aramaic-speaking Christian church.[14] But Mark also retains and then translates a number of Aramaic terms, primarily in the words of Jesus (3:17; 5:41; 7:11, 34; 14:36; 15:34; the two exceptions are 10:46 and 15:22). Although not impossible, it is a stretch to argue that the Aramaic-speaking church first used Aramaic words of healing (*talitha cumi, ephphatha*) and that from that point these words were passed on to the Greek-speaking church and simultaneously or later retrojected into Jesus' own speech. The case holds for Jesus' use of *abba* as well. On the whole, then, it is a more likely hypothesis that the Aramaic-speaking church cherished this form of address to God in prayer because of its origin in Jesus' own mode of address to God. Because it was known as Jesus' mode of address, it was also explained to and used by (at least some) Greek-speaking congregations as well.[15] John Meier's argument with respect to the language that Jesus spoke illuminates the current question:

> If Jesus regularly spoke in Greek, one is hard pressed to explain the tenacious survival of the Aramaic address to God, *abba,* even among Paul's Greek-speaking Gentile converts in Asia Minor (Gal. 4:6)—to say nothing of Gentile Christians in Rome who had never met Paul (Rom. 8:15). The most reasonable explanation is that *abba* represents a striking usage of the Aramaic-speaking Jesus, a usage that so impressed itself on and embedded itself in the minds of his first disciples that it was handed on as a fixed prayer-formula even to the first Gentile believers.[16]

But what can be inferred from Jesus' use of *abba* is less certain. As was pointed out earlier, it is common to attribute Jesus' use of *abba* to his experience of God. The following quotation is representative:

---

[13]Joseph A. Fitzmyer, "*Abba* and Jesus' Relation to God," in *À Cause de L'Évangile* (Études sur les Synoptiques et les Actes; Paris: Cerf, 1985), 28–30.
[14]This is essentially D'Angelo's conclusion.
[15]Fitzmyer, "*Abba* and Jesus' Relation to God," 31–32.
[16]Meier, *A Marginal Jew,* 1:266.

Jesus' experience of God was the experience of a person with his or her father. . . . [Jesus] came to experience God, to dwell in that experience with God, and out of that experience to point others to the kingdom. . . . It is probably this experience (not the teachings about *abba*), and the effects it had on his disciples, that led to the use of *abba* in early Christian worship.[17]

Feminist theologian Elizabeth A. Johnson similarly speaks of Jesus' "*abba* experience."

From the way Jesus talked about God and enacted the reign of God, it is obvious that he had a special and original experience of God as intimate, close, and tremendously compassionate over human suffering and sin. Out of that experience Jesus surfaced a name for God, namely *Abba*. . . . Jesus' own personal experience of God as close and compassionate led him to name God in this very intimate way, *Abba*. The name evokes the power of a very close relationship between Jesus and the One he names this way. Furthermore, Jesus teaches others to call God *Abba,* encouraging them to trust God the way little children trust a good parent to take care of them, be compassionate over their weakness, and stand guard against those who would harm them. Jesus' *Abba* experience is at the heart of the matter, the dynamism behind his preaching the reign of God and of his typical way of acting. God *Abba* was the passion of his life.[18]

Johnson thus places a portrait of a compassionate God at the heart and center of Jesus' experience, so that it also may serve as the center of his mission and proclamation and so become the way in which his followers relate to God as well.

But there is a serious difficulty with drawing too direct a line between *abba* and Jesus' experience of God.[19] In the first place, the statement that *abba* encapsulates Jesus' "experience of God" is a sheer assertion that could be neither verified nor falsified. If it were true, how would we know it? If one can assume that calling God Father means that one has a certain sort of experience of God, then can we also assume that every instance in the Old Testament or Jewish literature in which

[17]McKnight, *A New Vision for Israel,* 62.
[18]Elizabeth A. Johnson, *Consider Jesus: Waves of Renewal in Christology* (New York: Crossroad, 1990), 57.
[19]See also the discussion in chapter 1, 30–32.

God is spoken of as Father points to an "experience of God" and, if so, the same experience that Jesus had? As N. T. Wright puts it,

> It is doubtful whether one can actually *start* with the expression 'Abba', found as it is in only one gospel text, and build upon it a whole theory as to the uniqueness of Jesus' experience of, and teaching about, Israel's god. However, it should not be supposed that Jeremias has been disproved completely: there *is* a striking phenomenon to be observed in the prayers of Jesus, and, once we relieve it of the strain of being the load-bearing wall in a much larger construction, it can relax and make a valuable contribution to a different one.[20]

Even if Jesus' address to God as Father (or *abba*) reflects his practice and arises out of his own experience of God, that fact still does not tell us *how* Jesus "experienced" God, or why he used Father in the first place. The mode of address is not self-interpreting, and its significance cannot be derived from that address itself. In other words, we have too little specific data regarding Jesus' "experience" to make the category central in unpacking Jesus' use of Father for God or for coming to the conclusion that his experience was the *source* of his understanding of God as Father. The church's confession that Jesus is the Son of God rests not on Jesus' "*abba* experience," as though it were his "God-consciousness" that gave rise to such confession, but on the conviction that the entirety of Jesus' life, death, and resurrection bore witness to this fact.

While we do not have access to Jesus' experience, we do have the scriptures with which he was familiar and a number of Jewish texts that suggest how God's Fatherhood was understood in various contexts during Jesus' own lifetime. In the Old Testament and Jewish literature contemporary with Jesus, we have at least some data—and very important data at that—that shed light on the significance of Jesus' address to God as Father. These scriptures, and Jewish sources that reflect them in various ways, provide a framework for analyzing the Gospels that could easily suggest that the source of Jesus' convictions that God could be known and trusted as a Father was as much the scriptures of Israel as his own personal experience. Just as Jesus is elsewhere shown quoting from and interpreting the Old Testament as the framework for his own mission and work, and just as the core symbol of the "kingdom of God" has its roots in the language, piety, and hopes of the Old Testament, so

---

[20]Wright, *Jesus and the Victory of God,* 649.

also Jesus' usage of Father for God is consonant with the image of God as Father in the scripture. Jesus used the term Father not in spite of or because of its absence from the Old Testament but because of its presence in the texts that he knew and read as scripture.[21]

The following discussion is not a full-blown presentation of "the historical Jesus" or even of every aspect of the Father/Son language of the Gospels. Instead, the discussion intends to show how Jesus' use of Father language for God fits within the framework of "restoration eschatology," that understanding of first-century Jewish eschatological hope which has become central in recent reconstructions of the historical Jesus. In the Gospels, eschatological hopes are articulated in different ways, primarily but not exclusively in terms of the kingdom of God. One way of expressing the reality and hope of God's eschatological salvation is to speak of God as Father. To speak of God as Father and of God's fatherly provision and love is not somehow to tame the God of the kingdom but, rather, to offer another metaphor for speaking of God's saving activity with respect to Israel.

## Jesus and the Father

In spite of the frequent use of Father, in no Gospel does Jesus make the "Fatherhood of God" the subject of lengthy explanation. There are no exhortations urging people to think of God in a new way as a gracious and merciful Father. There are no antitheses in which Jesus introduces his own convictions regarding God in contrast with those generally or previously held: "You have heard it said . . . but I say to you that God is your heavenly Father." There are, of course, parables in which a father plays an important role, most notably Luke's parable of the prodigal son, and in this parable Jesus obviously intends his hearers to construe the Fatherhood of God in a particular way. But the fact that in the Gospels Jesus seems to assume, rather than to defend or explain, God's Fatherhood suggests that such address to God made sufficient contact with familiar ideas so as to be understandable to Jesus' original audiences.

With some confidence we can venture to say that these ideas were drawn from the Old Testament and that they also made contact with those views that are manifested in contemporary Jewish literature. Earlier we suggested three primary aspects of God's Fatherhood that come to expression in these sources: (1) God is the Father of Israel as

---

[21]So also John Riches, *Jesus and the Transformation of Judaism* (New York: Seabury, 1982), 149–50.

the one who called it into being and would give it its inheritance as his heir. (2) As the Father of Israel, God loves and cares for Israel. (3) God expects from Israel the honor and obedience appropriate to a parent, as even the Decalogue specifies; therefore, God also corrects and rebukes Israel when it is disobedient in order to nurture a more faithful obedience.

These three themes do not appear in the Gospels in the form of lists, any more than they do in the Old Testament. Rather, the evidence of the Gospels is that Jesus' use of Father for God testifies to his convictions that as the Father of Israel, God was now carrying out his promise to give Israel its inheritance, calling Israel to renewed obedience, and was prepared to discipline his people in preparing them to receive their inheritance. In a nutshell, Jesus' address to, and designation of, God as Father reflected his conviction that his mission was to announce the renewal and restoration of Israel, promised by God in the scriptures, and to call people to repent and reorient their lives to God. To turn in obedience to God, to honor God fully, to rely on God's provision—all as one would in relationship to one's father—was to seek the kingdom of God above all else. Although Jesus issued his call to all Israel, it is evident from the ample material in the Gospels, which includes warnings of judgment and of the division of Israel, of the separation of wheat and tares, sheep and goats, good and bad fish, good and bad fruit, that Jesus did not expect all Israel to respond to his call (Luke 12:49–53; Matt. 10:34; 11:23). The "renewal of Israel" would bring into being the "messianic remnant," the "core of the messianic people to be," the "remnant and first fruits of messianic Israel."[22]

The articulation of the hope for Israel's renewal found expression in the prophets in various ways, but at least sometimes it was expressed in terms of the relationship of God to Israel as a father relates to his children. The prophet Jeremiah laments the broken relationship of God and Israel with a sorrowful complaint:

> I thought
> > how I would set you among my children,
> and give you a pleasant land,
> > the most beautiful heritage of all the nations.
> And I thought you would call me, My Father,
> > and would not turn from following me.
> > > > > > > (Jer. 3:19)

---

[22]Ben F. Meyer, *The Aims of Jesus* (London: SCM, 1979), 210, 219.

Later Jeremiah celebrates the return of the exiles to Jerusalem in terms of God's becoming "a father to Israel" (Jer. 31:9), thus describing Israel's restoration as the act of God as Father. And Isaiah places "our father" and "our Redeemer" side by side (Isa. 63:15–16), imploring the Lord who is "our Father" to forgo his anger and forgive Israel's sin (64:8–9). Like Jeremiah, Isaiah pictures Israel's rescue from punishment with the image of a father's forgiving love. These two passages point to a future hope, a hope for restoration, and do so by calling upon God's mercy and forgiveness as Father and by inviting trust in God.

Jesus appropriates the prophetic language of God as Father to articulate his vision of God's faithfulness to Israel, as well as his call to repent and trust in the one who sustained Israel's very existence. In Jesus' call to Israel, the constancy of God's fatherly care and provision are assumed; but now Israel is called to respond with appropriate honor, obedience, and trust. By addressing God as Father, and instructing his disciples to do likewise, Jesus renews and reframes the prophetic vision with reference to those who would follow him. This, then, is in part what it means to speak of Jesus' appropriation of the eschatological vision of the prophets.

This is the same vision that Jesus articulates in his proclamation of the kingdom of God, the proclamation that God was now acting to call together a people who would live in renewed obedience to his sovereign will, expressed in love and mercy one to the other.[23] Jesus' ministry would gather together "the lost sheep of the house of Israel" in accordance with the prophetic promises of the Old Testament. Jesus spoke of God's imminent judgment in terms of division, winnowing, harvest, and separation. Because of the approaching judgment, the time for repentance and renewed obedience to God could not be postponed. Judgment would entail a reversal of status and of the situation of the

---

[23]This understanding of Jesus' ministry can be found in numerous proponents of the so-called Third Quest of the historical Jesus, including Ben F. Meyer, *The Aims of Jesus* (London: SCM, 1979); E. P. Sanders, *Jesus and Judaism* (Philadelphia: Fortress, 1985); N. T. Wright, *Jesus and the Victory of God* (Minneapolis: Fortress, 1996). Ben F. Witherington, *The Jesus Quest: The Third Search for the Jew of Nazareth* (Downers Grove: InterVarsity, 1995). Dale C. Allison, *Jesus of Nazareth: Millenarian Prophet* (Minneapolis: Fortress, 1998), and many other works. Not all these authors treat Jesus' eschatological expectations in exactly the same way, but they share the belief that Jesus is best understood as an "eschatological prophet" who promised God's imminent "restoration" of Israel and renewal of the covenant with it.

powerful and meek, the rich and the poor, suggesting a reordering of the values that would characterize life in God's kingdom. God's judgment would thus create a new people out of the old. Jesus chose twelve apostles as representatives of this new community, the restored Israel, and spoke of a new covenant, evoking both the exodus from Egypt and the giving of the law as the guide for life in the covenant community, as well as Jeremiah's promise of a renewed covenant. In light of the promise of that renewed covenant, Jesus interpreted the law, distilling its heart in the double love command, and so sketched the contours of the life that was expected of his followers. He expected the coming of the spirit of renewal; he promised a new world and told his followers that they would have a share in it.[24] Those who were his disciples would "inherit the kingdom," a hope whose realization lay yet in the future and hence could also be formulated in terms of the promise of eternal life. Such language does not consign the promised inheritance entirely to the future, but it does not allow it to be received fully in the present either.

What could be spoken of in terms of a promised kingdom or renewed covenant, the demand for obedience, and the warnings regarding judgment could also be expressed with reference to God as Father. Now the language is not that of kingdom but of a new family and of God's fatherly love and provision. The call for obedience issues not from an authoritarian eastern sovereign but expresses the parental right to honor, as well as the parental exhortation to love one's brothers and sisters, to live in community in such a way that mirrors the expectation of the one who is Father. Warnings regarding judgment and punishment belong in the context of parental discipline, correction, and nurture.

But the depiction of God as Father is not an alternative vision to be set over against that of God as sovereign or transcendent, as though to think of God as Father made God's sovereignty or transcendence tolerable. Rather, to speak of God's Fatherhood shows how God's sovereignty and transcendence were always expressed in relationship to Israel. Thus the Fatherhood of God is not to be understood primarily as an inner, personal, or "spiritual" reality experienced by Jesus or the believer. Instead, Jesus' references to God as Father are to be set within the eschatological and, consequently, soteriological orientation of his mission. N. T. Wright puts it this way:

---

[24]In *Jesus of Nazareth: Millenarian Prophet,* Dale Allison contends that all these features—and more— characterize both Jesus' own context and numerous millenarian movements throughout history.

Israel's god was to be seen as the "father" of his people. This, it must be emphasized, was not a new thought; it is found in the Old Testament and in a fair amount of subsequent Jewish writings. Nor is it simply a matter of "father" being one miscellaneous appellation among many for YHWH. Nor, yet, is it to be explained solely in terms of Jesus' "religious experience". . . . Jesus, in inviting his hearers, to think of their god explicitly in this way, was emphasizing a strand in Jewish tradition which implicitly carried forward his claim: those who possessed this "faith" in YHWH as "father" were defining themselves as the eschatological Israel.[25]

The response of repentance and obedience for which Jesus called could be articulated as turning to the God who is the Father of Israel. Not surprisingly, then, the parable that most prominently features a father, the (misnamed) parable of the "prodigal," justifies Jesus' outreach to those "in exile." But this time it is not Israel *per se* that is in exile, but, rather, the sinners and tax collectors who are cast out from the people of God and need to be included in the promised restoration of Israel. Jesus contends that by means of his table fellowship with sinners, God seeks to gather together disparate factions in Israel into a family or fictive kin group who collectively will receive the inheritance of God. In this family, the father ultimately inherits and disinherits. Thus the younger brother will be "reinherited" alongside his older brother. The family thus reconstituted by the father's love ought to honor the father and extend love, forgiveness, and mercy to each other, thus living by the double love command characteristic of Jesus' interpretation of the will of God for the people of Israel.

Other sayings of Jesus recorded in the Gospels link the kingdom and the Father. Most notable, perhaps, is the opening of the Lord's Prayer. With reference to both the address to God as Father and the opening petition, "thy kingdom come," John Meier writes:

The God whom the disciples are taught to address with the name "my own dear Father" (*abba*) is besought to reveal himself as Father once and for all at the end time. The eschatological thrust of the petition is clear.[26]

---

[25]Wright, *Jesus and the Victory of God,* 262–63; McKnight, *A New Vision for Israel,* 62–64.

[26]John Meier, *A Marginal Jew,* 2:297; so also McKnight, *A New Vision for Israel,* 62–65.

In other words, the petition is forward looking. Jesus instructs his disciples to call upon the one who is Father to bring his kingdom. Jesus speaks of this hope with assurance, admonishing his disciples not to be afraid but to trust in God's graciousness to provide: "Do not be afraid, little flock, for it is your Father's good pleasure to give you the kingdom." Equally forward looking is Matthew's parable of final judgment, which articulates an invitation to the faithful to "inherit the kingdom of my father" (25:34).

The centrality of "kingdom of God" does shed light on Jesus' use of Father. What was central in Jesus' proclamation was that *God's* kingdom was at hand. In keeping with the central place that Jesus gave to God and God's dominion, he identified the greatest commandment as the commandment to love God with all one's heart, soul, strength, and mind. Similarly, Jesus called people to trust and obey their heavenly Father and to imitate his love and mercy. It was the Father's will that was to be done on earth as it is in heaven. Through the juxtaposition of "kingdom" and "Father," Jesus forges a vision of God's kingdom that is given as an inheritance and lived out in the life of the community where the dictates of conduct are love, forgiveness, mercy, care, and kindness. "Father" and "king" are linked insofar as both express the authority and saving activity of God with respect to a particular people. The images of God as Father and God as king thus reinforce each other. Both are figures of authority; and both are figures of grace. Because as Father God is both powerful and gracious, God can be trusted to effect his purposes. "Father" and "king" are also the subject of Jesus' eschatological proclamation of the promise of the restoration of Israel and the renewal of its covenant with God. Jesus' convictions of God's graciousness and mercy are always joined with the conviction of God's authority and power to save. "Father" as a term for God is indeed "firmly anchored in a soteriological center."[27]

### Jesus: heir of the Father's promises

The hopes and expectations of "restoration eschatology" illumine the complex of sayings, parables, and admonitions regarding God as Father by shedding light on Jesus' own role and mission, as well as his

---

[27]Krentz, "God in the New Testament," 89–90. See also Markus Bockmuehl, *This Jesus: Martyr, Lord, Messiah* (Edinburgh: T. & T. Clark, 1994), 133: "Because God is Father, 'Your will be done' still means 'Your kingdom come.'"

understanding of the nature of the community that God sought to create through his call to his people. God's actions as Father are acknowledged and embodied first with respect to the community that Jesus gathers around himself. Jesus' own relationship to God as Father is to be located within that same framework. Jesus is the heir of the Father who inherits the promises of God on behalf of his people. According to Luke 22:29, at the Last Supper, Jesus says to his disciples, "I confer on you, just as my Father has conferred on me, a kingdom." These are not two separate kingdoms, but one and the same kingdom. As the heir of the Father, Jesus receives the kingdom on behalf of his brothers and sisters and in turn invites them to share his inheritance (Matt. 25:34). In the end, the inheritance of the kingdom is not the inheritance of some thing but a relationship with the one who grants the inheritance. Hence, to flesh out the picture of the kingdom of which he speaks, Jesus eats at table with sinners and outcasts, embodying in action his proclamation of their restoration to family status; he looks for those who "do the will of the father" and bear fruits appropriate to repentance; he urges love and mercy such as is befitting the children of God. Like Jeremiah, Jesus calls for an Israel that will call upon God as "my father" in trust, obedience, and in conduct that honors others as brothers and sisters.

In the portrayal of Jesus as the son of the Father in the Gospels, the status of the son as an *heir* plays an important role, for it is the son who receives an inheritance from the father. So, for example, in the parable of the wicked tenants and the vineyard, after the tenants have mistreated all the servants, they plot to kill the son, the heir, that they might have the inheritance for themselves (Matt. 21:33–46; Mark 12:1–12; Luke 20:9–19). All worries aside about the legal issues which the assumption of the tenants in the parable seems to raise, the parable does picture the *son* primarily as an *heir.* The land in question is a vineyard, and the vineyard is a symbol for Israel in the Old Testament (Isa. 5:1–6; cf. Ps. 80:8–14; Jer. 2:2; 6:9; 8:13; Ezek. 15:2–6; 17:7–8; Hos. 10:1). The parable turns on the son's inheritance, which others want to seize illegitimately. In his telling of this parable, Jesus evokes a picture of Israel as God's choice planting, God's vineyard. The son and heir of the landowner, who should legitimately inherit the vineyard, is rejected by its tenants, and that rejection prefigures Jesus' rejection at the hands of Israel's leaders and their subsequent removal from their positions. Because they do not treat the heir of the vineyard as they ought, they will have no continued share in it. Although Matthew alone gives Jesus' explanation regarding the "kingdom of God," the link between vineyard and kingdom through Israel reveals not only the fluid nature of such imagery but also the common link in the designation of Jesus as God's rightful heir.

Although Jesus speaks of God's kingdom or rule, he does not portray his own role or the nature of the kingdom with the royal imagery of the Old Testament or with hopes of the overthrow or replacement of Roman rule. Instead, he refers to his followers as a new family. To those who are his "mother and brothers and sisters" (Mark 3:33), he promises "houses, and brothers and sisters, and mothers and children, and fields"; that is, family and inheritance (Mark 10:30). He warns of judgment for those who have not shown mercy and kindness to the "very least" of his brothers and sisters (Matt. 25:31–46) and promises those who have extended such mercy that they will "inherit the kingdom." The designation of God as Father is particularly suited to designate the relationship of Jesus to God because it connotes a social and familial relationship in which others have a place. Jesus is the son who shares the inheritance of the kingdom freely with others, who invites them to have a share in it. The ways in which this happens are pictured in familial terms and events: people share meals together, they are to be reconciled to each other as those who are heirs together of the father's substance, and so on. Jesus is the heir who inherits on behalf of and in company with his brothers and sisters.

Jesus did not explicitly invite others to "know God as Father" or to "believe that God is near" or to "experience God's fatherhood through him."[28] Instead, he exhorts people to trust in God's provision, mercy, and care, precisely because of his convictions about the way in which God was now acting to give Israel its inheritance, its "kingdom." He calls upon those who know and acknowledge God as Father to put their convictions into practice. Hence, he calls his disciples to trust their heavenly father who feeds the birds of the air and clothes the grass of the field. Jesus pictures God as a father who desires to give his children bread, not stones.

This leads us to perhaps the most difficult question of all, namely, the source or genesis of Jesus' understanding of God as Father. Put most sharply, which came first—Jesus' understanding that God was, in some distinctive way, his Father, and that the relationship of his disciples to

---

[28]Thus I would not agree with Robert Hamerton-Kelly that "the intimacy and accessibility of Almighty God is *the essence of Jesus' 'good news'* " (emphasis mine). But I would agree that, for Jesus, "God is not distant, aloof, not anti-human, not angry, sullen and withdrawn: God draws near, very near; God is with us" ("God the Father in the Bible," 100).

God as Father grew out of and from his own; or Jesus' understanding that God was a Father to Israel, and that his own relationship grew out of that basic and prior relationship of God to Israel? The vast majority of New Testament scholars and theologians decide in favor of the former alternative. Jesus' sense of sonship and understanding of his relationship to God as Father are subsequently extended to include his own followers. Thus G. B. Caird asserts that "the further back we go, the more we discover the intense conviction of Jesus that God is his Father and he is His son."[29] Caird explicates this as "a profoundly personal religious experience" for Jesus, referring specifically to his complete trust in and obedience to God as Father.[30] In other words, Jesus' understanding of himself as Son and God as Father comes to expression in moral terms. For this reason, Jesus can also urge his disciples to imitate the love and forgiveness of God so that "you will be children of the Most High" (Luke 6:35).

While this is an appealing argument, the second alternative—that Jesus understood God first as the Father of the people of Israel, and his own relationship to God in and from that framework—has the merit of accounting for the biblical, historical, and Gospel evidence more fully. In support of this position, it should be noted first how rarely the Synoptic Gospels report that Jesus referred to himself as Son. On several occasions, the divine voice attests him to be "my Son" or "my beloved Son," and various figures hail him as Son of God, or inquire whether he is the Son of God. But outside the Gospel of John, Jesus never uses that designation for himself and seldom speaks of himself as Son or the Son. The notable exceptions are the saying about the mutual knowledge of Father and Son, the "bolt from the Johannine blue" (Matt. 11:27; Luke 10:22); Jesus' confession of the Son's ignorance of the hour of final judgment (Mark 13:32; Matt. 24:36); and the "Great Commission" (Matt. 28:20). By contrast, we have already noted the number of instances in which God is called upon or referred to as Father. In light of the shape of the evidence, Jeremias and others started with Father and reasoned to Jesus' sense of Sonship, since they argued—not illogically—that the two are connected and the one implies the other in some way. One who regards another as father must in some way think of himself as a son.

But Jesus' scant references to himself as Son, when placed alongside

---

[29]Caird, *New Testament Theology,* 400.
[30]Ibid., 402.

the more frequent references to God as Father, lead us directly to the Old Testament. There "son" has two referents. It refers to Israel (Exod. 4:22; Hos. 9:1) and to the king of Israel (2 Sam. 7:14; Ps. 2:7), and the first clearly finds greater resonance in the Gospel tradition, where Jesus speaks more often of his followers as children of the heavenly Father than of himself as the king on the Davidic throne! In other words, both the pattern of usage of Father and Son in the Old Testament, and the pattern of usage of Father and Son in the Gospels point decisively to the conclusion that in speaking of God as Father, Jesus wished first and foremost to say something about God's relationship to his people, what it meant to be children of God, and about his own confidence that this God could be trusted.[31] The contours of his assertions and promises in the Gospels trace the pattern already laid down in the Old Testament. God relates to Israel as a father to a son, and the relationship of God to the king is a specific instance of that relationship, not the other way round.[32]

A final argument for thinking that Jesus' understanding of God as the Father of Israel was foundational for his own sense of vocation is found in the overlap between the Old Testament image of God as king and father to the descendants of David. In spite of the appointment of a human king, God remains the king of Israel. The Davidic king in some way instantiates or replicates the rule of the divine sovereign. The king represents God's rule in Israel and, from the other direction, represents Israel before God. Similarly, a son represents and even replicates his father in some way. And if he is the eldest in a family, the son is the heir not only of the father's goods but also of the father's role as head of the family. He perpetuates the father's line. The king owes obedience to God, and many are the stories in the Old Testament of the disobedience and failures of kings and their subsequent punishment and downfall. Similarly, the son owes obedience to his father, and the "rebellious son" is one who is to be punished by the people (Deut. 21:18). There is a mutuality between God and the king of Israel which can be expressed in terms of the father/son dyad, as is, of course, already evident in the promise of 2 Samuel 7:12–14, where a kingdom is promised to the one

---

[31]Leander E. Keck, *A Future for the Historical Jesus: The Place of Jesus in Preaching and Theology* (Nashville and New York: Abingdon, 1971), 224, writes, "The motif of Jesus' mission can be understood as the trustworthiness of God." As Keck points out, this forces us to ask whether the root problem, then, is distrust (161).

[32]Cf. Wright, *Jesus and the Victory of God,* 649–50.

whom God regards as a son. Hence, the relationship and role of God and king, father and son, become mutually explanatory. There are expectations of obedience and honor, but there is also the promise of faithfulness and care, and of the bestowal of an inheritance.

The point is by no means to lessen the significance of Jesus' references to God as Father but, rather, to attempt to account for their origin and to underscore the difficulty of gaining access to Jesus' "sense of Sonship" through such references. Part of the difficulty comes in the fact that New Testament scholars tend to think of "Son of God" as a "title" and then find it difficult to understand how Jesus could have used such a "title" with reference to himself. Moreover, New Testament scholars are leery of reading back into Jesus' own references later Trinitarian confessions that speak of the Son as "the second person of the Trinity." In either case, whether "son" is some sort of messianic or christological title, or whether it refers to the second person of the Trinity, it is easier to imagine that Jesus had some strong religious sense of his own relationship to God as Father than that he went around applying titles and labels to himself. But assuming that he did speak of himself as "Son"—which we have seen occurs seldom in the Synoptic Gospels—we would do well to heed the caveat of George Caird that "son" is something of a wax nose, with a "supremely exploitable ambiguity" and can connote authority, agency, mutuality, uniqueness, or the identification of one with the many, all depending on the context in which it is used.[33]

In short, the Gospels indicate that Jesus spoke much more often of God as Father than of himself as Son. Along the same lines, the Gospels also indicate that Jesus spoke to his disciples of God as their heavenly Father, and that he spoke of God's commands, expectations, love, and provision as a heavenly Father. His own "Sonship" was not the centerpiece or content of his proclamation. In other words, the primary arena in which one finds references to God as Father is the community of Jesus' followers. Out of this context, the relationship of God as Father can be spoken of with reference to the people as a whole, or with reference to Jesus in particular. Both the corporate and individual references have a precedent in the Old Testament, although the references to God's relationship to an individual as Father are typically explicated with reference to the Davidic king. Such references do not feature prominently in the gospel tradition in the words of Jesus.

---

[33]Caird, *New Testament Theology,* 323.

The situation is much the same with "kingdom," where God is the king, but Jesus' role in the kingdom is seldom designated with the term "king" or "prince" or other royal imagery. In other words, Jesus' own relationship to God as Father or to God as King remains implicit rather than explicit. Insofar as Jesus spoke of God's kingdom and of God as Father, he placed himself with and among those who claimed allegiance to the one God of Israel, but he also claimed for himself a distinctive role of spokesman for the King, the heir of the Father who promised his brothers and sisters Israel's inheritance. The audacity of Jesus' proclamation lay not in what he claimed for himself so much as what he promised in the name of the Father.[34] In that regard, when speaking of Jesus' "sense of Sonship" we are dealing first with Jesus' awareness of vocation or convictions regarding his mission.[35] This is, in part, because kingdom and Sonship are closely linked, with the proclamation of the kingdom serving as the framework in which Jesus articulates his convictions regarding his own role. Just as Jesus' proclamation regarding the kingdom focuses on God's initiative and activity in bringing about God's reign, so any sense of "vocation" or "identity" which we can attribute to Jesus would do well to take as its starting point not Jesus' "sense of Sonship" but Jesus' references to God as Father.[36] What determines all else was Jesus' conviction that God was faithful, loving, and trustworthy, determined to bring Israel into obedient and loving relationship. The opening petition of the Lord's Prayer, "Father, hallowed be your name, your kingdom come" (Luke 11:2) and Jesus' confession of his own ignorance, "But about that day or hour no one knows, but . . . only the Father" (Mark 13:32) show that initiative for the coming of the kingdom lies with the Father and that Jesus trusts that God will bring these realities to pass.

---

[34]See E. P. Sanders, "Exegesis indicates that there were *specific issues* at stake between Jesus and the Jewish hierarchy, and that the specific issues revolved around a *basic question:* who spoke for God?" in *Jesus and Judaism,* 281.

[35]So also Wright, *Jesus and the Victory of God,* 652–53.

[36]Marinus de Jonge, *God's Final Envoy: Early Christology and Jesus' Own View of His Mission* (Grand Rapids/Cambridge: Eerdmans, 1998), 109: "Jesus not only announced the kingdom of God; he inaugurated it. This placed him in a unique relationship to God, and he was aware of it when he addressed God as Father . . . Jesus, then, had a 'christology.' But immediately we should add his christology was fundamentally *theocentric."*

### *"My mother, my brothers and sisters"*

Jesus couched his references to God's Fatherhood within the context of his ministry and mission to Israel and reserved the privilege of address to God as Father for his own disciples.[37] Father is both the way in which Jesus is shown directly addressing God and the way that God is known or addressed by those who acknowledge and trust in his goodness, as opposed to "the Gentiles," or those outside the covenant (Matt. 5:43–48, etc.). This usage somewhat parallels that in the Dead Sea Scrolls, where we find reference to God as a Father to "all the sons of thy truth," thereby appropriating a relationship to God as Father of the righteous to the covenant community. To be sure, however, Jesus defines "righteous" by quite different standards than did the covenanters of Qumran.

But Jesus' references to God as Father most often serve as the warrant for conduct within the community and particularly for the love and forgiveness that his followers are to demonstrate. They are to manifest God's indiscriminate love, a love not only for one's neighbor but also for one's enemy (Matt. 5:43; 19:19; 22:39; Mark 12:31; Luke 10:27). In such a way, they manifest the same sort of mercy that the heavenly Father manifests (Luke 6:37). Jesus' followers are called upon to exhibit a radical trust in God, which looks to him for provision of shelter, food, and clothing (6:25–32). They obey the commands of God and do the will of the Father (Matt. 12:50; 21:28–31). In Matthew's parable of judgment, those who "inherit the kingdom" do so on account of their love for "the least of these who are members of my family" (25:40).

Jesus' warning about judgment grows naturally out of his designation of the two great commandments as the commands to love God and to love one's neighbor. The first, in fact, entails and demands the second. To love God implies that one loves as God loves, that one loves the outsider, such as the Samaritan; the unjust, such as the tax collector; and the sinner, such as the lawbreaker or Gentile. Hence, it means to seek the one lost sheep and to rejoice when it is found, to eat at table with the lost, to proclaim justice to the captives, and to speak of God's revelation to "infants." Within this community, one is to use riches and goods for the sake of the poor and needy (Luke 16:20–27). They are to forgive, so that they will be forgiven (Luke 6:37). They are not to harm others either by action or by thoughts (Matt. 5:21–22, 27–28).

---

[37]So also Jeremias, *Prayers of Jesus,* 43; Bauckham, "Historical Jesus in Christology," 248–49; Caird, *New Testament Theology,* 398–99; McKnight, *A New Vision for Israel,* 58.

But this vision can be refocused in terms of God's Fatherhood, and then familial imagery becomes central. One is not to welcome the "lost," but the prodigal *brother.* One is not to behave as do the Gentiles, those outside the covenant of the children of Israel, but should instead be willing to become like children within Israel, refusing to lord authority or status over others, acknowledging that there is one Father in the community (Matt. 23:9). One is not to see the speck in the eye of the brother or sister (Matt. 7:3–5; Luke 6:41–42) or to insult a brother or sister or call another "fool" (Matt. 5:22). One is to forgive a brother or sister without keeping count of the number of offenses (Matt. 18:21).

There is both "cognitive" and "affective" content in Jesus' statements and parables that speak of or address God as Father. But the primary aim of such statements is neither to teach doctrine nor to evoke certain sorts of feelings about God. In their contexts in Jesus' teaching and mission, such statements call for trust, obedience, and specific behaviors from the gathered community called into being by God's initiative. Specifically, those who are children of the heavenly Father are to demonstrate the impartial love to the evil and the good, the just and the unjust, which God demonstrates. In this way they will live as children of the Father in heaven (Matt. 5:45). In other words, according to the Gospels, Jesus does not primarily teach new beliefs about God or offer an unparalleled experience of God, but on the basis of the scriptural conviction that God is a Father to Israel Jesus called together a people who would put their trust in, and offer their allegiance to, that God alone (Matt. 23:9). To trust God as Father is thus not to come to a new intimacy with God but, rather, to renew one's trust in the God of Israel.

### Summary Reflections: Jesus, the Father, and the Community

Jesus' address to God as Father and his designation of God as the Father of his disciples flows from his conviction that his mission was to gather Israel and to restore it as God's people. Indeed, his conviction of his mission to gather God's people together cannot be separated from his understanding of God as *abba,* the Father of the community that he was calling out, the community of the renewed people of God.

As God was the Father of Israel, so God would be the Father of the faithful who responded to Jesus' call. Jesus did not call upon *abba* to counteract Jewish views that God was distant, aloof, stern, or demanding but because he acknowledged God's authority and depended on God's mercy and goodness. While Jesus used other terms to speak of God, he is never shown addressing God by any of these terms, not even "king," although this is not uncommon in rabbinic prayers, and he never teaches his disciples another form of address. Jeremias was correct, then, to suggest that it would be direct address to God as Father that would prove most fruitful for understanding the significance of the term.

In speaking of God as "my Father" and "your Father," Jesus appropriates the relationship of Father and Son to himself, and of Father and children to his own community. Jesus did not proclaim that a relationship with God formerly unavailable was now possible. Rather, he revivified the reality of God's Fatherhood for Israel by speaking of God's mercy and faithfulness, calling for repentance, and insisting that there could be no devotion to that God without corollary commitment to one's brothers and sisters. Thus, Jesus did not invite his disciples to a share of his relationship with God but to a share of the inheritance that was theirs together. Trusting that God was indeed the Father of Israel, and so his Father as well as that of his disciples, Jesus called his disciples to renewed trust, obedience, and love. In this way, Jesus appropriated the prophetic vision of God as the Father of Israel both to call people to repentance and to promise the faithfulness of God. As Leander Keck writes,

> Jesus' whole career has to do with the trustworthiness of God and with the trusting response of man. He did not use this terminology, of course, but this is what his proclamation of the kingdom and the summons to repent (turn Godward), his deeds of mercy and his acceptance of death centrally mean.[38]

We might add that it is also what his appeal to God as Father and his promise of God's provision and salvation centrally mean. To speak of God as Father is to assume the trustworthiness of God. Jesus' invocation of God as *abba* does not mean that he *named* or *called* God Father but, rather, that he *called upon* God as Father. That he did so indicates his trust in the God of Israel.

Jesus called together a community that would renew its allegiance to God and allow its commitment to this merciful and gracious God to shape its life with each other. Jesus does not introduce to his hearers the idea that God is compassionate and merciful. Instead, he argues that those who know God in this way are expected to show such compassion to others. Accordingly, Jesus spoke of the First Commandment as the

---

[38]Keck, *A Future for the Historical Jesus*, 183.

command to love God with all one's heart, soul, and mind, and the Second Commandment as requiring love of neighbor. Jesus' use of Father for God is not intended to answer the question "what do we call God?" or "what is God's name?" or "how do we conceive of God?" Rather, Jesus adapts the notion that God is the Father of Israel and, more specifically, the Father of the faithful (whether individuals or a community) to his own mission and situation. Jesus both adopts and adapts the Old Testament presentation of God as the Father of Israel in speaking of himself as Son and of the community that he gathers together as his family. When Jesus speaks of God as Father, he does not primarily give expression to his own intuition or experience of God as near, loving, intimate, and accessible, nor does he intend first to articulate his own relationship to God. Jesus' boldness lay not in speaking to God as Father, but in promising others, on God's behalf, that God would be their Father. The promise that God was and would be a merciful and faithful Father is one way in which Jesus articulates his conviction of God's saving purposes for Israel and the world, which are to be embodied in his (filial) mission and subsequently also through those who follow him.

# 4

# Jesus and the Father
# in the Synoptic Gospels

While Jesus' own use of the term Father or *abba* remains a contested issue, the Gospels' presentation of God as the Father of Jesus, and of Jesus as the Son of the Father, is a matter of simple observation. To be sure, Father is not the only image or appellation for God that occurs in the Gospels. Alongside references to God as Father, one also finds imagery for God as judge, master, landowner, employer, farmer, and king. All this imagery together becomes the content of Jesus' understanding of God. And yet a distinctive portrait of God as Father emerges from the Gospels through the associations that Father draws to itself and the contexts in which Jesus' words, parables, and exhortations are found. The point of this chapter is to describe the picture of God as Father that is found in each of the Synoptic Gospels by paying attention to the narrative of each of the Gospels and the way in which that narrative renders God as Father.[1]

In earlier chapters, we highlighted three aspects of the presentation of God as Father in the Old Testament and Jewish literature. We may repeat these themes briefly: (1) God is the Father of Israel as the one who called it into being and would give it its inheritance as his heir. (2) As Father of Israel, God loves and cares for Israel. (3) God expects from Israel the honor and obedience appropriate to a parent. None of the

---

[1]That the discussion is here limited to the Synoptic Gospels is due to John's well-known differences from the Synoptic tradition, perhaps nowhere as evident as in the central position he assigns to God as "the Father" and Jesus as "the Son." John's portrait will be taken up in a separate chapter.

Gospels explicitly enumerates these themes, nor would one expect a list of them, inasmuch as they are simply the warp and woof of God's Fatherhood as pictured in the scriptures. To speak of God's Fatherhood would naturally entail describing God's activity in one or all of these ways. Yet while distinguishing these aspects of God's Fatherhood, it is also important to note that the distinction is rather artificial. It is impossible, for example, to conceive of God as the Father of Israel without simultaneously considering the obligation that Israel owes to God. And God's very creation of Israel expresses God's love and goodness. In other words, the three aspects are integrally related, although here or there, both in the Old Testament and in the Gospels, one may be emphasized more than the other.

In Mark's Gospel, there is particular emphasis on the third aspect of God's Fatherhood. God is a figure of authority to whom honor and obedience are due. Mark, however, plays down the particular place of Israel and highlights instead the obedience that Jesus, the faithful Son, offers to God the Father. Nowhere is this more evident than in Jesus' prayer in the Garden of Gethsemane. While Jesus appeals to God to deliver him from what lies ahead, he also accepts the way of the cross as the will of the Father. Mark thus focuses his gaze intently on the relationship between Jesus and God as Son and Father.

Luke and Matthew overlap a good deal, not only in the actual material in which God is presented as a Father but also in the fundamental lineaments of the portrait of God as Father. One can say that all three of those themes specified above find a place in Matthew and in Luke. In both Gospels, God is pictured as a Father who grants Israel its inheritance. But this is Israel conceived of as a remnant of those who are obedient to the one who is their Father. There is a narrowing of the scope of God's Fatherhood in both Matthew and Luke from "the children of Abraham" to "the children of Abraham who bear fruit that befits repentance." Luke stresses the *inclusion* of the outcasts and sinners in this inheritance, whereas Matthew warns of the *exclusion* of those who do not live as the children of the Father. In keeping with the third aspect of God's Fatherhood, both Matthew and Luke accentuate the importance of obedient response to God's commands and filial imitation of God's actions. Both Matthew and Luke speak of God's love and care for the faithful, of God's provision, and of God's mercy.

What emerges as distinctive in all the Gospels is the singling out of the relationship of Jesus to the Father as an exceptional instance of the Father/Son relationship. All three themes itemized above apply not only to the people of God but also to Jesus himself and, when they do, Jesus is shown to embody them more completely than anyone else. Because God is the Father of Jesus, he is the heir of the Father's inheritance. He receives what the Father promises and in turn bestows it on others. The Gospels present him as willingly and faithfully obedient to the commands of God, withstanding temptation from devil and disciple alike to follow the difficult path of the costly will of God. Thus he expresses his reliance on God's good provision for him. In every way, Jesus' relationship as Son to God as Father is exemplary. Yet in none of the Gospels is he simply an exemplary or typical "child" of God. Others use the language of Father for God not by imitation of Jesus or his mode of address but because they are among his followers.[2] This is amply demonstrated by the distinction between Jesus' reference to God as "*my* Father" on the one hand and the community's acknowledgment of God as "*our* Father" on the other. Hence, in the Synoptic Gospels there are two particular manifestations of God's Fatherhood. God is the Father of the faithful people of God; and God is the Father of Jesus, the faithful and obedient Son.

But a Gospel is a narrative account, not a list of themes and ideas. It is the embodiment of these convictions, promises, and admonitions in the narratives of the Gospels that gives texture to the portraits presented there. These accounts of Jesus' ministry help us imagine what it might mean to speak and think of God as Father, not theoretically, but in the concrete situations in which would-be followers of Jesus find themselves. We turn, then, to a brief examination of each of the Synoptic narratives and the presentation of God as Father embodied within them.

### Mark: The Beloved Son of the Father

Mark uses Father four times. Jesus speaks once of the Son of Man coming "in the glory of his Father" (8:38); once of unique knowledge which "the Father" has of "the hour" (13:32); once of the need to forgive others so that "your Father in heaven may also forgive you your trespasses" (11:25); and once Jesus prays "*Abba,* Father," in the Garden of Gethsemane (14:36), the only passage in all the Gospels that contains the Aramaic term *abba.* The well-known prayer runs, "*Abba,* Father, for you all things are possible; remove this cup from me; yet, not what I want, but what you want." Coming as it does in the scene in the garden, where Jesus will soon be arrested, Jesus' prayer assumes a

---

[2]Donald Juel, "The Lord's Prayer in the Gospels of Matthew and Luke," in *The Lord's Prayer: Perspectives for Reclaiming Christian Prayer* (Grand Rapids: Eerdmans, 1993), 60.

particularly prominent place and might well figure as the most important disclosure of Jesus' address and relationship to God as Father for Mark. What convictions undergird Mark's presentation of Jesus' prayer to God as *Abba*?

If the stress falls on the intimacy so often attributed to the sense of *abba,* then perhaps Mark intends to show Jesus communing with one whom he knew to be very near to him in the garden. But the rest of the Gospel of Mark gives little room for drawing such a conclusion. In fact, in order for Jesus' address to be meaningful to Mark's first readers, one must assume either that the term *abba* was well known to them, perhaps from their own use of the term in prayer or worship, or that the addition of Father (Greek, *patēr;* πατήρ) adequately explained it for non-Aramaic speaking readers. Mark's practice of translating certain Aramaic phrases is attested throughout the Gospel (3:17; 5:41; 7:11, 34; 10:46; 14:36; 15:22, 34). Here his immediate translation of the term *abba* shows how he wished his readers to understand it, or what he thought its nearest Greek equivalent was. It is therefore interesting that Mark uses not a term of endearment or familial intimacy but, rather, the most common and generic word for father.

The rest of Jesus' prayer glosses the invocation of *abba.* Jesus calls on the Father for whom "all things are possible." Jesus' acknowledgment of God's power echoes his earlier promises to his disciples that "all things can be done [are possible] for the one who believes" (9:23) and "for God all things are possible" (10:27). In both these passages, Jesus is shown as speaking of God's great power, explicated in terms of the capacity to accomplish "all things" (πάντα). Accordingly, one interpreter has aptly paraphrased Jesus' prayer in the garden as follows: *"Abba,* You all-powerful One!"[3] To acknowledge God as Father is to acknowledge God's power not as abstract sovereignty but as the disposition to help in situations of distress and peril. For Mark, Jesus' calling upon God at the hour of his deepest distress indicates that Jesus not only acknowledges God's ultimate sovereignty but trusts God's ultimate goodness as well. The other uses of Father in Mark reinforce this same understanding. The Son of man will come "in the glory of the Father," and it is only the Father who knows the hour when this will occur. The consummation of all things lies in the hands of the Father. The Father holds the power to forgive sin (11:25). This is a starkly etched portrait of the authority of the Father.

---

[3]J. M. Oesterreicher, "Abba, Father! On the Humanity of Jesus," *The Lord's Prayer and the Jewish Liturgy* (ed. J. J. Petuchowski and M. Brocke; New York: Seabury, 1978), 132.

The other side of Mark's portrayal of God as Father is his portrayal of Jesus as the Son of God. Jesus is introduced this way in the opening verses of the Gospel. And at three other crucial points he is again presented as the Son of God, if not necessarily by that designation. At baptism, a heavenly voice announces, "You are my Son, the Beloved, with you I am well pleased" (1:11). Later, in the Transfiguration, a voice again speaks of Jesus as Son: "This is my Son, the Beloved, listen to him" (9:7). Finally, the Roman centurion at the foot of the cross affirms, "Truly this man was God's Son!" (15:39). The designation Son of God or Son is thus linked with key moments in the life of Jesus—baptism, transfiguration, death. From beginning to end he is Son of God, the Beloved.

But merely to assert that Jesus is the beloved Son of the Father does not yet fully explicate the significance of that relationship for Mark. The designations Son and Father cannot be torn apart from each other or from the narrative in which they are embodied and made to stand on their own, as though they carry their own significance. The best access to understanding these terms is not through an analysis of their "meaning" apart from the narratives and contexts in which they appear but through investigation of their function and placement within the narratives in which we find them. In the narrative of Mark we find that as the beloved Son Jesus' pathway seems to be marked as much by humiliation as it is by honor. In his book *The Death and Resurrection of the Beloved Son,* Jon Levenson wryly reminds us that in Jewish tradition to be a beloved Son carried with it not only the promise of privilege and inheritance but always ominous overtones as well.[4] As Levenson notes, "The beloved son is marked for both exaltation and for humiliation. In his life the two are seldom far apart."[5] This characterization aptly suits Mark's presentation of Jesus as the beloved Son.

From the outset of the Gospel, Jesus and God are identified by this way of speaking of their relationship. The designation of Jesus as Son and God as Father serves to validate Jesus' mission as the chosen one of God. Jesus is first introduced as Messiah or Christ, which is elaborated by Son of God (1:1). The baptismal announcement of Jesus as Beloved Son presents Jesus as the one loved by God, anointed by the

---

[4]Jon Levenson, *The Death and Resurrection of the Beloved Son: The Transformation of Child Sacrifice in Judaism and Christianity* (New Haven: Yale University Press, 1993).

[5]Ibid., 59.

Spirit for a yet undisclosed mission. This is Mark's presentation of Jesus as Israel's Messiah. Son and Messiah are linked via the promise that God would be a Father to the one who occupies David's throne. Then, in the summary opening proclamation, Jesus announces, "The time is fulfilled, the kingdom of God has come near; repent, and believe in the good news" (1:15). The one who is the Messiah, the Son of God, now announces the nearness of God's own kingdom. Later he is transfigured in glory, again presented as the Son of God. And at Jesus' trial, the high priest asks whether he is "the Messiah, the Son of the Blessed One"(14:61). Finally, at the moment of Jesus' death on the cross, a Roman centurion announces what the Evangelist had made clear at the outset: "Truly this man was God's Son!" (15:39) The entire narrative thus discloses what it means for Jesus to be the Messiah, the Son of God. Although that title is assigned to Jesus in the beginning, its significance is spelled out through the course of the narrative, which reaches its climactic moment in the death of Jesus, clearly signaling that apart from Jesus' crucifixion, one cannot understand what it means to be "the Messiah, the Son of God." But the open disclosure of his coming "in glory" remains yet in the future (13:26). In other words, there is an inevitable hiddenness to the relationship of Father and Son, an orientation toward the future when the full significance of that relationship is manifested.

Yet while Mark presents Jesus as the Messiah and Son of God, those terms cannot be isolated from the account that presents Jesus as the beloved Son of the Father. The narrative of the life, death, and resurrection of Jesus explicates Jesus' Sonship and Messiahship. At the opening of the Gospel, God presents Jesus as his beloved Son; toward the close of the Gospel, Jesus prays to God as his beloved Father. In Mark's account, Jesus thus enunciates the conviction that the Father who leads the Son on this mysterious path of suffering and death can yet be known and trusted as *Abba.* Thus not only does the Father introduce the Son as his beloved; but the Son introduces the Father as the trustworthy Father. Even as the full unveiling of the identity of the Son awaits the future, so also does the vindication of the trustworthiness of the Father.

## Luke: "Be Merciful, as Your Heavenly Father Is Merciful"

Luke uses "God" (θεός) 122 times in the Gospel and 168 times in Acts. He uses Father (for God) about twenty times in the Gospel and only three times in Acts (1:4, 7; 2:33). Since all the references to the Father in

Luke are in Jesus' own speech, the lack of references to God as Father in Acts is naturally explained by the fact that Jesus is not a regular character in the narrative.[6] But the limitation of Father for God to Jesus' own speech clearly also tells us a good deal about Luke's understanding of God as Father. In Luke, Jesus refers to God as "my Father" and "your Father," and in direct address he refers to God simply as "Father." This is of course identical with the invocation with which the Lukan Jesus begins the Lord's Prayer: "Father, hallowed be your name" (11:2).

Of the seventeen references to God as Father in Luke, six passages are unique to Luke, and these show Jesus speaking about "my Father" and "your Father," or simply addressing God as Father (2:49; 12:32; 22:29; 23:34, 46; 24:49).[7] One could say, then, that passages in Luke that reflect his unique material, the so-called "L" source, tend to stress Jesus' filial relationship to God. The rest of Luke's nine references to God as Father come from Q, the source common to Matthew and Luke.[8] In these passages emphasis falls primarily on God's mercy, care, generosity, and providence.

Overall these passages display a fairly even distribution of usage: "my Father" (4 times), "your Father" (3 times), "the Father" (4 times), and "Father" (6 times). Luke might be said to show a slight preference for forms *without* personal pronouns (the vocative "Father" or the absolute "the Father"), especially when compared with Matthew, but the sample is probably too small to be significant. One might surmise that Luke has removed the personal pronouns (my, our) precisely to include the disciples in Jesus' own prayers and address to God.

---

[6]The first two references in Acts (1:4, 7) are in Jesus' indirect and direct discourse; the third is in Peter's speech at Pentecost, referring to the Spirit as the Father's promise (see Luke 24:49). See also Robert L. Mowery, "The Disappearance of the Father: The References to God the Father in Luke-Acts," *Enc* 55 (1994): 353.

[7]Two passages come from Mark, with slight changes: Mark's statement that the Son of Man will come "in the glory of *his* Father" (Mark 8:34; cf. Matt. 16:27) becomes in Luke "in the glory of *the* Father" (9:26). The address to God in the prayer in Gethsemane omits Mark's *abba* (Luke 22:42; Mark 14:36; contrast Matt. 26:39).

[8]6:36, your Father; 10:21–22, Father, 2x; my Father, 1x; the Father, 2x; 11:2, Father; 11:13, the heavenly Father; 12:30, your father. For a discussion of the material in this source, see Antoinette Clark Wire, "The God of Jesus in the Gospel Sayings Source," in *Reading from this Place* (ed. Fernando F. Segovia and Mary Ann Tolbert; vol. 1 of *Social Location and Biblical Interpretation in the United States;* Minneapolis: Fortress, 1995), 277–303.

This brief statistical overview points to three facets of Luke's presentation of the Fatherhood of God: (1) Jesus' relationship to God as Father is distinctive. Jesus' regular use of "my Father" points to his unique knowledge of the Father (10:21–22), to his function as the one who mediates the kingdom (11:2; 12:32; 22:29), and to his promise to bestow the Spirit from the Father (11:13; 24:49; Acts 1:4). (2) Jesus' disciples are included in his relationship to God as Father because Jesus' mission is to mediate the kingdom of his Father and to bestow the Spirit of his Father. Through Jesus' mission, then, the disciples may also call God Father. As Father, God cares for, watches over, and shows mercy and forgiveness to those whom Jesus characterizes as "the little ones" or "the little flock." (3) Jesus teaches that this same mercy ought to shape the lives of that little flock. Jesus' actions and teaching, embodied in his table fellowship with sinners and justified in the parable of the prodigal son, drive home the point of filial and familial obligation in light of God's mercy. In his own life, Jesus exemplifies the forgiving grace that he calls for from his followers. Subsequently, Luke depicts the community, particularly in Acts, gathered in the name of the Father and Son as empowered by the Spirit to live out the commands Jesus taught in the Gospels. We will look briefly at each of these three points.

### Jesus' relationship to God as Father

Luke introduces us to Jesus by means of the so-called birth narratives. Interestingly, in these narratives three different figures are called Father in relationship to Jesus. First, Gabriel announces to Mary that she will bear a child and that the Lord God "will give to him the throne of his *father David*" (1:32; RSV). Second, after Simeon's prophecy over the child Jesus, Luke comments that Jesus' "father and mother were amazed at what was being said about him" (2:33). This note is picked up later when the worried Mary scolds Jesus after he stays behind in Jerusalem, "your father and I have been looking for you in great anxiety" (2:48). Upon Mary's reprimand, Jesus in turn reproves Mary with the words, "Did you not know that I must be in my Father's house?" (2:49). Jesus is, of course, speaking of God as his Father. Ultimately, then, it is neither David nor Joseph who is the father of Jesus. The genealogy of Jesus, which is traced in Luke through "the son of Adam, the son of God," demonstrates that in the final analysis it is God who is the Father of Jesus. God's paternity cannot be construed in physical terms with respect to Jesus any more than with respect to Adam. While Luke then underscores the fact that Jesus' one true Father is God, within the narrative it is Jesus himself who *first* speaks of God as his Father and *only* Jesus who speaks of God as Father, facts perfectly in keeping with the later pronouncement that "no one knows the Son except the Father, and no one knows the Father except the Son" (10:22).

Both in what he says and in what he does, Jesus shows his true status as the Son of the Father. Where "my Father" indicates a distinctive relationship between Jesus and God, it points to his function of mediating the kingdom (12:32; 22:29). Several passages in Luke point to this role which Jesus exercises. Both Matthew and Luke show Jesus speaking of "my Father's kingdom," rather than of the "kingdom of heaven" or "kingdom of God." Luke alone has the poignant admonition: "Do not be afraid, little flock; for it is your Father's good pleasure to give you the kingdom." Jesus thus promises the kingdom to his followers on behalf of the Father. In the rather difficult parable of the ten pounds, which apparently contains a thinly veiled allusion to Jesus' own departure and promised return, a nobleman is said to go into a "far country to receive a kingdom" and to return when he has received it (19:12, 15; RSV). At the Last Supper, Jesus tells his disciples, "I confer on you, just as my Father has conferred on me, a kingdom" (22:29). The verb translated "confer" comes from the Greek *diatithēmi* (διατίθημι), meaning to "dispose of property by a will."[9] It has the same root as the Greek word *diathēkē* (διαθήκη), "testament" or "will." The emphasis here, as well as in other passages regarding the Father's "giving" the kingdom, falls on the Father's initiative in "bequeathing" a kingdom to Jesus and his followers. Jesus inherits the kingdom from his Father and in turn confers it on his followers. Not without reason, one commentator has suggested that all references to the "kingdom" in the Gospels ought to be rendered as "inheritance," which captures something of the flavor of the present passages.[10] God is now giving Israel its kingdom through Jesus; the Father is now giving the Son his inheritance.

The heart of Luke's Gospel underscores Jesus' distinctive relationship to God as Father, as well as the way in which that relationship is

---

[9]It is used in this sense, with the word kingdom, in Josephus, *Ant.* 13.407: "Now although Alexander had left two sons, Hyrcanus and Aristobulus, he had bequeathed the royal power to Alexandra" (βασιλείαν διέθετο).

[10]Antoinette Clark Wire's translation of *basileia* as "inheritance," while playing down too much the sense of "dominion" inherent in the term, captures the emphasis on God's bestowing a kingdom or inheritance and provides a connection between the image of God as king and God as Father ("The God of Jesus in the Gospel Sayings Source," 281).

mediated to or available to others, even to those least likely to be called children of Abraham. A well-known passage, once dubbed the "bolt from the Johannine blue," highlights Jesus' distinctive relationship to God as Father. It reads as follows:

> In that same hour, [Jesus] rejoiced in the Holy Spirit, saying "I thank you, Father, Lord of heaven and earth, because you have hidden these things from the wise and the intelligent and have revealed them to infants; yes, Father, for such was your gracious will. All things have been handed over to me by my Father; and no one knows who the Son is except the Father, or who the Father is except the Son and anyone to whom the Son chooses to reveal him." (10:21–22)

Two distinguishing characteristics of God's Fatherhood in the Old Testament, authority and graciousness, are thus brought together in Luke's presentation of Jesus' own mission. The embodiment of God's authority in the revelation to "infants," rather than to the wise and intelligent, gives sharper definition to the gracious disclosure of his will. This passage shows the sorts of people who receive the Father's revelation through the Son and thus the sorts of people who call on God as Father. What stands out is that Jesus aligns himself with the "infants" rather than the wise and intelligent and thus speaks of himself also as the recipient of God's revelation, which he in turn mediates to others.

The passage is followed in Luke by accounts that exemplify the nature of the "infants," those who are not wise and intelligent by human standards. First, the parable of the Good Samaritan demonstrates how the unlikely Samaritan—one of the "infants" rather than the wise and intelligent—lives by the command to "be merciful, just as your Father is merciful" (6:36). The good Samaritan manifests the sort of mercy God manifests; the Samaritan—not the priest, not the Levite—thus shows himself to be a true son of the Father, who lives by Jesus' teaching. The Samaritan is one of those "to whom the Son chooses to reveal [the Father]."

Similarly, in the account that follows the parable of the Samaritan, Mary does the "one thing needful": she hears the word of God. And those who "hear the word of God and do it" are those whom Jesus calls his mother and brothers and sisters (cf. 8:21). Following the accounts of the Good Samaritan, and Mary and Martha, Jesus teaches his disciples to pray, "Father, your kingdom come." The merciful Samaritan and the faithful Mary exemplify the kind of people Jesus gathers around him to pray to God as Father. To persons such as these, Jesus says, "Do not be afraid, little flock; it is your Father's good pleasure to give you the king-dom" (12:32).

### The Father and the little flock

Jesus' assurance that it is "your Father's good pleasure to give you the kingdom," is situated in a passage in which Jesus promises his hearers that God will provide for his children even as he cares for the lilies and the birds of the air. Luke 12:30–34 reads as follows:

> [I]t is the nations of the world that strive after all these things, and your *Father* knows that you need them. Instead, strive for his *kingdom,* and these things will be given to you as well.
> Do not be afraid, little flock, for it is your *Father's good pleasure to give you the kingdom.* Sell your possessions, and give alms. Make purses for yourselves that do not wear out, an unfailing treasure in heaven, where no thief comes near and no moth destroys. For where your treasure is, there your heart will be also.

The juxtaposition of ideas here is striking. After telling his disciples to "strive for the kingdom of God," he assures them that "it is your Father's good pleasure to give you the kingdom." It is in light of the promise of what the Father will give that Jesus couches his exhortation to his disciples to "strive for the kingdom of God." Their striving or seeking is neither endless nor impossible, for ultimately the kingdom is the gift of the Father to them. But then follows Jesus' admonition to "sell your possessions and give alms." If God is indeed a Father who provides, a Father who desires to give the little flock their inheritance, then they may sell their possessions and give alms.

Other passages in Luke regularly link together the gift of the kingdom and the gift of the Spirit as God's good fatherly provision. In the Lukan version of the Lord's Prayer, for example, Jesus teaches his disciples to pray, "Father, hallowed be your name. Your kingdom come" (11:2–3). Following the prayer there are some additional instructions and a parable on prayer, which culminates in this way:

> Is there anyone among you who, if your child asks for a fish, will give a snake instead of a fish? Or if the child asks for an egg, will give a scorpion? If you then, who are evil, know how to give good gifts to your children, how much more will the heavenly Father give the Holy Spirit to those who ask him! (11:11–13)

Among the good gifts that the Father gives his children is the Holy
Spirit. Following his resurrection, Jesus renews his promise: "See, I am
sending upon you what my Father promised; so stay here in the city until
you have been clothed with power from on high" (24:49), a promise that
is reiterated early in the pages of Acts (1:4). The Spirit is the gift of "my
Father" (cf. Matt. 10:20). Ultimately it is the Father's gift of the Holy
Spirit that empowers the conduct that Jesus calls for. Thus Luke depicts
the community in Acts, gathered in the name of the Father and Son as
empowered by the Spirit to live out the commands Jesus taught in the
Gospels. It is through the Spirit that they can sell their possessions and
give alms, and through the Spirit that their lives may be oriented toward
God's good gift of the kingdom and that the realities of God's kingdom
may be embodied in their corporate lives.

### Living together in the kingdom of the Father

If Luke then wishes to make it clear that Jesus' true Father is God, it
is equally apparent that he presents Jesus himself as proclaiming God as
the true Father of all the faithful. As John the Baptist preaches in the
wilderness, he warns the people against claiming the privilege of having
Abraham as Father. It is not enough. They are to "bear fruits that befit
repentance," giving food and clothing to those who have none, and for-
going ill-gotten gain and profit (3:11–14). Jesus sounds these notes later
in his own teaching. In the so-called Sermon on the Plain, one encounters Jesus' first public reference to God as Father, when Jesus admonishes his hearers, "Be merciful as your heavenly father is merciful."[11]

> If you love those who love you, what credit is that to you? For
> even sinners love those who love them. If you do good to those
> who do good to you, what credit is that to you? For even sin-
> ners do the same. If you lend to those from whom you hope to
> receive, what credit is that to you? Even sinners lend to sinners,
> to receive as much again. But love your enemies, do good, and
> lend, expecting nothing in return. Your reward will be great,
> and you will be *children of the Most High;* for he is kind to the

---

[11]As noted in the previous chapter, the *Jerusalem Targum I* on Lev. 22:28
reads, "My people, children of Israel, as our Father is merciful in heaven, so you
shall be merciful on earth." Similarly, the *Isaiah Targum* renders "father" in Isaiah 63:16 and 64:8 with the phrase "he whose mercies upon us are more than a
father's upon sons." Mercy is virtually inherent in the understanding of God as
"father" in Jewish tradition.

ungrateful and the wicked. Be merciful, just as your *Father is merciful.* (Luke 6:32–36)

Just as Luke showed that Jesus' true Father is God, he goes on to show that Jesus calls his people to live as those whose true father is not Abraham, but God. If it is not enough to say "we have Abraham as our father," neither is it enough to *say* "we have God as our Father." Those who make this claim are to live it out. They do this by bearing the "fruits that befit repentance," by exercising mercy, compassion, and forgiveness, by loving God and neighbor. They are to live in this way because this is the way of God. They are to be merciful because God is merciful. To name God as Father implies not only privilege but an obligation to all those who likewise regard God as Father—and beyond them, even to those who do not. The admonition to extend God's mercy to others becomes an important theme in the parable of the prodigal son.

New Testament scholars have often made Jesus' parable of the prodigal son the centerpiece for determining Jesus' views of God, and particularly Jesus' understanding of God as Father. Joachim Jeremias, well known for both his work on the parables of Jesus and on Jesus' use of the Aramaic *abba* for God, calls this parable "The Parable of the Father's Love." Helmut Thielicke titled the parable "The Waiting Father," which places the emphasis on the father's attitude and actions. Undoubtedly one of the most provocative titles in recent years is to be found in the commentary of Eduard Schweizer, who names it, "The Powerless Almighty Father."[12] Still other interpreters have seen the parable in terms of the younger son, as in the classic designation, "The Prodigal Son," or, in the traditional German title, "The Lost Son" (*Der verlorene Sohn*). Many have seen the parable in terms of both sons, hence, designations such as "The Two Lost Sons."

Few see the elder son as the key to the parable. Yet according to Luke, Jesus tells this parable, as well as the parables of the lost sheep and the lost coin, in response to the grumbling of the scribes and Pharisees that he ate with tax collectors and sinners (15:1–3). Since it is widely acknowledged that the "older son" represents the scribes and Pharisees, it may plausibly be assumed that if Jesus' parable answers their complaint at all, then the older son's reactions and actions are

---

[12]Eduard Schweizer, *The Good News According to Luke* (Atlanta: John Knox, 1984), 246; and idem, *Luke: A Challenge to Present Theology* (Atlanta: John Knox, 1982), 75–80.

key to understanding the parable. It is virtually impossible for Christian readers today, who identify "Pharisees" as self-righteous hypocrites, to think that their complaint that Jesus "eats with tax collectors and sinners" has any sort of merit at all. Similarly, it is nearly impossible to credit the older brother with anything other than pettiness and selfishness.

In order to hear the parable freshly, we need to be reminded that the Pharisees were a group of laypersons, particularly zealous for the study of the law and its practice, and interested in preserving and fostering the purity and holiness of Israel in keeping with the Old Testament vision that Israel was to be "a priestly kingdom and a holy nation" (Exod. 19:6). Israel was to be "holy," as God is holy. "Holiness" was understood as separation "from all that is unclean" (Lev. 20:22–26). In keeping apart from uncleanness as the law commanded, the holiness of God's people was preserved, simultaneously honoring God's law and holiness as well. In short, the Pharisees were a movement that sought to bring all of life under the "sacred canopy" of God's law.

Against this backdrop we may place Jesus' deliberate invitation to his table of those who were not particularly known for their scrupulous purity. As a teacher and interpreter of scripture, Jesus manifested his actual understanding of the law by eating with those who showed little regard for keeping the dictates of the law.

> Jesus' willingness to welcome to his table those whose lives demonstrate contempt for God's law conjures up the real possibility of undermining moral seriousness and determination. The possibility of bringing all life under the sacred canopy of God's law is threatened by actions that suggest God is not serious about the law.[13]

This is what bothers the Pharisees; in the parable, it is the father's similar disregard for moral seriousness and accountability that so troubles the older son. While he has been at work minding the family business, his younger brother has been disgracing the family name and squandering the family's heritage. The father seems completely unconcerned by all of this. Oblivious to the work that needs to be done, unconcerned about the well-being of his family, its business, and property, and apparently completely uninterested in his own reputation, he welcomes the prodigal home.

---

[13]Juel, "The Lord's Prayer," 68.

This, then, leads to the question of who the central character of the parable really is. A typical reading of the parable features the younger son, or perhaps the younger son and father together, as the heroes of the parable. The younger son repents, and returns home; the father graciously welcomes him. Thus either it is the younger son's recognition of his guilt and shame that prompts him to cast himself on the mercy of his father or it is the father's astonishing forgiveness that become the point of the parable. But on virtually any reading the older son is the villain, alienated from both of the central figures of the parable.

But crucial to the parable are the facts that its central characters are a father and his sons, and that the parable opens and the story is set in motion by the younger son's demand for "his share of the inheritance." The father gives it to him, and then the younger son proceeds to squander it, so that in the end he is left with nothing. This pattern sounds familiar. Numerous stories in the Old Testament feature a younger son usurping the older son's privileged place and right of inheritance—Cain and Abel, Esau and Jacob, Joseph and his brothers, Manasseh and Ephraim. The blessing intended for the older in some way falls on the younger. Sarah demands that Abraham expel Ishmael, the son of the slave woman Hagar, so that he will not inherit along with Isaac (Gen. 21:9–13). This theme of inheritance was one of the dominant themes running throughout the Old Testament picture of a father. The father provides an inheritance to his firstborn; Israel is God's own firstborn; and hence, God is the father of Israel or of the righteous individuals within it; and God grants them an inheritance.

The image of the Father as one who provides an inheritance is crucial to understanding the parable of the prodigal son. In this parable, the younger son receives and then squanders his inheritance, signaling that he has effectively disinherited himself from his own family. Not only has he thrown away his inheritance, but also he has essentially forfeited the right of sonship. The older son did not do this; the father did not do this; the younger son does it to himself. He is no longer worthy to be called a son of his father; he is no longer an heir. This is most graphically depicted when the prodigal finds himself "in a far country" eating the food of pigs. Clearly he is among those who are not "holy as God is holy." "To tend the pigs of a Gentile is about as alienated as a Jew could imagine being."[14] Although the older brother, standing in for the

---

[14]Luke T. Johnson, *The Gospel of Luke* (SP 3; Collegeville, Minn.: Liturgical Press, 1991), 237.

Pharisees, is often made the "bad guy" in this parable, it is not the older brother who took away the younger son's inheritance. The conception of the Father as the one who grants an inheritance explains the older son's reaction to what his brother had done: having disinherited himself, he has cut himself off from his family, the land, his heritage. He is like those who, in the command of Leviticus and Exodus, have defiled themselves by committing acts of impurity: they shall be "cut off."

But when the prodigal returns, the father not only welcomes his younger son home, he apparently "reinherits" him as well. This is the meaning of his initial words to the older brother: "*This son of mine* was dead and is alive again; he was lost and is found." The younger brother is indeed again a son, an heir. But later the father tells the older son, "We had to celebrate and rejoice, because *this brother of yours* was dead and has come to life; he was lost and has been found." The point is obvious. The elder brother should show himself a true son of his father by welcoming his brother back. The father is not simply a waiting father, nor simply a forgiving father, but also a reconciling father. He attempts to reconcile the two brothers. To do that, the father takes the great risk of alienating the older brother. The "powerless almighty father" can, but does not, force either son to act in either appropriately filial or fraternal ways. The father runs the risk of letting them alienate themselves from him and from each other. As Schweizer writes,

> The end of the story grips the hearts of the hearers, because there is no solution given. Jesus leaves us with the picture of the powerless father out there. And over against him stands that righteous elder son who is so thoroughly convinced that, if there were an almighty father, he would have to act in a quite different way.[15]

We must not lose the specific context in which this parable is set. The parables of Luke 15 are presented as explaining why Jesus welcomes sinners and eats with them. According to Luke, Jesus explained his ministry as giving the lost their inheritance and asking for the "joint heirs" of that inheritance to extend to each other the mercy, forgiveness, and charity that their Father had extended to them. In Luke's Gospel, Jesus is shown practicing the forgiveness to which he called others. This is amply embodied in his table fellowship with sinners. He extends forgiveness to a woman who weeps at his feet. On the cross, he welcomes

---

[15]Schweizer, *Luke: A Challenge to Present Theology,* 80.

the repentant thief to Paradise. And there he also prays, "Father, forgive them, for they know not what they do." Luke thus shows Jesus "loving his enemies" even unto the end. Unlike the older brother, who cannot forgive his younger brother, Jesus presumes that the father's forgiveness extends to his enemies. Jesus lives out his own command to "be merciful, as your heavenly father is merciful."

## The community of the Spirit in Acts

The early chapters of Acts portray the Christian community as a community empowered by the Spirit of God to proclaim the Word but also to live together in fellowship, in breaking bread, listening to the apostles' teaching, and in sharing their goods. The sharing of goods is as much a product of the Holy Spirit's guidance as is the proclamation of the Word of God. Indeed, the dispute between the Hellenists and Hebrews is a communal matter which must be settled by selecting seven persons "full of the Holy Spirit." Because the Spirit engenders the life of this community, that community fulfills Jesus' admonition in Luke to "sell what you have and give alms." They serve God, not mammon (Luke 16:13). They avoid the avaricious self-seeking of the "rich fool" and do not "store up treasure for themselves" but, rather, are "rich toward God" (Luke 12:16–21). They avoid the mistake of the rich man who ignored the ailing Lazarus at his doorstep. Though the rich man called upon "Father Abraham" to have mercy, it is clear that he had not borne the "fruits that befit repentance" (3:8), without which no appeal to Abraham as father will avail before God's judgment. Luke thus indicates that it is by the power of the Spirit of the Father that people live out Jesus' commands regarding riches in community. Such community was an ideal sought by many in the ancient world, as is evident from various attempts at communal living, such as the covenanters at Qumran.[16] According to Luke, it is the Spirit, the gift of the Father, by which such self-giving is enabled.

Another way to put it is that the community empowered by the Spirit can do what the "older brother" could not do: extend mercy in such a way that fosters the life of the community and shows its members to be "children of their Father who is in heaven." This mercy is tangibly

---

[16]See the discussion in Martin Hengel, *Property and Riches in the Early Church: Aspects of a Social History of Early Christianity* (Philadelphia: Fortress, 1974), 33–34; and Luke T. Johnson, *The Literary Function of Possessions in Luke-Acts* (SBLDS 39; Atlanta: Scholars Press, 1977), especially 26–28.

shown in the embrace of the other and in tangible acts of generosity. As one commentator notes, "God is presented by Luke as the Father who *cares* for his children and *acts redemptively* on their behalf."[17] And it is no less true that God is presented by Luke as the Father who expects those who are the children of God to care for each other and thus to embody God's redemptive acts to each other. The redemptive love of the Father is socially embodied in the community's life together.

Luke portrays God as a Father who acts redemptively by giving "even to the Gentiles the repentance that leads to life" (Acts 11:18). While the inclusion of the Gentiles seems to come as an enormous surprise to the disciples, within Luke-Acts it is the working out of the implications of the parables of the lost sheep, lost coin, and the prodigal son of Luke 15. The first two of these parables end with a similar refrain: "There will be more joy in heaven over one sinner who repents than over ninety-nine righteous persons who need no repentance" (15:7; cf. 15:10). The parable of the prodigal gives a graphic portrayal of that joy and celebration, inviting the righteous to celebrate along with the father. In the book of Acts, the "sinners" are the Gentiles, and their inclusion poses the question to the early Jewish Christian community whether they will celebrate with the Father. That the celebration did not come without some great effort is clear from the so-called Jerusalem Council of Acts 15, as well as from the letters of Paul. It is also the letters of Paul that illustrate that the fear of the older brother was not unfounded, that to sit loose to the law might well lead to immorality, confusion, and a squandering of Israel's good heritage and name. No more graphic demonstration that the older brother's complaint was justified could be offered than the Corinthian congregation!

Luke thus pictures God as a Father whose mercy and compassion for his children imply that in God's kingdom they must manifest to each other the same sort of mercy and forgiveness. The Father's conduct is exemplary; just as the father forgives and reclaims the prodigal, so the siblings in the family must go and do likewise. But the Father also makes possible, through the gift of the kingdom and the gift of the Spirit, precisely the sort of conduct to which Jesus calls his followers. Indeed, this is just the sort of conduct that Jesus himself demonstrates, ultimately showing that he is the true Son of the Father and that it is only he who truly knows the Father.

---

[17]Joel B. Green, *The Gospel According to Luke* (NICNT; Grand Rapids: Eerdmans, 1997), 438.

## Matthew: "You Have One Father"

Matthew uses Father language for God more often than Mark and Luke combined. Whereas Luke showed some preference for the simple "Father," Matthew prefers possessive formulations. Thus Matthew has some form of "my Father" about fifteen times,[18] and "your Father" about fifteen times as well.[19] Matthew thus emphasizes both that God is the Father of Jesus and that God is the Father of those who follow Jesus. When held together, these twin convictions disclose Matthew's vision of the Fatherhood of God.

### *"Your heavenly Father"*

It is telling that when Jesus speaks of "your Father," the audience is typically his disciples.[20] Seldom does he use Father language when larger crowds are in view. A few instances will illustrate Matthew's usage.

> They neither sow nor reap nor gather into barns, and yet *your heavenly Father* feeds them. (Matt. 6:26)
> They neither sow nor reap, they have neither storehouse nor barn, and yet *God* feeds them. (Luke 12:24)

> It is not you who speak, but the *Spirit of your Father* speaking through you (Matt. 10:20).
> For the *Holy Spirit* will teach you at that very hour what you ought to say (Luke 12:12).

> Whoever does the will of *my Father in heaven* is my brother and sister and mother (Matt. 12:50).
> Whoever does the will of *God* is my brother and sister and mother (Mark 3:35; cf. Luke 8:21).

> When I drink it new with you in *my Father's kingdom . . .* (Matt. 26:29).
> When I drink it new in the *kingdom of God . . .* (Mark 14:25; Luke 22:18).

---

[18]Compared to four times in Luke; never in Mark.

[19]Three times in Luke; once in Mark.

[20]A. W. Argyle, *God in the New Testament* (Philadelphia: Lippincott, 1965), 65.

*My Father,* if it is possible, let this cup pass from me. . . . (Matt. 26:39)
*Abba, Father,* for you all things are possible. . . . (Mark 14:36)
*Father,* if you are willing, remove this cup from me. (Luke 22:42)

Matthew's frequent personal references to "your Father" or "your heavenly Father" highlight his emphasis on God as a Father who knows and provides for the needs of his children.

Look at the birds of the air; they neither sow nor reap nor gather into barns, and yet your heavenly Father feeds them. . . . Therefore do not worry, saying, "What will we eat?" or "What will we drink?" or "What will we wear?" For it is the Gentiles who strive for all these things; and indeed your heavenly Father knows that you need all these things. (Matt. 6:25–26, 31–32)

In this passage, Jesus does not appeal to his hearers to believe that God is their heavenly Father but, rather, calls on them to trust in the one whom they, in contrast to "Gentiles," acknowledge as Father. Like a father who provides and cares for his own, God provides and cares for those who are his own (Matt. 7:7–11//Luke 11:9–13).[21] To be sure, this Father is the God who cares for all creation, but Jesus tells his followers that this God is "your heavenly Father." When Jesus in the Gospels speaks of God as "your Father," the accent falls on God as one who provides and cares for his children.[22] The response called for is the response of trust.[23]

---

[21]Luke's version reads "*the* heavenly Father" instead of "*your* father in heaven," making the designation of God as Father somewhat less particular.

[22]As Stephen C. Barton states, "For Matthew, God's presence is experienced as fatherly" (*The Spirituality of the Gospels* [London: SPCK, 1992], 12). Barton further explicates the experience of "God's fatherly presence" in terms of (1) a recognition of the providence of God as creator and sustainer of the world; (2) acknowledgment of the final authority of God in humble dependence; and (3) the reciprocity of the relationship, albeit not as a relationship of peers (12–14).

[23]Johanna van Wijk-Bos (*Reimagining God,* 43–44) argues that paternal imagery for God assigns a "childlike posture to the believer, which is particularly damaging for women, who need to free themselves from such stereotypes." Much, of course, depends upon what valence one assigns to "childlike posture," but that Jesus called for trust in and dependence upon God, and that in this capacity he invoked the image of God as Father, is not an incidental part of his teaching or call to his people. Those who have been called into being as a family by God are to relate to him in trust and dependence.

Jesus states that the Father expects those within this family to have the kind of regard for each other that mirrors God's own character (5:16, 45, 58; 7:21; 12:50; 21:31; 25:34, 41). The Beatitudes reflect such an expectation. When Jesus says, "Blessed are the peacemakers, for they shall be called children of God" (5:9), the underlying assumption is that as God is a peacemaker, so the children of God are to be as well. Similarly, Jesus' command to love one's enemies takes as its norm the love of God:

> Love your enemies and pray for those who persecute you, so that you may be children of your Father in heaven; for he makes his sun rise on the evil and on the good, and sends rain on the righteous and on the unrighteous. For if you love those who love you, what reward do you have? Do not even the tax collectors do the same? And if you greet only your brothers and sisters, what more are you doing than others? Do not even the Gentiles do the same? Be perfect, therefore, as your heavenly Father is perfect. (Matt. 5:43–48)[24]

In this passage, Jesus not only speaks of God as Father, but of others as "brothers and sisters." "Gentiles" refers to those outside of Israel, to whom the "brothers and sisters" are contrasted. But those who are truly children of their heavenly Father will manifest it through the way in which they reflect God's impartial mercy to others. They are to act as their heavenly Father does. In a later account, this point is made in another way. When Jesus' family comes to look for him, Jesus redefines his family as those who do the will of his Father.

> Someone told him, "Look, your mother and your brothers are standing outside, wanting to speak to you." But to the one who had told him this, Jesus replied, "Who is my mother, and who are my brothers?" And pointing to his disciples, he said, "Here are my mother and my brothers! For whoever does the will of my Father in heaven is my brother and sister and mother." (12:47–50)

Mark's version speaks of doing "the will of God" (3:35), and Luke's of "those who hear the word of God and do it" (8:21). While the ultimate point is the same, Matthew's reference to doing the will of Jesus' Father

---

[24]Luke's version of this saying, "Be merciful as your heavenly father is merciful" (Luke 6:36) makes it clear whereof "perfection" consists.

in heaven emphasizes the familial imagery even more strongly than do the other Synoptic Gospels. He speaks of "doing the will of my Father who is in heaven." In Matthew, the word "will" is always connected with the Father, rather than with God. Disciples are to pray, "Our Father . . . your will be done" (6:10), a prayer that Jesus prays in Gethsemane, "My Father . . . your will be done" (26:39, 42). It is the "gracious will" of the Father to reveal hidden things to infants (11:25).[25] Whoever "does the will of my Father in heaven is my brother and sister and mother" (12:50).[26] It is "not the will of your Father in heaven that one of these little ones be lost" (18:14). A Matthean parable about two sons, one who said he would go to work in the vineyard, but did not, and one who said he would not, but in the end did, raises the question, "which of the two did the will of his father?" (21:31) and so followed in "the way of righteousness" (21:32).

Matthew also emphasizes Jesus' role as teacher of the Father's will. Those who do "the will of my Father" are kin to Jesus. Jesus relocates the primary sphere of faithful obedience from the home to the community. In that community, brothers and sisters are to live together in humility and mutual honor of each other. There is no pulling rank in this family. All allegiance is directed toward God, the only one properly designated Father, that is to say, the only one who exercises the role or authority which the term "father" implies.

> But you are not to be called rabbi, for you have one teacher, and you are all students. And call no one your father on earth, for you have one Father—the one in heaven. Nor are you to be called instructors, for you have one instructor, the Messiah. (23:8–10)

These words are found in Jesus' long tirade against the Pharisees and scribes. Inasmuch as the prohibition against calling any human being Father is sandwiched between the warnings that there is only one teacher (*didaskalos;* διδάσκαλος) and only instructor or tutor (kathēgētēs; καθηγητής),[27] the prohibition against calling another human being

---

[25]Here, however, the Greek word is *eudokia* (good pleasure) rather than *thelēma* (will).

[26]In Mark 3:35, a parallel statement reads, "Whoever does the *will of God* . . . ." Luke's parallel reads, "My mother and my brothers are those who hear the word of God and do it" (8:21). The thought is of course similar, but the phrase "will of my father" is decidedly Matthean.

[27]Bruce W. Winter argues for this meaning in "The Messiah as Tutor: The Meaning of καθηγητής in Matthew 23:10," in *TynBul* 42 (1991): 151–57.

"father" refers to putting any human instructor or teacher in the place of God, the "one Father" in heaven.[28] Through the Messiah, the Father teaches and instructs. No human being may usurp the roles of the Father and Messiah in the community. They may neither usurp God's prerogative to demand obedience and honor, nor may they take his place as ultimate authority.[29] Those who follow the way of Jesus to the cross are not to "lord it over each other" (20:25), as do those outside the family. Instead, they are to treat each other as kin, and in the family they are not to pull rank. For all call God Father, and no one else properly merits that term.[30]

There are standards of behavior for life within the family. The brothers and sisters of Jesus' family are to forgive each other. Even as Jesus instructed his disciples to petition God for their own forgiveness, so he exhorted them to forgive others and warned them of the consequences of failing to do so (Matt. 6:14–15). In Matthew, moreover, the Father and the Father's response are of particular concern when Jesus is addressing issues of piety and practice, such as prayer, almsgiving, and fasting (Matt. 6:1–16). This focus might seem to radically individualize the relationship between God and the individual: people are to pray alone, in secret; they are to give alms without trumpeting them before others; they are to fast without making it known. While such admonitions can be taken to foster a personal and private piety, in fact there are repercussions for the life of the community. To carry out the required

---

[28]The historical context of the prohibition in Matthew 23:9 is unclear. Commentators typically suggest that the prohibition opposes either calling Jewish synagogue leaders or Christian leaders Father as a reverential or honorific form of address. The use of Father in direct address for a contemporary rabbi is rare in rabbinic literature, although it does refer to the earlier great scholars of the tradition (such as Hillel and Shammai). In Hellenistic moral philosophy, a philosopher could be addressed as Father by his disciples; see Abraham Malherbe, "Paul: Hellenistic Philosopher or Christian Pastor?" *ATR* 67 (1985): 9, and idem, *Paul and the Thessalonians: The Philosophic Tradition of Pastoral Care* (Philadelphia: Fortress, 1987), 40. For a reading that understands the protest against calling anyone Father as directed against Roman authority vested in the emperor who was known as Father, see Mary Rose D'Angelo, "*Abba* and 'Father.' "

[29]The following prayer, attributed to Akiba (*b. Ta'an.* 25b), provides a partial parallel to Matthew's admonition: "Our father our king, we have no king but you; Our father our king, for your own sake have mercy on us." John 19:15 ("We have no king but Caesar") clearly reverberates off such acclamations.

[30]On this point, see particularly the comments of Schüssler Fiorenza, *In Memory of Her,* 150–51, cited in the Introduction to the present volume, p. 12.

actions of true piety in secrecy, rather than openly, means that no one can ever attain to a public status based on achievement or merit in their piety. In communal life, no one's piety becomes celebrated. The hiddenness of certain acts of obedience thus promotes the life of the community because it ensures that no person can lord it over another.

It is precisely the fact that the community knows and calls upon God as "our Father in heaven" that obligates them in turn to treat each other with familial love and care. In this light, the traditional understanding of Matthew 18 as a chapter on "church discipline" would better be viewed as a chapter that seeks to show how brothers and sisters in a family are to treat each other and to make sure that their life together functions as the heavenly Father desires. Again, the Father's own actions provide the warrant for the life of the community. No one is to despise "the little ones," because "it is not the will of your Father in heaven that one of these little ones should be lost" (18:14; cf. 18:11).

No parable or saying in Matthew drives home the point of family obligation so emphatically as the famous parable of the last judgment, a parable that at first glance might appear to have nothing to do with family ties (25:31–46). For although Jesus tells his disciples early on in Matthew that their heavenly Father provides for and cares for his children, here, toward the end of the Gospel, he depicts the judgment of those who did not provide and care for the needy.

> When the Son of Man comes in his glory, and all the angels with him, then he will sit on the throne of his glory. All the nations will be gathered before him, and he will separate people one from another as a shepherd separates the sheep from the goats, and he will put the sheep at his right hand and the goats at the left. Then the king will say to those at his right hand, "Come, you that are *blessed by my Father, inherit the kingdom* prepared for you from the foundation of the world; for I was hungry and you gave me food, I was thirsty and you gave me something to drink, I was a stranger and you welcomed me, I was naked and you gave me clothing, I was sick and you took care of me, I was in prison and you visited me." (25:31–36)

Those who are characterized as "the righteous of my Father" are those who fed the hungry, clothed the naked, and visited those in prison. They are those who, like God the Father, provided for the needy (6:25–34), because they understood the twofold covenant obligation to love God and neighbor. They are those who have indeed learned that they cannot serve two masters (6:24) and that when one serves God, others are necessarily to be served as well. While in Matthew Jesus urges the disciples to trust in God's provision, to rely on "their heavenly Father," who so graciously feeds the birds of the air and clothes the grass of the field, God's fatherly provision for his children nevertheless does not excuse them from being part of the way in which God provides for the needy. Indeed, God's fatherly goodness obligates those who are children of God: those who have learned faithfulness in the family of God must live it out. If God clothes the grass, God's children are to clothe the naked; if God feeds the birds, God's children are to feed the hungry.

### *"My Father in heaven"*

In spite of the emphasis on the new family of the heavenly Father, gathered around Jesus in the way of discipleship, Matthew still retains the singularity of Jesus' address to God as "my Father" and his admonitions to his disciples regarding obedience to "your Father." Clearly there is a distinction between the way in which Jesus relates to God as Father and the way in which the disciples do. Matthew's manifest predilection for the formulation "my Father" reflects his understanding of the distinctive character of Jesus' Sonship and the relationship of the Father and the Son. A distinctive relationship is summarized in the saying regarding the mutual knowledge of Father and Son, also found in Luke, and already discussed above.[31] In Matthew, as in Luke, Jesus' saying follows the pronouncement of judgment on Chorazin, Bethsaida, and Capernaum. But in Matthew, it precedes the invitation for all those who are burdened and oppressed to come to Jesus for rest. Jesus' statement regarding the reflexive and distinctive knowledge of Father and Son thus serves as a pivot between the pronouncement of judgment and the invitation to follow Jesus, both of which are effected through the hiding and revealing of the "Father, Lord of heaven and earth." The passage celebrates the unexpected manifestation of God's grace to "the little ones," "the least of these," those whom Jesus takes pains elsewhere to identify as the members of his family (Matt. 10:42; 18:6, 10, 14; 25:40, 45). Here, as elsewhere in Matthew, Jesus thus subverts rather than supports worldly standards of value, worth, and power. But this

---

[31]So Chilton, "God as Father," 69–70. Jesus' references to "my Father" appear regularly in material unique to Matthew (M), as well as in Matthean redaction of Mark and, possibly, of Q as well.

happens specifically in the context of Jesus' own mission. By creating division among those who hear him, Jesus' very words effect the judgments and promises of which he speaks. In this saying in Matthew regarding the mutual knowledge of Father and Son, the emphasis falls not on the metaphysical relationship of Father and Son, or even so much on the intimacy and mutuality of their knowledge, but rather on the way in which God's hiding and revealing are effected through and in the ministry of Jesus.

Jesus' address to God as "my Father" coheres with Matthew's stress on Jesus' messianic status, although it is clear that not every aspect of Jesus' Sonship can be derived from it. In the passage just discussed, for example, there is no explicit indication that the relationship of the Son and Father is to be construed as "messianic." Still, Jesus' identity as "son of David" is reiterated often in Matthew, and Jesus is unquestionably identified as the Messiah of Israel. As Messiah, Jesus is the Son of God, even as Nathan's prophecy had promised; Matthew's formulation of Peter's confession, "You are the Christ, the son of the living God," virtually equates messianic and filial identity. Because he is Son and Messiah, Jesus may speak with confidence about the reality of his Father's coming kingdom and address God as "my Father." Although Luke also specifically links the gift of the kingdom with the Father (e.g., 12:32), Matthew lays the accent on the kingdom as the "kingdom of *my* Father."

> Then Peter said in reply, "Look, we have left everything and followed you. What then will we have?" Jesus said to them, "Truly I tell you, at the renewal of all things, when the Son of Man is seated on the throne of his glory, you who have followed me will also sit on twelve thrones, judging the twelve tribes of Israel. And everyone who has left houses or brothers or sisters or father or mother or children or fields, for my name's sake, will receive a hundredfold, and will inherit eternal life. (19:27–29)

For Matthew, as for Luke, the kingdom belongs to the Father. Jesus teaches his disciples to pray, "Our Father . . . thy kingdom come." At the end of the Matthean parable of the wheat and the weeds, Jesus says that "the righteous will shine like the sun in the kingdom of their Father" (13:43). The parable of the sheep and the goats ends with the invitation, "Come, you that are blessed by my Father, inherit the kingdom prepared for you . . ." And at the Last Supper, Jesus promises not to drink "of this fruit of the vine until that day when I drink it new with you in my Father's kingdom" (26:29). Matthew apparently considered Father a particularly apt designation for God on the lips of the one who, as Messiah and "the Son of the living God," issued a call to people to show themselves to be children "of your Father who is in heaven."

In Matthew, then, Jesus speaks of God as "my Father" and to his disciples of God as "your Father." This dual usage mirrors that of the Old Testament, where God is the father of the king, as well as of the people of Israel. Matthew draws from the Old Testament both the motif of the Messiah as the Son of God, and of the people of Israel as the children of God. The question with which he is concerned is not, How shall we think of God? or What shall we call God? Rather, Matthew's question is, Whose conduct acknowledges God as Father? In contrasting the behavior of those who are children of the heavenly Father with the behavior of "the Gentiles," Matthew's Jesus appeals to the righteous to show themselves to be true children of that Father.

Matthew's account, in which Jesus speaks of God as "my Father" and his disciples are invited to pray to God as "our Father," may be read against God's lament in Jeremiah 3:19:

> I thought
>> how I would set you among my children,
> and give you a pleasant land,
>> the most beautiful heritage of all the nations.
> And I thought you would call me, My Father,
>> and would not turn from following me.

In Jeremiah, God laments that he desired to give Israel its "most beautiful heritage," and hoped for Israel to call upon God as "My Father." Yet there is the hope for a reestablishment of such a relationship.

> With weeping they shall come,
>> and with consolations I will lead them back,
> I will let them walk by brooks of water,
>> in a straight path in which they shall not stumble;
> for I have become a father to Israel,
>> and Ephraim is my firstborn.
>
> (Jer. 31:9)

Later in Jeremiah 31 one finds the promise of the new covenant that God will make with those of Israel. There are several features of the covenant:

- The law will be written on the hearts of the people.
- The house of Israel will be God's people.
- There shall be no need for them to "teach one another," for they shall all know the LORD.
- God will forgive their sins. (31:31–35)

According to Matthew, the time has come for God to make this new covenant with Israel. The one who is son of Abraham and son of David, the true Israelite, calls upon God as "my Father." This Messiah teaches an interpretation of the law that calls for obedience from "the abundance of the heart," as expressed in love of God and neighbor (Matt. 12:34). This Messiah gathers together "the lost sheep of the house of Israel" as God's people (Matt. 15:24). Because they have the Messiah as teacher and the new covenant written in their hearts, they have no need for any other authoritative teacher (23:10). Because God has "become a Father to Israel," they are to call no one "Father" but God (23:9). But through the Messiah they have the knowledge of the LORD which Jeremiah promised. And finally, the new covenant is sealed by Jesus' "innocent blood" (cf. Jer. 26:15; Matt. 27:4, 24), the "blood of the covenant, which is poured out for many for the forgiveness of sins" (Matt. 26:28). In short, Matthew portrays Jesus' mission as the outworking of Jeremiah's promise of a new covenant. The renewed covenant entails knowing the Lord and returning to God as Father in obedience and trust.

## Summary Reflections: Jesus and the Father in the Synoptic Gospels

Mark's portrait of God as Father focuses almost exclusively on God's relationship to Jesus himself. Although Mark provides the sparest picture of God as Father, the identification of Jesus as the Son of God figures as an important Markan theme. Because the few references are spaced throughout the narrative in conjunction with key events which disclose the mission and mystery of Jesus, they provide the substance of the Gospel's portrait of Jesus as the Son of God. The other strand of Father language, which has to do with the disciples' relationship to God, plays a very minor role in Mark. Rather, what is emphasized is Jesus' distinctive relationship to God.

By contrast, for Luke the relationship of God as Father to Jesus' own followers looms large. The Father gives Jesus' "little flock" the kingdom and the Spirit; from them God expects the sort of merciful behavior appropriate to the kingdom and empowered by the Spirit. To be sure, the emphasis on the relationship of Jesus' followers to God the heavenly Father is not purchased at the expense of Jesus' distinctive relationship to God. From the very beginning of the Gospel, Jesus is presented to the reader as the unique Son of God. Furthermore, as the envoy of the kingdom, the recipient of the kingdom, and the one who baptizes with the Spirit, Jesus has the status of the Father's Son in a singular way. Matthew emphasizes the filial strand as much as, if not more than, Luke, repeatedly showing Jesus as the Son of the one he calls "my Father." Through Jesus' teaching and through his death, he gathers a new community, who know God as the only Father and Jesus as the Son, the one through whom God's inheritance is given and God's promised covenant is sealed.

While Matthew and Luke do show an increase in the *frequency* of the use of Father for God vis-à-vis Mark, the distinctive material in Matthew and Luke is not uniformly more christological in its focus. In direct continuity with Mark's portrait of God as Father, both Matthew and Luke assume that God is the Father of Jesus. What Matthew and Luke—and Q—contain, and which Mark does not, is quite a lot of material with a decidedly communal and ethical focus, material that spells out the implications of God as Father for those who would be disciples of the Son. Hence, the increase of language for God as Father is coupled with the increased emphasis on the shape of discipleship. God is Father of the community gathered around Jesus; and this relationship creates and shapes the commitment that those in the community owe not only to God but also to each other.

Luke and Matthew particularly reflect the view that to speak of God as Father means to point to the one who has called this community into being. As children of that one God, those within the community are obligated to each other. Ultimately, then, God's Fatherhood serves not as a model for the behavior of a human father, nor does it in some way give shape to the nuclear family. Rather, God's Fatherhood serves as the model for the life of the faithful community together. All are called to reflect God's mercy and love. No one reflects God's Fatherhood more or less by virtue of status, birth, gender, or class. All are to call on God, and only on God, as Father, and together all are family, brothers and sisters, children of God.

Not only does God's grace and mercy provide the model for the community's conduct, but God's initiative and active love provide the *raison d'être* for it. Thus the community lives together in ways that reflect the gracious activity of God in calling them together. Its corporate conduct reflects God's gracious behavior toward it. As God brings redemption, justice, and forgiveness to the poor, the outcast, and the sinner, so, too, the community that claims allegiance to that God demonstrates it through the same sorts of actions. And although this is the obedience of faith that God asks for, that obedience is lived out within the reality created by God's gift of the kingdom to and through the Son of the Father.

# 5

# "Heirs of God, Heirs with Christ"

The epistles of the New Testament have provided the church with language that has become deeply embedded in its confessions and liturgy. Among the formulations of the New Testament are a number of variations on phrases such as "the God and Father of our Lord Jesus Christ," in which God is designated as the Father of Jesus. One also finds formula in the epistles in which God is referred to as the Father of those who are followers of Jesus Christ. So, for example, we find "our God and Father" or "God our Father." And in two of Paul's letters Christians are said to call upon God as *"Abba,"* the Aramaic term that is ascribed to Jesus in Mark. In speaking of God as the Father of Jesus on the one hand and believers on the other, Paul evinces the same pattern of references that we found in the Synoptic Gospels, especially Matthew and Luke. But the question legitimately arises whether the continuity of this pattern reflects an underlying continuity of content.

In earlier chapters we have argued that several aspects of a father's role in Israelite and Jewish culture particularly illumine the relationship of God to Israel. First and foremost among these features of fatherhood is the notion of the father as the founder of a clan or head of a family who bestows an inheritance on his son and so also on subsequent generations. This aspect of a father's role plays a part in the relatively infrequent references to God as Father in the Old Testament, where God bequeaths an inheritance to Israel (Deut. 32:4–6; cf. Deut. 32:18; Jer. 3:19; 31:9; Isa. 61:7–10; 63:16; 64:8; Zech. 9:12). It is this very notion of God as a Father who gives his children an inheritance that is crucial to Paul's argument in Romans and Galatians. God the Father has, through the Spirit, made Jews and Gentiles together "heirs of God and joint heirs with Christ" (Rom. 8:16–17; cf. Gal. 4:6). Through the Spirit, those who are "heirs with Christ" share the same mode of address to God that Jesus used. They call upon God as "*Abba,* Father."

Because of this shared form of address, Joachim Jeremias's arguments regarding the significance of *abba* in Jesus' ministry are often taken to be applicable to believers as well. In other words, Jeremias's arguments that Jesus' use of the reverent and familial term *abba* revealed his own consciousness of a special relationship to God are now taken to describe the believer's *experience* and *sense of intimacy* in relationship to God. In this manner, Jeremias's argument regarding *Jesus'* sense of Sonship has been transferred wholesale to believers, a move with two fateful consequences. First, it eviscerates Jeremias's hypothesis regarding Jesus' *distinctive* filial consciousness; second, it also virtually ignores the *eschatological* context that Jeremias posited as the basis of Jesus' mission. For Jeremias argued not only that Jesus' use of *abba* arose from his distinctive sense of relationship to God but that this personal and direct address to God revealed his conviction that "the expressions of God's fatherly goodness are *eschatological events.*"[1] Too often this aspect of Jeremias's argument has been lost sight of in discussions of Jesus' use of *abba* and, by extension, in Paul's understanding of God's Fatherhood as well.

But although the eschatological framework of the confession of God as Father has disappeared in some modern interpretations, it remains crucial for Paul. For Paul, confession of God as Father rests on the conviction that, in Christ, God's purposes for the salvation of all the world are being brought to their completion.[2] Jew and Gentile together call on God as Father. The invocation of God as Father acknowledges the divine initiative in salvation. God has now graciously bestowed the promised inheritance on Jesus Christ, the heir of all things; and through Jesus, others become "joint heirs" of the Father's promised inheritance. Through the Spirit, those in Christ enter into their inheritance, calling upon God as Father. But this work remains to be completed in the future, when all things will be handed over by the Son to the Father, when the adoption promised to Israel (Rom. 9:4) will be sealed in the salvation of "all Israel." These are fundamentally eschatological convictions for Paul. These affirmations, and not the filial sensibilities of believers or some newly benign view of God, comprise the substance of

---

[1]Jeremias, *Prayers of Jesus,* 43, 63; emphasis added.
[2]Edgar Krentz, "God in the New Testament," 89–90.

the invocation of God as *"Abba*! Father" in Paul's thought. Because Paul's argument is most fully traced out in Romans, we shall follow it here, noting some similarities with and differences from other epistles along the way.

### "God our Father and the Lord Jesus Christ"

God is explicitly called Father only four times in the 15 chapters of the epistle to the Romans (1:7; 6:4; 8:15; 15:6). There are just over 40 references to God as Father in all the letters of the Pauline corpus. Every letter in the Pauline canon begins with some form of greeting or opening blessing in which God is designated at least once, and sometimes several times, as "our father,"[3] "the father,"[4] or "the father of our Lord Jesus Christ."[5] Some letters (including 1 Timothy, 2 Timothy, Titus, and Philemon) contain no other references to God as Father. Some contain only a few. For example, outside of the opening greetings, in Galatians Paul refers to God as Father only once, in reporting the invocation of God by believers as *"Abba*, Father" (Gal. 4:6). Philippians contains two other references to God as Father, one in the final line of the so-called Christ hymn (Phil. 2:11, "to the glory of God the Father") and one in a closing benediction. Again, not including the opening greetings, Romans has three references to God as Father; 1 Corinthians, two references; 2 Corinthians, three references. Obviously, these statistics cannot be interpreted to mean that the designation of God as Father is theologically or pastorally unimportant for Paul. But they are worth mentioning simply because sweeping claims have been made for the status of the term Father in the New Testament. But it is clear that Father is not the preferred designation for God in the Pauline writings. The most common term for God is simply the Greek term *theos* (θεός), which occurs about five hundred times.

But what is more illuminating is the pattern of the references to God as Father. Paul's most common way of referring to God as Father includes the plural possessive pronoun; hence, some form of "our Father." And although all references to God as "our Father" stand in

---

[3]Rom. 1:7; 1 Cor. 1:3; 2 Cor. 1:2; Gal. 1:3–4; Eph. 1:2, Phil. 1:2; Col. 1:2, 1 Thess. 1:3; 2 Thess. 1:1–2; Phlm. 3.

[4]Gal. 1:1; 1 Thess. 1:1; 1 Tim. 1:2; 2 Tim. 1:2; Titus 1:4.

[5]2 Cor. 1:3; Eph. 1:3; Col. 1:3.

some sort of benediction or prayer, "our Father" never stands alone, as it does, for example, in Matthew's version of the Lord's Prayer. Rather, it is always coupled with "God." For example, one finds "our God and Father"[6] and "God our father."[7]

We can make these observations even more precise. Although the first phrase, "our God and Father," always stands alone, the second phrase, "God our Father" is regularly followed by some variation on "and the Lord Jesus Christ." In other words, one typically finds "God our Father and the Lord Jesus Christ." Indeed, "God our Father" and "the Lord Jesus Christ" have come to be inseparably linked in the minds of many Christians today, by virtue of having the formula repeated so often. For modern readers of the New Testament, God is "our Father" and "the Lord" is Jesus Christ. "Our Father" thus serves to qualify and identify the rather open-ended term "god", just as "Jesus Christ" serves to qualify and identify "the Lord."

As Paul writes elsewhere, "Even though there may be so-called gods in heaven or on earth—as in fact there are many gods and many lords—yet for us there is one God, the Father, from whom are all things and for whom we exist, and one Lord, Jesus Christ, through whom are all things and through whom we exist" (1 Cor. 8:5–6). Paul thus reflects the habits of Old Testament and Jewish authors, who regularly add explanatory phrases to "God" in order to make clear which deity is being referred to: "The LORD God Almighty," "the God of Abraham, Isaac and Jacob," "The God of Israel," or "the Most High God." In Paul's writings, a common explanatory phrase includes the plural possessive pronoun—God is "our" God; God is "our" Father.

In other instances in the Pauline epistles, we find the absolute "the Father."[8] Outside of the opening greetings and prescripts, there are two references to God as "the Father of our Lord Jesus Christ."[9] But what one never finds is a dual reference to God as the Father of Jesus Christ and of believers. There is "God our Father *and* the Lord Jesus Christ" or "the God and Father of our Lord Jesus Christ," but never "God, Father

---

[6]Gal. 1:4; Phil. 4:20; Col. 1:2; 1 Thess. 1:3; 3:11, 13.

[7]Rom. 1:7; 1 Cor. 1:3; 2 Cor. 2:2, passim.

[8]"The Father" is found in Rom. 6:4; 1 Cor. 8:6; 15:24; 2 Cor. 1:3 ("the father of mercies," or "the merciful father"); Phil 2:11. The various "disputed" Paulines show a preference for "the Father" for God: six times in Ephesians, not including the prescript (1:17, "the father of glory"; 2:18; 3:14; 4:6; 5:20; 6:23); twice in Colossians (1:12; 3:17); once each in 1 Timothy, 2 Timothy, and Titus.

[9]Rom. 15:6; 2 Cor. 11:31 ("the Father of the Lord Jesus").

of us all and of our Lord Jesus Christ" or "the God and Father of our Lord Jesus Christ and of all those in Christ." In other words, Paul never links Jesus together with believers in formula that refer to God as Father. Is this just accidental? Perhaps so. But more likely it preserves the distinction between affirmations regarding God as the Father of Jesus and God as the Father of believers, a distinction found also in the Gospels. To say that God is the Father of Jesus Christ makes a somewhat different predication than the assertion that God is the Father of Christians.

In any case, all Paul's references to God as "our Father" are found in some sort of benediction or prayer.[10] This pattern suggests that already by the time of the writing of the earliest Pauline epistle, "our Father" had become a characterization of God in the Christian community, particularly in various sorts of prayer. This may suggest a direct link to the pattern of prayer that was apparently characteristic of both Jesus' practice and instruction. Both for Jesus and for Paul, the designation of God as Father was particularly appropriate in prayer. However, it should also be noted that invocation of God as Father can be found in Jewish literature and prayers as well and, indeed, is frequently lodged in those contexts. The practice of Jesus and Paul may not be novel; that does not mean that it is insignificant or irrelevant to considering the New Testament understanding of God as Father.

The patterns referred to above are found in the reference to God as Father in Romans, namely in Paul's opening greeting and blessing: "To all God's beloved in Rome, who are called to be saints: Grace to you and peace from God our Father and the Lord Jesus Christ" (1:7). This pithy opening adumbrates three key elements of Paul's understanding of God as Father.

(1) Nowhere in Paul's letters does he call upon, or refer to, God as "my Father." This stands in stark contract to Jesus' regular references in the Gospels to God as "my Father," a way of referring to God particularly emphasized in Matthew and John. The Gospels also picture Jesus as speaking to his disciples of God as "your Father," which the Pauline epistles mirror in regularly designating God as "our Father." In Matthew's Gospel the plural pronoun clearly refers to Jesus' own disciples. Matthew maintains a strong sense of the difference between Jesus'

---

[10]Other references to God as "our father" in the Pauline epistles include the following: Phil. 4:20 ( a closing benediction); 1 Thess. 3:11, 13 (in a prayer or benediction); 2 Thess. 2:16 (again, in a prayer or benediction).

day and his own, underscoring that Jesus' mission was directed to "the lost sheep of the house of Israel" (15:24) and that in Jesus' own day his followers were to "go nowhere among the Gentiles" (Matt. 10:5). When Jesus speaks of "your heavenly Father," the referent is clearly to Jesus' own immediate Jewish audience. But by the time Matthew was written, Jesus' followers and Matthew's addressees may have been a mixed group of Jews and Gentiles, so that "your heavenly Father" now encompassed a different group. For Paul, it is programmatic that the church composed of Jews and Gentiles in Christ speaks to God as "our Father." The affirmation that God is the Father of Jew and Gentile is critical to understanding God as Father (Rom. 3:29–30; cf. 1:16). Already at the outset, the epistle's inclusive emphasis is distilled in its address to *all* those who are in Rome, and its affirmation of God is as "*our* Father."

(2) Those who know God as Father are "God's beloved." For Paul, it is through the Spirit that "God's love has been poured into our hearts" (5:5). It is through that Spirit that the adoption of the children of God is effected. This adoption is permanent, so that nothing is "able to separate us from the love of God in Christ Jesus our Lord" (8:39). Paul does not claim that God's love has been transferred from Jews to Gentiles, or from Jews to Christians. Israel remains "*beloved,* for the sake of their ancestors" (11:28).[11] But the very love and mercy of God that elected Israel now elects all those in Christ, including the Gentiles. The Gentiles are grafted into the tree; they are adopted in the household of God. The result is that those who were "not my people" have been called "my people," and those who were "not beloved" have been called "my beloved" by God (9:14–18; 10:25–26; 11:29–32; 12:1–2). The terms previously applied to Israel—"my people," "my beloved," "children of the living God"—now include the Gentiles as well. This, then, is a redefinition of the people of God which can be expressed by reconstruing those of whom God is Father.

No epistle in the Pauline corpus celebrates the unity of Jew and Gentile in Christ so much as the epistle to the Ephesians. Perhaps, then, it is no coincidence that Ephesians also has more references to

---

[11]See N. T. Wright, "Romans and the Theology of Paul," in *Pauline Theology,* vol. 3: *Romans* (ed. David M. Hay and E. Elizabeth Johnson; Minneapolis: Fortress, 1995), 54: "Paul is careful not to say, or imply, that the privileges of Israel are simply 'transferred to the church,' even though, for him, the church means Jews-and-Gentiles-together-in-Christ. . . . All that the new family inherit, they inherit in him."

God as Father than any other Pauline letter. Outside of references to God as Father in the opening and closing blessings, which is typical of Paul, there are several references to God as Father, all of which are linked with the theme of the unity of believers. In Ephesians 2:16–19, we read of the reconciliation of "both groups to God in one body" and of the "access in one Spirit to the Father" granted to those who were once "strangers and aliens" but who are now "citizens with the saints and also members of the household of God." Later, in a celebration of the unity of believers in Christ, there is a catalog of the things that they share—one body, one Spirit, one hope, one Lord, one faith, one baptism—culminating in "one God and Father of all, who is above all and through all and in all" (Eph. 4:4–6). That God is Father implies that there are "children," and in the Pauline letters it is the family of Jew and Gentile together in Christ who are called by and respond to God as Father. Few other terms can substitute for Father here, although elsewhere Paul also speaks of "one God" of Jew and Gentile, as in Romans 3:29–30: "Is God the God of Jews only? Is he not the God of Gentiles also? Yes, of Gentiles also, since God is one." Not surprisingly, God and Father are often linked together. "Our Father" identifies who this God is.

(3) Those who are God's beloved are *"called* to be saints." This phrase echoes the description of Paul as one *"called* to be an apostle" (1:1) and of believers as those *"called* to belong to Christ Jesus" (1:6). It also accentuates God's initiative: God has called them to be saints, to belong to Christ.[12] "Called" does not simply mean "renamed." Those who were "not my people" and "not beloved" have been *called* "my people," "children of the living God," and "my beloved." This does not mean that God has given the Gentiles a new *name;* but, rather, that in adopting them as heirs God has granted them a new *status* as part of a new family or clan (cf. 8:28; 9:7, 11, 26).

These three elements—the corporate identification of God as "our Father" and of believers both as "beloved" and as "called"—lead us to the heart of Paul's understanding of the "Fatherhood of God." For Paul, to speak of God as Father now means to include the Gentiles in the household of faith. In order to make his point, Paul demonstrates that both Jew and Gentile alike are descended from Abraham, the honored forefather of the people of Israel. But when he asserts that God is the

---

[12]C. E. B. Cranfield, *A Critical and Exegetical Commentary on the Epistle to the Romans* (2 vols.; ICC; Edinburgh: T. & T. Clark, 1975), 1:69.

Father of Jew and Gentile, Paul appeals not first to what God is but what God has done. To be sure, Paul talks about God's mercy and righteousness, but these are aspects of the way in which God relates to the world, not simply "attributes" of God that can be pondered in isolation from God's saving actions through Christ. Paul's argument is that in Christ, God has gathered together a people of Jew and Gentile. This activity discloses God to be Father, not apart from, but precisely in and through, that activity. Paul makes this argument both in Galatians and, most fully and somewhat differently, in Romans. As we shall see, Romans 4 and Romans 8 together comprise a diptych: Romans 4 names *Abraham* as the father of Jew and Gentile, while Romans 8 names *God* as the Father of Jew and Gentile. Thus to establish that God is the Father of both Jew and Gentile, Paul first argues that Abraham is the forefather of both Jew and Gentile.

### "Our Forefather Abraham"

In Romans 4, Abraham serves as the prime example of one who is justified by God's grace through faith (4:3) and not by works (4:2). To score the point, Paul quotes Genesis 15:6, "Abraham believed God, and it was reckoned to him as righteousness." But while Abraham serves as an instance of exemplary trust in the promises of God, his designation as "our forefather" points to his role as the progenitor of many people who, as his offspring, are also his heirs.[13] If Abraham were only an *example* of faith, then Paul would not need to argue that Abraham was *the father* of all who believe (4:11–12, 16–18) and that Abraham's *descendants* (4:13, 16, 18) would inherit the promises made to him (4:13–14). Abraham could merely be an exemplary instance of radical trust in God; and, indeed, he is often taken in that way. The epistle of James leans in that direction. But Paul persistently uses metaphors of family and inheritance, arguing that Gentile believers are true heirs and descendants of Abraham. In this way Paul indicates that not only do the Gentiles share Abraham's faith but that "their destiny is prefigured in

---

[13]On Abraham as example of faith and forefather of the Jewish people, see James D. G. Dunn, *Romans* (2 vols.; WBC; Dallas, Tex.: Word, 1988), 1:200, for discussion and references to primary literature; J. C. Beker, *Paul the Apostle: The Triumph of God in Life and Thought* (Philadelphia: Fortress, 1988), 99; and Leander Keck, "What Makes Romans Tick?" in *Pauline Theology*, vol. 3: *Romans*, 25.

him."[14] Gentiles who receive and trust the promise of God do not simply *imitate* Abraham; they *belong* to Abraham's family. The Gentiles have in Abraham a forefather, not by virtue of physical descent from him—which they cannot claim—but because they are heirs of the promise made to him who trusted in the promises of God.

But this is exactly the way in which Paul envisions Abraham to be the forefather of the Jews as well: he is their forefather as the recipient of a promise given to him by the God in whom he trusted (cf. 9:6–8).[15] Abraham is "the father of us all" (4:16), because Jew and Gentile alike are heirs through the promise made to Abraham and his seed (4:13), *not* because Jews are descended from Abraham "according to the flesh."[16] Accordingly, there are not two ways of becoming part of Abraham's family: there is only one, and it is according to grace (4:16), not according to fleshly descent (4:1), for Abraham is "the father of us all" (4:16).[17] While Jews might appear to have a "natural" claim on Abraham's inheritance, they inherit in precisely the same way as do the Gentiles: by means of the promise made to Abraham. Paul establishes the equal status of Jew and Gentile before God by contending that all who trust in God's promises are true heirs of Abraham.[18] That this promise has been carried out through Christ testifies to the faithfulness of God, the one who gives life to the dead.

Indeed, underlying the whole argument about Abraham is the view of the father as the one who gives life. The contrast between death and life figures in important ways throughout Romans. In Romans 4:17 God is described as the one who "gives life to the dead" and "calls into existence the things that do not exist." God's life-giving power allows Abraham, whose body "was as good as dead," to become a father first of Isaac and subsequently "of many nations." So also God's life-giving

---

[14]Richard B. Hays, *Echoes of Scripture in the Letters of Paul* (New Haven: Yale University Press, 1989), 56; idem, " 'Have We Found Abraham to Be Our Forefather According to the Flesh?' A Reconsideration of Romans 4:1," *NovT* 27 (1985): 76–98; and Wright, "Romans and the Theology of Paul," 40. But for salient objections against Hays's way of punctuating Romans 4:1, see Dunn, *Romans,* 1:199.

[15]See Wright, "Romans and the Theology of Paul," 39–42.

[16]Andrew T. Lincoln, "From Wrath to Justification: Tradition, Gospel, and Audience in the Theology of Romans 1:18—4:25," in *Pauline Theology,* vol. 3: *Romans,* 152.

[17]Wright, "Romans and the Theology of Paul," 40.

[18]See here N. T. Wright, *The Climax of the Covenant: Christ and the Law in Pauline Theology* (Minneapolis: Fortress, 1992), 167.

power raises Jesus from the dead. Similarly, Abraham "is the father of us all" (4:16), the "father of many nations" (4:17), because he gave life to a son and, through him, to many offspring. God is the Father of Jesus Christ, whom he raised from the dead, and through whom believers "walk in newness of life" (6:4; cf. 10:9).[19] With the designation of God as Father, Paul underscores with one stroke both the life-giving power of God and the ways in which believers find their destiny prefigured in the death and resurrection of Jesus, the ultimate heir of the promise made to Abraham.

### *"Abba*, Father!"

The promise made to Abraham was fulfilled, first, through the birth of a son and heir, "our forefather Isaac" (9:10), who in turn becomes the forefather of those who are children of the promise (9:6–9). But ultimately it is through the birth, death, and resurrection of God's own Son (8:3), through whom one receives adoption and so enters into the promised inheritance. This is the narrative underlying Paul's argument in Romans. It begins with Abraham and the birth of Isaac; moves to the life, death, and resurrection of Jesus; and concludes in the adoption of Abraham's many descendants in Christ. This narrative explains the varying designations of God as simply "the Father" (Rom. 6:4; 1 Cor. 8:6; Gal. 1:1), "the God and Father of our Lord Jesus Christ" (Rom. 15:6; 2 Cor. 1:3; 11:31), and "God our Father and the Lord Jesus Christ" (Rom. 1:7; 1 Cor. 1:3; 2 Cor. 1:2; Gal. 1:3, passim*).* God is "our Father" because God is "the Father of our Lord Jesus Christ," the Son and heir, through whom his offspring also become heirs of God's inheritance. Thus those who are in Christ are "heirs of God" and "fellow heirs with Christ" (Rom. 8:17; Gal. 4:15–18). Because they are heirs, they call upon God as Father.

Paul explicitly locates the believer's address to God as *"Abba!* Father!" in the work of the Holy Spirit (8:15). This passage, together

---

[19]Dunn, *Romans,* 1:315, comments that usually in resurrection formula, agency is not specified, whereas here it is. It is not surprising that the agent of raising Jesus to life is the *Father,* for in Romans "fatherhood" is particularly associated with the creation and procreation of life. See also the comments of Andrew T. Lincoln, "Abraham Goes to Rome: Paul's Treatment of Abraham in Romans 4," in *Worship, Theology and Ministry in the Early Church: Essays in Honor of Ralph P. Martin* (ed. Michael J. Wilkins and Terence Paige; JSNTSup 87; Sheffield: Sheffield Academic Press, 1992), 176–78.

with Galatians 4:6, is the *locus classicus* for understanding the Fatherhood of God in Paul. Unfortunately, discussion of this invocation has
been too quickly severed from its context in the argument of Romans
regarding the revelation of God's righteousness to Jew and Gentile alike
and moved into the realm of the believer's subjective experience of God.
As we shall see, Paul's use of the unusual verb "to cry" (*krazein*) has
been taken to point to the emotional, enthusiastic, or spontaneous
prayers of believers. At the same time, the address to God as *abba* has
been read, in light of Jeremias's arguments about Jesus' use of the term,
to refer to the believer's sense of intimacy in relationship with God. On
this reading, the Spirit "bears witness" to the reality of this intimate relationship within the realm of the individual's experience or faith. It is
telling, for example, that in J. D. G. Dunn's massive tome on the theology of Paul, discussion of God as Father finds its place under the heading of "God in experience."[20] Such interpretations find a natural home
in those outlines of Romans that posit a sharp break between the argument for "justification by faith" in Romans 1—4 and the description of
the life of faith in Romans 5—8.[21] In this view of the structure of
Romans, once Paul has made the argument for "justification by faith"
apart from the law (1—4), he then moves on to describe the reality and
benefit of life in Christ (5—8). The argument that by the Spirit those in
Christ know and experience God as Father both fits with and reinforces
this reading of Romans.

Such factors have contributed to reading Romans 8 primarily in *individualistic, subjective,* and *experiential* terms. But this misses the heart
of Paul's argument, which should be read first in *cosmic, corporate,
eschatological,* and *theocentric* terms. When Romans 5—8 is made a
distinctive unit, it is effectively severed both from what precedes and
from what follows. On the one hand, this division separates Paul's statement that through the Spirit believers cry out to God as Father from his
argument that God's righteousness has been revealed in adopting Jew
and Gentile together into one family in fulfillment of the promise to

<hr />

[20]See James D. G. Dunn, *The Theology of Paul the Apostle* (Grand Rapids:
Eerdmans, 1998), 49.

[21]See, for example, the magisterial commentary by Cranfield, which follows
just this division, with appropriate labels: "The revelation of the righteousness
which is from God by faith alone—'He who is righteous by faith' expounded
(1:18—4:25)"; "The life promised for those who are righteous by faith—'shall
live' expounded (5:1—8:39)."

Abraham. The narrative thread from Abraham, to Christ, to the Spirit is thus cut. And if the affirmations about calling on God as Father refer entirely to individual experience, then the eschatological aspect of Paul's theology is diluted. No longer is Paul's argument a statement of the eschatological work of God in Christ. It is rather a declaration of the affective results of that work of God in Christ. This is not to deny that Paul has concerns with the individual and with response to God in Christ, but it is to argue that these are not the formative concerns in material dealing with God as Father.

On the other hand, when Romans 5—8 is made an independent unit within the larger structure of Romans, then chapter 8, with its assertions of the adoption of the children of God, is severed from the argument in Romans 9—11. There, of course, Paul takes up the issue of God's faithfulness to Israel in part because of the fact that the "adoption" rightly belongs to it. A typical way to solve the problem of the relationship of Romans 5—8 and 9—11 is to see chapters 9—11 as something of an excursus or virtual afterthought: what happens to Israel, to whom the adoption belongs, once the Gentiles are adopted as God's heirs? And to some extent these chapters do deal with exactly that question. But confession of God as Father highlights God's mercy to Israel as well as to the Gentiles. Jew and Gentile together are adopted into one family who, as descendants of Abraham, inherit together in Jesus Christ (15:8–9). God's creation of that one family finds its proper place within the larger narrative of God's redemption of the whole world.

In Romans, Paul places particular emphasis on the agency of the Spirit in the creation of that people. It is also through the Spirit that God gives life, and in Paul that theme is associated with the Father as the source of life. Here Paul writes that through the Spirit believers call out to God as Father. The verb Paul uses is *krazein* (κράζειν; "cry out"), a term whose sense is disputed. How one takes it depends to a large extent on how one reconstructs the character of early Christian worship. Taking the lead from the apparent disarray that seems to characterize Corinthian worship, some interpreters imagine a rather free-form and spontaneous gathering. That believers "cry out" fits the context well. Thus *krazein* is taken as pointing to the "deeply emotional or enthusiastic character of earliest Christian experience and worship."[22] Other

---

[22]Dunn, *Romans,* 1:453.

interpreters construe *krazein* as a technical term, the proper setting of which is a liturgical event within the life of the congregation.[23]

Paul's use of *krazein,* rather than a word for confess, speak, or pray, is indeed striking.[24] One does not *confess* that God *is* Father; one does not even *pray* to God as Father. Rather, they "cry" to God as Father. The term *krazein* is also found in Galatians 4:6 where, however, the subject of the verb is not the believer, but the Spirit. There Paul writes, "God has sent the Spirit of his Son into our hearts, crying, '*Abba!* Father!'" Romans 9:27 contains the only other use of *krazein* in the Pauline correspondence: "And Isaiah cries out concerning Israel, 'Though the number of the children of Israel were like the sand of the sea, only a remnant of them will be saved.' In that passage, the verb refers to Isaiah's prophetic speech. It is used interchangeably with *proeirēken* (predict, foretell) in 9:29, indicating the Spirit-inspired nature of Isaiah's speech. It seems likely, therefore, that the verb *krazein* is used because the Spirit is the ultimate source of these words, rather than because they signify the interior or emotional state of those who are speaking or a particular setting of prayer or worship.[25] The verb may point to the power of the Spirit at work in believers. Thus when Dunn writes that "in Rom. 8:16 Paul speaks *explicitly* of a *sense of sonship* to God as Father," one hears the echoes of Jeremias's contention that Jesus' distinctive filial consciousness found expression in his prayer to God as *Abba.*[26] But Romans 8:16 speaks *explicitly* of the work of the Spirit, not of the "sense of sonship" which believers have. In Romans 8, Paul celebrates the work of the Spirit in enabling Gentiles to acknowledge God as the source of their life and salvation.

While Paul's discussions elsewhere of the Spirit may well suggest that the setting for such Spirit-inspired speech lies within the context of corporate worship, it is the *corporate* dimension of acknowledging God as Father that sheds further light on Paul's use of the term and his argument in Romans 8. Paul's concern is not merely with the individual's

---

[23]Ernst Käsemann, *Commentary on Romans* (ET Grand Rapids: Eerdmans, 1980), 228.

[24]But see Mark 14:36: "[and] he said, 'Abba, Father. . .'"

[25]See also Gordon D. Fee, *God's Empowering Presence: The Holy Spirit in the Letters of Paul* (Peabody, Mass: Hendrickson, 1994), 567. Moreover, it is not at all clear that even if Jeremias's arguments regarding Jesus' use of *abba* were correct that one can legitimately transfer Jesus' sense of consciousness to believers.

[26]Dunn, *Theology of Paul,* 49; my emphasis.

experience of God, nor with the Spirit's activity within the individual, but with the unity of Jew and Gentile. In Christ, both call out to the one God with the same acclamation: "*Abba*! Father!"[27] Three factors testify decisively to the corporate, rather than individualistic, dimension implicit in Paul's assumptions about the significance of this address to God.

(1) First, the pronouns and verbs from Romans 8:1 through the end of the chapter are almost all plural. For example, "the Spirit of God dwells in you" (8:9, 11); "you have received a spirit of adoption" (8:15); the spirit bears witness with "our spirits" that "we are children of God" (8:16); "the Spirit helps us in our weakness, for we do not know how to pray as we ought." This is the same "us" and "our" that Paul has in mind when he speaks of God as "our Father."

(2) Second, the family imagery points not to an agglomeration of individuals but to a greater, corporate reality. The family is a fictive kin group, not simply a group of relatives. It is the family or clan *qua* distinct entity that Paul has in view.

(3) Third, the link between becoming part of Abraham's family (ch. 4) and God's family (ch. 8) underscores the point that just as the Gentiles are Abraham's heirs, so, too, they are "heirs of God and joint heirs with Christ" (8:17). Those who are heirs are all in Christ, now including all the Gentiles in Christ. In short, Paul's declaration that through the Spirit those in Christ know and acknowledge God as Father does not speak only of one of the benefits of being in Christ but, rather, further advances the whole thrust of the argument in Romans that in Christ God has abolished the divisions between Jew and Gentile and adopted them together into one family.

In this light, it can scarcely be forgotten that the whole of Romans 8 is framed, on the one side, by chapter 7, with its exposition of the power of sin and the consequent limitations of law, and, on the other side, by chapters 9—11, with their impassioned demonstration of God's ongoing faithfulness to Israel. It is in fact the whole discussion of Romans 1—8, with its argument that God has brought the Gentiles into the elect family of God, along with Israel, to whom "the adoption properly belongs," which then requires that Paul establish that God has actually confirmed "the promises given to the patriarchs . . . in order that the Gentiles might glorify God for his mercy" (15:8–9). The evidence that God has now also adopted the Gentiles into the family to share the

---

[27]See Fee, *Empowering Presence,* 569.

inheritance of Israel lies in the empowering presence of the Spirit by which believers, Jew and Gentile alike, acknowledge God as Father. The ultimate question of how God brings people into right relationship is answered in two ways: positively, in terms of adoption as children; and negatively, in terms of the law. To paraphrase Paul, God has done what the law could not do: by sending his own Son he created a family of Jew and Gentile together, adopting them as his own, not through the law, which could not effect unity, but through the Spirit. Calling God Father cannot, therefore, be reduced to the characterization of an internal experience; rather, the accent falls, as it does throughout Romans, "not on the subjective experience of believers but on God's saving power through Christ's act *pro nobis.*"[28] Put differently, in Paul's argument, the use of Father for God is not simply expressive of the knowing subject's experience but of the activity of the God who is experienced. Paul's statements have more to do with what God has done than how God is experienced.[29] For Paul, God's gracious actions as Father are played out as much in the moral and social spheres as in the personal, individualistic sphere of piety.

Paul sets this whole argument within a larger cosmic framework. The human dilemma, described in Romans 7—8 in terms of slavery and bondage, cannot be isolated and analyzed apart from the cosmic sweep of the power and effects of sin, death, and decay. "We know that the whole creation has been groaning in labor pains until now; and not only the creation, but we ourselves" (8:22–23). Human beings will and do participate in God's liberation of *all* creation, of which the adoption of the children of God is but one facet. "The glorious liberty of the children of God" belongs in the cosmic frame of God's intent and promise that "the creation itself will be set free from its bondage to decay" (8:21).[30] Moving out from this sweeping cosmic framework, Paul contends that in the human realm God has dealt with slavery to sin through the emancipation of the slaves—not only obtaining their freedom but further adopting them into one family as his own children.[31] As J. Louis Martyn sharply phrases

---

[28]Richard B. Hays, "Adam, Israel, Christ: The Question of Covenant in the Theology of Romans: A Response to Leander E. Keck and N. T. Wright," in *Pauline Theology,* vol. 3: *Romans,* 75.

[29]See Francis Martin, *The Feminist Question,* 166.

[30]The universal scope of God's redemption is emphasized by Ernst Käsemann in his commentary on Romans; cf. the comments of Hays, "Adam, Israel, Christ," 74.

[31]Dunn, *Romans,* 1:452.

it, "The gospel is about the divine invasion of the cosmos (theology), not about human movement into blessedness (religion)."[32]

Paul also speaks of the freedom for all creation in the context of eschatological hope, even as he does of the "glorious liberty of the children of God." While he writes "you *have received* the spirit of adoption" (Rom. 8:15) and "we *are* children of God" (8:16), and while he testifies to the freedom of the children of God who are heirs and not slaves (Rom. 8:2, 15), he also speaks of groaning "as we *wait for* adoption" (8:23). Present adoption nevertheless anticipates full adoption in the future. Similarly, while in Romans 9:6 Paul speaks of "adoption" as properly belonging to the Israelites, he has already stated that this privilege now belongs to those who receive their inheritance through the one true heir, Jesus, rather than by virtue of genealogy. And yet, contending that the gifts and the call of God are irrevocable (Rom. 11:29), Paul holds on to the hope of the future "adoption" of Israel as children of God. He envisions the gathering of Jew and Gentile together who "may with one voice glorify the God and Father of our Lord Jesus Christ" (15:6; cf. 15:7–13). Ultimately the harmonious glorification of "the God and Father of *our* Lord Jesus Christ" summarizes the purpose of the Gospel, the revelation of the righteousness of God for all who believe, both Jew and Gentile (1:16–17; 15:8–9).

## Summary: Mercy Upon All

The adoption of Jew and Gentile as heirs of the promise made to Christ should not be construed simply as a result or "benefit" of the cosmic, theocentric, Pauline Gospel—although adoption is surely not less than that. Rather, the adoption of the children of God is the Gospel, now expressed in language of family and inheritance. This Gospel speaks of God's faithfulness to the Jews, the children of Abraham, and God's mercy to the Gentiles, also the children of Abraham. To speak of God as Father is to underscore God's faithfulness to Israel, "to whom belongs the adoption," and God's mercy toward the Gentiles who, as the heirs of God through Christ, have received adoption as children and the promised inheritance—an inheritance sealed to believers by the Spirit of God. What lies at the core of Paul's convictions that God is the Father of all who are children of Abraham and heirs with Christ is the belief that, in Christ, God has had "mercy upon all" (Rom. 11:32).

Consistent with the Old Testament picture of God's Fatherhood, Paul

---

[32]J. Louis Martyn, "The Abrahamic Covenant, Christ, and the Church," in *Theological Issues in the Letters of Paul* (Nashville: Abingdon, 1997), 170.

describes the faithfulness of God to Israel, which is manifested through steadfast love, and by which God's purposes are worked out in the world. The twist in Paul is that God's faithfulness to Israel is now being worked out through mercy toward the Gentiles. As heirs through Christ, they have received adoption as children and the promised inheritance, an inheritance sealed to believers by the Spirit of God. To borrow a phrase from Paul, God's Fatherhood can be summarized as "faithfulness working through love." The community is in turn to be a community of faithfulness working through love. Even as the "mercies of God" are manifested through the adoption of the Gentiles to be God's children, so Paul implores them "by the mercies of God" (12:1) to live together in the unity appropriate to a family created by God's gracious act.

That God is Father and Jesus is the Son of the Father are not abstract statements but, rather, find their proper place in the narrative of God's faithfulness to Israel, which comes to its climax when, "at the right time, God sent forth his Son." Because of the particularity of the biblical narrative, and of Jesus' relationship to God as Father, any abstraction of the language from the narrative itself runs the risk of losing sight of the promise of God's faithfulness and God's mercy. Father will become a dysfunctional metaphor if we insist on the form of the term without lodging it in the biblical narrative of God's faithfulness, care, and provision, and if we abstract it from the particular promises made to and through Jesus, the Son, in whom and through whom the faithful have their inheritance.

If this movement from promise to fulfillment is lost, then God's initiative, faithfulness, and mercy in adopting the heirs of Abraham in Christ all become mere ciphers, without the evidence in human life of which Paul speaks: the confession of the community that the Father, through the Spirit, has adopted heirs of the Son. And the underlying narrative does not cease with the movement from promise to fulfillment. For Paul, the fulfillment of the promise opens up, rather than forecloses, the orientation toward the future. God's fulfillment of the promise to Abraham becomes the ground for hope that God will complete this act of adoption. That future orientation precludes any triumphalist claim of an assured status that is vested in the individual believer, rather than in the God who brings the dead to life and calls believers together into one family. The very narrative that moves from promise to fulfillment unfolds toward the future with hope as its leitmotif—hope that by the mercy shown to the Gentiles, the Jews also may receive mercy (11:30–31). The questions raised by Paul's use of Father for God are whether God is faithful and can be trusted to fulfill those promises made to Abraham. As Paul answers it elsewhere, all the promises of God find their "yes" in Jesus Christ (2 Cor. 1:20).

# 6

# "The Living Father"

The most common designation for God in John is Father. John uses Father about 120 times, more often than all the other Gospels combined. By comparison, "God" (θεός) appears in John 108 times. But the pattern of the references is even more revealing of the significance of Father in John. The first references to God as Father are found in the prologue, a designation commonly attached to the first eighteen verses of the Gospel. Twice in those introductory verses, God is specifically depicted as the Father of the only Son, Jesus.

> And the Word became flesh and dwelt among us, full of grace and truth; we have beheld his glory, glory as of the only Son from the Father (John 1:14; RSV).

> No one has ever seen God; the only Son, who is in the bosom of the Father, he has made him known (1:18; RSV).

In both passages the term *monogenēs* (μονογενής), which later came to be laden with heavy theological freight, is used. Jesus is the only Son of the Father. Even more than the other Gospels or than the Pauline epistles, John emphasizes the unique relationship of the Son and the Father.

Subsequent references to God as Father occur in the Gospel almost exclusively in the words of Jesus. Jesus refers to God as "my Father," "the Father," and most distinctively as "the Father who sent me." A few references to God as Father are found in editorial comments, where again Jesus' unique Sonship is in view. For example, in John 5:18, the author states that the Jews were pursuing Jesus because he called "God his own Father, thereby making himself equal to God" (5:18; 8:27).

John also exemplifies the pattern, found in the other Gospels as well, that almost all the references to God as Father occur in sayings of Jesus, and *only* Jesus *addresses* God as Father. Over 85 times we have simply "the Father" in the words of Jesus in John. Jesus speaks of "my Father" about two dozen times, and he addresses God simply as "Father" nine times (once, "holy Father"). Once he speaks to his disciples of God as "your Father" (20:17). Nowhere in the Gospel does Jesus speak of God as "our Father" in a way that either includes the disciples with him in such a designation or in a form of address commended to the disciples as their own. There are but one or two exceptions to this pattern. In John 8, "the Jews" argue that they have God as Father (8:41), but this is a claim that Jesus disputes (8:42). Apparently, then, only Jesus may properly speak of and to God as Father.

Given the frequency of the term Father in the Gospel of John, one might naturally conclude that it has simply become a substitute for the term God, functioning as do a variety of epithets for God, such as "the Blessed" or "the Most High" or "the Almighty" in other New Testament texts, as well as in the literature of Judaism. And yet this is not the case. The terms God and Father are not simply interchangeable. For example, formulations that refer to the Son as being "sent" belong primarily to the Gospel's Father terminology. It is the Father who sends the Son. Likewise, Jesus is said not to do "the will of *God,*" but the "will of the *Father.*" Thus there are distinct patterns of usage that illumine the meaning of Father in the Gospel and suggest why it has become the most important term, other than *theos* (θεός) itself, to refer to God. It is these patterns of usage, the particular formulations and contexts in which Father appears, which give shape and content to God's Fatherhood in the Gospel of John. What is particularly telling in the depiction of God as Father is the way in which God's actions as Father are focused on Jesus himself. It is Jesus who speaks of, and addresses, God as Father. Jesus speaks but rarely even to his own disciples of God as their father, and then only after the resurrection. In short, according to the Gospel it is the prerogative of Jesus to address God as Father and to speak of God in these terms.

The pattern of the references to God as Father in the New Testament can be illumined by parallels in the Old Testament and Jewish literature. Of the characteristic descriptions of the activity or attributes of a Father, and particularly of God as Father, three figure most prominently and importantly: (1) The father is the head of a clan or family, and hence is the "ancestor" who gives life to and bequeaths an inheritance to his heirs. (2) The father is a figure of authority, who is worthy of obedience and honor. (3) The father is one who loves and cares for his children. Broadly speaking, these three marks of a father characterize God's relationship to Israel, or to a faithful core within Israel, both in the Old Testament and Jewish literature. These three characteristic behaviors and obligations of a father are pressed into service in the New Testament in order to characterize certain aspects of God's relationship both to Jesus himself and to the disciples of Jesus Christ.

While the Gospel of John particularly reflects the view of God as the source of life and as a figure of authority, worthy of obedience and honor, John modifies these themes more than any other book in the New Testament. Most notably, John uses these themes to bring to the fore the peculiar relationship of Jesus the Son to God the Father, so much so that God's relationship to Jesus is constitutive of God's Fatherhood. One also notices that some of the recurrent Synoptic emphases are missing in John. For example, the typically Matthean note that as Father God provides for his own is not sounded so clearly in John. The Father loves the Son, but the emphasis on provision and care recedes from view. So, also, the Synoptic emphasis on the imitation or reflection of God in the life and community of the disciples and in their conduct toward outsiders is treated by John in quite a different way. Now the disciples are to imitate Jesus' own self-giving love and, as is well known, the emphasis on "loving one's enemies" no longer takes center stage. Instead, the Johannine accent falls on the Father as the source and giver of life, a note that plays little role in the Synoptic Gospels, although it figures more importantly in the Pauline literature. As we turn to the Gospel of John, that most distinctive and in many ways enigmatic of Gospels, we will scarcely be surprised to uncover a distinctive pattern of the use of Father for God.

### Father and Son in the Gospel of John

In the Gospel of John we find that Jesus is the Son who receives life from the Father and in turn gives it to others (5:25–26). Jesus receives the Father's inheritance (8:31–38). Jesus manifests the obedience to which God calls his children (8:39–50). And Jesus is the object of the Father's love. Indeed, the mutual love of the Father and the Son lies at the heart of their relationship (3:35; 5:20; 10:17). Although the Gospel does speak of God's love for the world (3:16), it does so only once, just as only once does Jesus speak to his disciples of the Father's love for *them* (16:27). Similarly, believers are called "children of *God*" or those who are "born of *God*," but never "children of the Father" or those "born of the Father." Jesus, on the other hand, comes from God, but is not said to be "born of God" or even "born of the Father." If we jump to the Johannine epistles, we find this assertion, "See what love the Father has given us, that we should be called children of God; and so we are" (1 John 3:1). Even in such an assertion, the Father's love has made us into "children of *God,*" rather than children of the Father. Perhaps that seems to be splitting the hairs too finely. But we note also in John that the vocabulary for "children" distinguishes Jesus and believers in their relationship to God. Jesus is always called Son, *huios* (υἱός), whereas believers are always designated children, *tekna* (τέκνα).[1] While there are many "children" of God, there is only *one* Son. The Johannine tradition enshrines a genuine distinction not only in the terminology for Jesus as *Son* of God, or the Son of the Father, and believers as *children* of God, but also in the terminology used of God in each instance. As already noted, Jesus speaks not of "our Father" but of "my Father" and "the Father who sent me." Jesus speaks to the disciples of God as "your Father" only after the resurrection (20:17), itself a crucial datum for construing the nature of God's Fatherhood.[2] Thus there are two ways of construing relationship to God as Father, embodied in and through two different terms, "children" and "Son."

The "kinship" of God and Jesus as Father and Son becomes the basis for a number of claims made for Jesus. These claims include his authority to judge, to give life, to mediate knowledge of the Father and to reveal him, to do the works and will of the Father, and therefore to receive honor, as even the Father does. The assertions that are made regarding the Father and Son depend on the unity and love between them, unity and love that are construed in terms of kinship. It is this basic relationship, the relationship of parent and child, father and son, and not any specific characteristic behavior or obligation of a father, that forms the basis for delineating the relationship of Jesus and God in the Fourth Gospel. That is, in John it is not a particular characteristic of God that shapes understanding of him as Father. The fundamental reality is that a father's relationship to his children consists first in terms simply of giving them life. What it means to be a father is to be the origin or source of the life of one's children. For John, this pertains particularly

---

[1]This distinction is maintained in the Gospel and in 1 John. It is not found, however, in Paul or other literature of the New Testament.

[2]So also Paul W. Meyer, " 'The Father': The Presentation of God in the Fourth Gospel," in *Exploring the Gospel of John: in Honor of D. Moody Smith* (ed. R. Alan Culpepper and C. Clifton Black; Louisville: Westminster John Knox, 1996), 260.

to the way in which the Father has given life to the Son and through the Son mediated life to others, who become "children of God" (1:12; 11:52; see 1 John 3:1–2).

Indeed, John so emphasizes the unique character of the relationship between the Son and the Father that it is not unreasonable to ask whether it is even possible to talk about God as Father apart from talking of Jesus as the Son.[3] There is no Father without the Son. Father is not something that God is apart from relationship to the Son. It is not merely the designation of God as Father but the corollary reference to Jesus as Son that delineates the meaning of each.[4]

### "The Father Loves the Son"

Both in Matthew and Luke, Jesus speaks to his disciples of the mercy, provision, forgiveness, and care of God the heavenly Father for them. But curiously, none of the Synoptic Gospels ever speaks explicitly either of God's love for Jesus or of God's love for his disciples. Jesus, of course, calls upon people to love God, to love their neighbors as themselves, and to love their enemies. He also speaks of loving him (Matt. 10:37). But even in contexts in which one might expect Jesus to speak of God's love for humankind or the disciples, such a note is explicitly missing. For example, according to Luke, Jesus speaks these words: "Love your enemies, do good, and lend, expecting nothing in return and Your reward will be great, and you will be children of the Most High; for he is kind to the ungrateful and the wicked. Be merciful, just as your Father is merciful" (6:35–36). While Jesus commands his disciples to "love your enemies," he speaks of "the Most High" as "kind" and of "your Father" as "merciful." The words of Matthew 5:46–48 reflect a similar pattern. There Jesus commands his disciples to love their enemies because even tax collectors "love those who love them." Instead, Jesus' disciples are to show the indiscriminate love of the one who "makes the sun rise on the evil and the good" and so to be perfect, as their heavenly Father is perfect.

Obviously while the implication is that God's way of loving ought to be imitated by the disciples, it remains the case that in none of the

---

[3]Meyer, "The Presentation of God," 255.

[4]As Meyer makes clear in his very fine essay "The Presentation of God."

Synoptic Gospels does Jesus ever speak directly of God's love for the disciples. In the announcement at Jesus' baptism, "This is my Beloved Son" (Mark 1:11), one finds the sole Synoptic reference to Jesus' being loved by God. And in the comment in Mark that Jesus looked at the rich young man and "loved him," one finds the only statement that Jesus is said to love anyone (Mark 10:21). In short, love is what people express toward God, toward their neighbors, and toward their enemies. But it is not used explicitly of God's posture toward human beings, and it is used only once of God's relationship to Jesus, once of Jesus' posture toward an individual, and never of Jesus' attitude toward God. This is not to say that the Synoptic Gospels deny these attitudes to God or Jesus but that explicit statements to that fact are simply lacking.

By contrast, the Father's love for the Son and the Son's love for the Father, as well as the Son's love for the disciples and their love for him and for each other, are programmatic in John. Given the centrality of the relationship of the Father and Son, the emphasis on their reciprocal love is scarcely surprising. Father and Son point to the relationship of God to Jesus in terms of a familial metaphor, with all the privileges and obligations entailed by it, including the rights of inheritance and the obligation of honor and obedience on the part of the son. While the primary characteristic of the Father–Son relationship is the life that constitutes their relationship, that relationship is further characterized in John in terms of love. Even as the life of the Father is given to the Son and so through him to others, so, too, the love of the Father is bestowed on the Son and through him to others. Again we note the striking concentration of the Father's activity, here expressed as the fundamental relationship of love, in and through the Son. The Father loves the Son (3:35; 5:20; 10:17), so much so that the Father has "given all things into his hands." The Father will love those who love Jesus (14:21, 23; 16:27). Because Jesus has made God known to his own, the Father's love for the Son is said to be in them (17:26). Even as those with faith receive life from the Father through the Son, and so are taken up into the relationship of the Father to the Son, so do they participate in the relationship of mutuality and love of the Father and the Son.

Love is not one of many possible attitudes or actions that the Father may express toward the Son, the Son toward the Father and believers, and so on. Rather, it is the fundamental way of relating among those who find their very life and existence determined by the relationship of Father and Son to each other. The Father gives the Son life, who in turn gives it to others, and much the same may be said of love. There are, however, striking differences. Most notably, while Jesus commands his disciples to love one another as he has loved them, there is no similar command to give or extend life to each other. And yet both the Father's love and life are embodied in the Son and through him in the community gathered around him. The command to love each other extends the relationship of Father and Son, expressed both as life and love, and it is through the reception of the Father's love and life in the Son that those of faith participate in the reality of that relationship.

## "The Living Father" in the Gospel of John

As already noted, the term Father tends to stand on its own, but it is once modified by the adjective "holy"; a number of times by the personal pronoun "my"; frequently by the relative clause "who sent me"; and only once, but tellingly, by the adjective "living." God is "the living Father." This phrase mirrors the common designation of God as "the living God," which had become quite common by the first century. The phrase occurs about a dozen times in the New Testament. It is found, for example, in Matthew's version of Peter's confession of Jesus: "You are the Messiah, the Son of the living God" (Matt. 16:16; 26:63; Acts 14:15; Rom. 9:26; 2 Cor. 3:3; 6:16; 1 Thess. 1:9; 3:15; 1 Tim. 4:10; Heb. 3:12; 9:14; 10:31; 12:22). In Old Testament polemic, the epithet "living God" contrasts the Lord who creates with "dead idols" made by human hands (1 Sam. 17:26, 36; 2 Kgs. 19:4, 16; Jer. 23:36; Deut. 5:26; Josh. 3:10; Ps. 42:3; 84:3; Isa. 40:18–20; 41:21–24; 44:9–20, 24; 45:16–22; 46:5–7). "[Idols] are the work of the artisan and of the hands of the goldsmith; . . . they are all the product of skilled workers. But the LORD is the true God; he is the living God and the everlasting King" (Jer. 10:9–10). The contrast thus also emphasizes that the living God is not a created artifact but, rather, the creator and source of life (Ps. 36:9; Jer. 2:13; Ezek. 37:1–4).

This designation of God as "the living God" later also serves in Jewish monotheistic polemic to underscore the unity and uniqueness of God. One of the clear corollaries of belief in the uniqueness of the living God, or in God's eternal existence, is the affirmation of God as Creator of the world. Consequently, where some variation of the phrase "living God" or "everlasting God" is absent, one often finds instead a description of God as Creator, or as the source of all life. Sirach explicitly joins together God's eternal existence with God's creation of the world: "He who lives for ever created the whole universe" (18:1). For Philo, of course, God's eternity is the self-evident truth about God; God is "the one who is" (ὁ ὤν). God is the sole uncreated—hence eternal—being, and so necessarily the source of the life of the world (*Her.*

42.206); Creator and Maker (*Spec.* 1.30; *Somn.* 1.76; *Mut.* 29; *Decal.* 61); planter of the world (*Conf.* 196); Father;[5] Parent *(Spec.* 2.198); "Cause of all things" (*Somn.* 1.67);[6] Fountain of life (*Fug.* 198).[7] That God creates all that is rests on the assumption that God is the only ungenerated being. For Philo, in other words, God is the "unmoved mover." Eternal existence and creation go together. To be sure, Philo has interpreted these biblical themes in light of his Platonism, but nevertheless they are biblical themes that he both affirms and develops.

Similar views are found throughout Josephus' writings. Josephus writes that God is "the beginning, the middle, and the end of all things," who created the world "not with hands, not with toil, not with assistants of whom He had no need" (*Ag. Ap.* 2.190–192; cf. *Ant.* 8.280, "the beginning and end of all things"). In fact, Josephus argues that the etymology of the Greek word Zeus shows the proper understanding of deity, for the name comes from the fact that "he breathes life (ζῆν) into all creatures" (*Ant.* 12.22). Once Josephus asserts that "the only true God is ὁ ὤν" (the one who is; *Ant.* 8.350). Josephus likewise assumes that the God of Israel is "the God who made heaven and earth and sea" (*Ag. Ap.* 2.121, 190–192).[8] In describing the zealous piety of the Essenes, Josephus states that they pray before and after meals in order "to do homage to God as the bountiful giver of life" (*J.W.* 2.131).

One could easily multiply texts that assume God's eternity and, particularly, God's creation of all that is to show that for Jewish authors of the period, the uniqueness of Israel's God was lodged in God's creation of all the world. God is "the Lord God who gives life to all things" (*Jos. Asen.* 8:4), the "Creator of all things" who, in his mercy, gives "life and breath" (2 Macc. 1:24; 7:23). Precisely in this life-giving activity, God is unique. Echoing the words of Isaiah, one of the Scrolls from Qumran reads, "You are the living God, you alone, and there is no other besides you" (4Q504—4Q Words of the Luminaries V, 9).

---

[5]The Father: *Spec.* 2.197; *Opif.* 74, 76; *Mut.* 29; "Father of all things, for he begat them," *Cher.* 49; "Father and Maker," *Opif.* 77; "Father and Maker of all," *Decal.* 51.

[6]See *Decal.* 52: "The transcendent source of all that exists is God."

[7]"God is the most ancient of all fountains. . . . God alone is the cause of animation and of that life which is in union with prudence; for the matter is dead. But God is something more than life; he is, as he himself has said, the everlasting fountain of living."

[8]See also Jdt. 9:12; *Jub.* 2:31–32; 12:19; 16:26–27; 22:5, 66–67; 2 Macc. 1:24; 7:28.

There is only one God who, in contrast to idols and false gods, is the living God; and that living God is the source of all life. The phrase "the living God" does not occur in the Gospel of John. But the interesting variation, "the living Father," does occur. The occurrence of the phrase "living Father," rather than "living God," is not simply an incidental variant. Rather, the epithet embodies within it the conviction that as the eternally existent, living God, God alone is the source of all life. But since life is bestowed by the Father through the Son, the life-giving aspect of God's activity is illuminated by an image drawn from the human sphere of paternal relationship. The affirmation that God is Father cannot be separated from the affirmation that God is the source of life, nor from the conviction that the life of the Father has been given to, and comes to human beings through, the Son. Consequently, within the Gospel of John, the commonplace that God is "the living God" appears within polemic contexts (chs. 5 and 6) precisely as the warrant for the claims about the life-giving work of Jesus, the Son.

Indeed, the Johannine emphasis on God as "the living Father" goes a long way toward explaining the prominence of the theme of life in the Gospel.[9] Taken together, the ideas of God as Father, and hence the source of life, and of God as the living God, the creator of all that is, account for the belief that God gives *life* through the Son, who derives his life from the Father. A father gives life to his son; indeed, a son by definition is one who has life from his father. So also, the Father gives life to his Son; the Son by definition has life from his Father. And therefore through him life can be given to others as well. These virtually tautologous statements can be unpacked by looking briefly at the fundamental assertion that the Son has life *even as* the Father has it, and that through faith in the Son one *has* life in the present.

### "As the Father Has Life in Himself"

Against this backdrop, let us look briefly at what I take to be one of the most theologically important statements in the Fourth Gospel: "Truly, truly, I say to you, the hour is coming, and now is, when the dead will hear the voice of the Son of God, and those who hear will live. For as the Father has life in himself, so he has granted the Son also to have life in himself"

---

[9]John Ashton calls "life" the core or central symbol, around which all other symbols cluster (*Understanding the Fourth Gospel* [Oxford: Clarendon, 1991], 219 n.28).

(John 5:25–26). According to these verses, those who hear the voice of the Son of God will live, because the Son "has life in himself" even as the Father does. The parallel clauses in these verses assert life-giving prerogatives of both the Father and the Son. These predications are striking, for in biblical thought the power to give life is attributed to God alone. As the eminent Johannine scholar C.K. Barrett comments, "This expression, denoting *exact parallelism* between the Father and the Son, is the keynote of this paragraph." But the question remains wherein this "exact parallelism" consists. Barrett himself explicates it as "the complete continuity between the *work* of the Father and the *work* of the Son."[10] Hence the emphasis is on the functional unity of Father and Son. Raymond Brown asserts that the life in view is not the inner life of the Godhead but rather God's "creative life-giving power exercised."[11]

On this view, the Gospel is not addressing the question of the nature of the relationship or of the unity of Father and Son but, rather, is characterizing the unity of their work. The Father's work and prerogative are to grant life; and because he grants this prerogative to the Son, the Son participates in the Father's work. These assertions are clearly true and have much to commend them. For in this passage, as throughout the Gospel, there is a concerted effort to argue that the work of the Son is indeed the very work of the Father and that the Father does his work through the Son. Hence the most famous of all the Johannine assertions regarding the unity of the Father and Son, namely, "I and the Father are one" (10:30), actually refers in context to Jesus' promise that the Father and Son are one in the work of preserving the sheep of the fold from loss or harm. "I give them eternal life, and they shall never perish, and no one shall snatch them out of my hand. My Father, who has given them to me, is greater than all, and no one is able to snatch them out of the Father's hand" (10:28–29).

But the statements in 5:25–26 press further. The life-giving prerogative does not remain external to the Son. He does not receive it merely as a mission to be undertaken. It is not simply some power he has been given. Rather, the Son *partakes* of the very life of the Father: the Son has life in himself. Therefore, when Jesus *confers* life on those who believe, they also participate in and have to do with the life of the Father, because the Father has given the Son to have life *in himself,* even as he

[10]C. K. Barrett, *The Gospel according to St. John: an Introduction with Commentary and Notes on the Greek Text* (2d ed.; Philadelphia: Westminster, !978), 260; emphasis added.

[11]Raymond E. Brown, *The Gospel according to John: Introduction, Translation, and Notes* (2 vols.; AB 29AB; New York: Doubleday, 1966, 1970), 1:215.

has it.[12] Such predications assume and are dependent upon the conviction that there is but one God, one source of life. The Son confers the Father's life, which he *has in himself*.[13] Hence the formulation assumes the unity of the life-giving *work* of Father and Son, but it also predicates a remarkable status of the Son, one which is not made of any other creature or entity. The Son "has life in himself."

Yet it is important to note that this statement does not stand on its own. The Son has life in himself *because* "the Father has granted" it to him. Precisely in holding together the affirmations that the Son has "life in himself" with the affirmation that he has been *given* such life by the Father, we find the uniquely Johannine characterization of the relationship of the Father and the Son. The Father does not give the Son something, power, or gift; the Father gives the Son life. Because he has life from the Father, the Son has the power to confer life.

But we have not yet looked at the one verse in John that actually uses the phrase "the living Father." That verse reads as follows: "As the living Father sent me, and I live because of (διὰ) the Father, so whoever eats me will live because of (διὰ) me."[14] Here again the Father is described as the one who gives life, and the Son is the one who receives it. In 5:26, Jesus asserts that the Father has given him "life in himself." Here, Jesus says, "I live because of the Father." Unless Jesus' life were granted to him from the Father, he would have no life; unless he came from the "living Father," he would be unable to confer life.

Both verses do speak of Jesus' power and authority to give life to others. In chapter 5, Jesus says that "those who hear the voice of the Son of God will live." In the "bread of life" discourse in chapter 6, Jesus states that whoever "eats me will live *because of* me." These two verses make it clear that Jesus confers the life he has from the Father on others. While there is an analogy between the way in which God gives life to Jesus, and Jesus in turn confers it on others, there is not perfect

---

[12]Kenneth Grayston, *The Gospel of John,* (Philadelphia: Trinity, 1990), 51.

[13]"Just as the Father as Creator and Consummator possesses life, he has given that possession also to the Son, not merely as the executor of incidental assignments but in the absolute sense of sharing in the Father's power" (Herman Ridderbos, *The Gospel of John: A Theological Commentary* [trans. John Vriend; Grand Rapids: Eerdmans, 1997], 198).

[14]One might expect the use of *dia* plus the genitive in order to convey the idea of "source," as in 1 John 4:9, "God has sent his only Son into the world that we may have life through him" (*dia autou*). Yet, as Brown points out, the context seems to indicate the "chain of sources of life," as is also implied by John 5:26 (*John,* 1:283).

parallelism. On the one hand, there is analogy: Just as the Father has life and gives life to the Son, so the Son has life and gives life to those who have faith.[15] Jesus lives because of the Father's determination that he should have life in himself (cf. 5:21, 24–27), even as believers live because of Jesus' determination that they should have life. And yet there is a difference, a breach of the parallelism as well.[16] Believers always have mediated life, never "life in themselves." They cannot pass on their "life" to others; they have no offspring or heirs. If others live, it is because they receive the Father's life through the Son. These differences are expressed in the terminological distinctions noted earlier: believers are *children of God,* but Jesus is the *Son,* indeed the "only Son." Furthermore, Jesus is not "*born* of God," or "*born* from above." Rather, he *is* from God; he *comes* from above. He has life in himself, just as the Father does. Jesus is unique because he has power in himself to mediate life to others.

The scope of these assertions encompasses God's life-giving work from creation to resurrection. God is the living and life-giving Creator, who exercises sovereignty over all life. The work of creation, the universal sovereignty over creation, and its expected final redemption are all carried on in the Gospel through the Son and are all expressed in terms of life. At the outset, in the prologue of the Gospel, we read the affirmation that "All things were made through [the Logos], and without him was not anything made that was made. In him was life" (1:3–4; RSV). These verses underscore the presence and agency of the Logos in creation. That same word "became flesh" in Jesus of Nazareth, to whom has been given the power to give life in works and words. Jesus acts and speaks, and the dead come forth from their tombs (5:28–29). His words are "spirit and life" (6:63); in fact, he is life (11:25; 14:6). God grants the gift of life through Jesus. And Jesus' life-giving works also anticipate the final resurrection at the last day, which he himself effects (6:39, 40, 44, 54; 7:37; 11:24; 12:48). In short, the life-giving work of the Father in the Son does not refer to a single event but to the all-encompassing creative and sustaining work of God, which has past, present, and future reference points.

---

[15]Ernst Haenchen, *A Commentary on the Gospel of John* (2 vols.; Hermeneia; Philadelphia: Fortress, 1984), 1:296. Bultmann translates, "As (i.e., correspondingly as) I have life because of the Father, so too he who eats me will live through me," thus effacing the parallelism (*The Gospel of John* [trans G. R. Beasley-Murray et al.; Philadelphia: Westminster, 1971], 236, n.8).

[16]D. A. Carson, *The Gospel according to John* (Grand Rapids: Eerdmans, 1991), 299.

## The Work of the Father
## in the Work of the Son

In light of these observations, we may look briefly at the "signs" of Jesus in the Gospel of John. As is probably well known, John's terminology for the "miracles" or "mighty works" of Jesus differs from that found in the Synoptic Gospels. Whereas the Synoptic Gospels use a variety of terms, including terms that are translated "mighty works," "marvels," and "wonders," John always uses two terms: signs (*sēmeia*) and works (*erga*). Moreover, these tend to be further distinguished in the following way: For others, the deeds of Jesus are "signs"; but Jesus himself characterizes his deeds as his "works" and, more specifically, the "works of the Father." And from this very terminology, two questions arise: (1) If the deeds of Jesus are "signs," what are they "signs" of? (2) If the deeds of Jesus are the work of the Father, what then is the work of the Father?

A typical answer to the first question is that the signs—the deeds of healing, feeding, raising the dead—are "signs" of another level of reality, another sort of power that Jesus has and gives. If he raises the dead, this is a sign of his power to bring life to the spiritually dead; if he feeds the hungry, this is actually a sign of his power to bring spiritual nurture and sustenance to people; and so on. The significance of the signs is that they point beyond themselves to the "spiritual" meaning that is inherent in them. Because they bestow life in this world, they point beyond themselves to the spiritual or eternal life which Jesus can confer. On this reading of the signs, the "work of the Father" through the Son, Jesus, consists primarily in the work of salvation construed as giving "eternal life." Put differently, the signs point to the presence of God in another realm or sphere, but they do not themselves embody or manifest that presence.

But this understanding of the sign needs to be altered. The signs of Jesus are the work of God as Father because they are life-giving. The living Father grants life through these works, and it is the character and work of God—and of God alone—to give life. Because the signs confer life, then Jesus' works are the works of God. Because Jesus' signs impart life and embody God's life-giving character, one should "believe the works" (10:38; 14:11), that is, see in them God's own works of healing and restoration (5:19–21, 36; 6:32; 9:3, 33; 10:25, 32, 37–38; 14:8–11; 15:24). God's Fatherhood, God's life-giving power, is thus actually effected through the work of the Son. It is as the one who gives life that God is Father. Through the work of the Son, the Father's life-giving power becomes embodied, rather than remaining merely a cipher or idea, and thus God's identity as

Father is concretely realized through the work of the Son.[17] To put it most sharply, "I am working and my father is working" are not two parallel statements but, rather, one and the same statement.[18]

Perhaps no account underscores this more clearly than the narrative of the healing of the man at the pool of Bethesda. Several features in this account stand out. First, in the midst of this story, Jesus speaks these words, "The hour is coming, and is now here, when the dead will hear the voice of the Son of God, and those who hear will live" (5:25). This promise will be graphically illustrated in the raising of Lazarus; but the man at the pool is neither dead nor dying. The fact, however, that Jesus speaks of the dead "living" in the context of this healing miracle already suggests something of the breadth of the Johannine understanding of "life." But the giving of life is God's prerogative and solely in God's power. Second, the healing of the man at the pool takes place on the Sabbath. Such an act, or at least the man's carrying his mat on the Sabbath day, apparently violates the law against working on the Sabbath. And yet Jesus defends his healing on the Sabbath with the assertion that "the Father is working, and I am working." With this statement, Jesus argues that he performs the kind of work reserved for God alone—he gives life—and that he does it on the day reserved for God to work—the Sabbath.

According to the book of Genesis, however, God did not work but rested on the Sabbath. This not only suggested a troubling anthropomorphic view of God, as though God needed a siesta, but it raised an interesting question. If God did not work on the Sabbath, who kept the world going? In a play on words, Philo argued that God "rested" or "paused" (*katepausen*) in his work, but did not "cease" (*epausato*) from it. The rabbis argued that God could work on the Sabbath without violating the Torah since (1) the whole world was God's private residence (Isa. 6:3), and (2) God fills the whole world (Jer. 23:24).[19] However the argument was framed, the point was clear: this exception pertains to God alone. The discourse of John 5 invokes a traditional argument, which is found also in

---

[17]On the enactment of identity, see Hans Frei, *The Identity of Jesus Christ: The Hermeneutical Bases of Dogmatic Theology* (Philadelphia: Fortress, 1975).

[18]David A. Fennema, "Jesus and God According to John: An Analysis of the Fourth Gospel's Father/Son Christology" (Ph.D. diss., Duke University, 1979), 142.

[19]See the discussion and references in C. H. Dodd, *The Interpretation of the Fourth Gospel* (Cambridge: Cambridge University Press, 1953), 320–23; Barrett, *Gospel of John,* 256.

Philo and the rabbis, that God worked on the Sabbath without violating the law. Even on the Sabbath, God sustains the creation in life.

Thus when Jesus states, "I am working and my Father is working," he usurps to himself the prerogatives of God: he gives life, and he exercises his power to do so on the Sabbath day. Note that Jesus' argument with his adversaries is framed in terms of his continuing the work of his *Father* in giving life: "My Father is working and I am working still." Not incidentally is this relationship summarized most emphatically in John 5 in terms of the life-giving work of the Son; and not accidentally do Jesus' adversaries reject him because of his apparent arrogant claim that God is "his own father," for by claiming such unity he "makes himself equal to God." The equality of the Son with the Father is of course precisely the point of John 5, in which the Son claims to have "life in himself," as does also the Father. In keeping with the emphasis on the Father's character as one who gives life, God is referred to as "Father" nine times in this chapter; and only twice as "God," in contexts where Jesus challenges his opponents that they do not have God's life within them, nor do they seek the glory that comes from God. In other words, they do not know God as Father, in that they do not have life in him.

Thus two stories where someone has "heard Jesus' word" and been granted life are used to introduce the claim that Jesus grants eternal life.[20] But what is the relationship between the gift of physical life and the granting of eternal life? Are the healings merely illustrations of the gift of eternal life? The interpretation of signs as "symbols" suggests that physical life serves as a symbol or figure of eternal or spiritual life. But on what basis can the claim be made that the one guarantees the other? The answer that John supplies is the answer of the Old Testament prophets and of basic Jewish belief: there is one God who provides and sustains life. If we turn to the Gospel of John, we are reminded that the world was created by God through the Logos (1:10), and there is "life in

---

[20]On the significance of "hearing Jesus' word," see the study by Craig Koester, "Hearing, Seeing, and Believing in the Gospel of John," *Bib* 70 (1989): 327–48. Koester argues that authentic faith in the Gospel of John is based on hearing, but never on seeing; signs confirm faith that is engendered through hearing (332). One wonders whether Koester does not dismiss too quickly (1) the problem of those who will not see (20:30–31) and (2) the summary statements in 12:37–38 and 20:30–31, which draw a direct link between signs and believing. 12:37–38 especially asserts the guilt of those who do not believe. This is hard to understand unless the signs were to lead them to faith and not merely to confirm faith they already had.

him" (1:4). The Word is the agent or instrument of bringing the world to life. Subsequently, Jesus' healing of the official's son and of the man at the pool confer physical life. Thus the Son is the agent of bringing life to the world, sustaining the world even on the Sabbath as does his Father, the Lord God of Israel. The Son also has the authority to pass judgment and raise people in the resurrection to eternal life. From beginning to end, his work is characterized as bestowing life from God. John portrays the Word, as both the agent of creation and, as incarnate in Jesus, the mediator of life.[21] The signs, then, are not simply illustrations or figures of another kind of life-giving power Jesus has; the power to give life is singular and all-encompassing. Jesus' deeds are ultimately wrought by the one God (5:19, 21, 26; 10:38; 14:11) who is the source of all life. The life-giving signs of Jesus are ultimately the life-giving work of God.[22] This conviction underlies the emphasis in the Gospel on God as Father and Jesus as the Son. The Father, by definition, gives life to the Son; the Son is one who has received life from his Father. Jesus' works are the tangible manifestation and embodiment of the Father's life-giving power, in and through him, the embodiment of God's presence.

### "The Father Who Sent Me"

On the lips of Jesus, God is repeatedly designated not only as Father but as "the Father who sent me." This description underscores the distinctiveness of Jesus' relationship to God as Father in several ways. First, the expression highlights the unique way in which God is the Father of Jesus. God is "the Father who sent *me*." When John the Baptist is said to be "sent by God" the designation "Father" is conspicuous by its absence. The only other figure sent by the Father, is the Paraclete, the Holy Spirit.[23] Second, the very use of the relative clause, in Greek a participial form (ὁ πέμψας με πατήρ), designates the Father as *the one who sends*. It makes the Father the subject and initiator of the Son's activity,[24] and thus the participial phrase identifies the Father by means of his action with respect to the Son. Third, the emphasis on God as the Father who

---

[21]C. F. D. Moule, "The Meaning of 'Life' in the Gospels and Epistles of St. John: A Study in the Story of Lazarus, John 11:1–44," *Theology* 78 (1975): 122.

[22]Gerd Theissen, *The Miracle Stories of the Early Christian Tradition* (ET Philadelphia: Fortress, 1983), 226–27 writes, "There is no relativisation of miracles in John; on the contrary, they are a continuation of God's work of creation (5:17), and indeed surpass it (5:20). They are unique. No one else can perform them (15:24; 3:2)."

[23]Of the other Gospels, Luke particularly stresses that the Spirit is the gift of the *Father.*

[24]Fennema, "Jesus and God," 4.

has "sent" the Son introduces a new element into the description of the
relationship of Father and Son. Not only is God Father, but God is "the
Father who *sent* me." The language of *sending* reflects a view of the Son
as an emissary or agent who is sent by another to carry out a task or fulfill a commission. Indeed, the Son is identified primarily in terms of the
one sent to carry out that mission, and the Father as the one who sends
the Son.[25]

This aspect of sonship did not come up in the survey of the role of the
father in the Old Testament and Jewish literature because, although a son
may be one who ably serves as an agent or emissary of his father in trans-
acting business, the father is not equally identified as one who authorizes
his son to carry out certain commissions.[26] A father may do so, but this
scarcely constitutes a distinguishing characteristic of a *father*. It is, therefore, all the more significant that, although on numerous occasions John
states that God, or the Father, has sent Jesus, he never speaks of Jesus as
"the sent one," which would be the corresponding equivalent to "the one
who sent me." The fact of Jesus' being sent has not become crystallized
into a title or name. But often the participial phrase "the one who sent
me" is appended to "the Father," so that the Father becomes identified
primarily with and through the act of sending the Son. As Paul Meyer
comments,

> There is not so much a *Gesandtenchristologie* [a Christology
> of the one who is sent] in the Gospel as there is a *Senderthe-*
> *ologie* [theology of the one who sends]. . . . The language of
> "sending" is *theo*logical language that undergirds Christology
> but refuses to be absorbed into it.[27]

John's Christology is often understood against the background of the
role of the "agent." This refers to a business or legal relationship or role,

---

[25]Ashton, *Understanding the Fourth Gospel,* 314, distinguishes between the
Gospel's language of *mission,* reminiscent of the sending of prophets in the Old
Testament, and the nonreligious language of *agency.* With respect to the latter,
Ashton comments: "Here for the first time we appear to have an authentic tradition capable under the right conditions of generating the high christology according to which the man who has listened to the words of Jesus has heard the
voice of God and, more strikingly, in Jesus' own words to Philip, 'He who has
seen me has seen the Father.' "

[26]Ashton, *Understanding the Fourth Gospel,* 318, argues in a somewhat different direction when he asserts that sons are "rarely *sent*" by their fathers.

[27]Meyer, "The Presentation of God," 264. See also Bultmann, *Theology of*
*the New Testament,* 2:34.

rather than to a specifically "religious" function or figure, like a prophet. In the rabbinic writings, one often finds this statement: "The one who is sent is like the one who sent him." Hence, if one transacts any business with the agent, the one who is sent, it is as though one had transacted it with the one who sent that agent. For all practical purposes, there is a functional, albeit limited and temporary, equality. This category of agency is often deemed helpful in interpreting certain passages in John, such as "Whoever has seen me has seen the Father."

But John takes this tradition in a somewhat different direction when, in addition to predicating the virtual equality of the one who is sent with the one who sends, he tends to stress that the one who sends is *greater* than the one who is sent. So, for example, in John 13:16, Jesus asserts, "Truly, truly, I say to you, a servant is not greater than his master; nor is he who is sent greater than he who sent him," a statement that certainly does not stress the equality of the one who is sent and the one who sent him. And then there is the well-known statement, "The Father is greater than I" (14:28). Such formulations in the Gospel are typically labeled as examples of John's "subordinationism." But this label is at best misleading, inasmuch as it conceives of the relationship of Father and Son primarily in hierarchical terms. Because John stresses the function of the Father as the one who gives life to his offspring, rather than the role of the Father as the one who instructs or disciplines, statements such as "the Father is greater than I" ought not to be read against a backdrop of patriarchal hierarchy. The Father is the source of the Son's life; it is as the origin of the Son's very being that "the Father is greater than I." This is clear even from the context of that statement, in which Jesus asserts that he returns to the Father, because the Father is greater; that is, he has his origins in the Father (14:28). In the Fourth Gospel, then, the emphasis on the Son as the "agent" who is sent actually serves to shift attention to the Father who sends the Son; and the notion of hierarchy or "superiority" is actually subsumed into the Father's life-giving, not "command-giving," persona.

The case is much the same in considering the theme of a son's obedience to his father. While maintaining the typical view that a true Son is one who "does the will of the Father," John nevertheless stresses rather dramatically the harmony of the Son's will with the Father's, interpreting the Son's obedience as an *enactment* or *expression* of the Father's will, rather than as submission or acquiescence to it. For although the Son is often said to "do the will" (4:34; 5:30; 6:38–39) or to "do the works" of the Father (5:36; 10:25, 37), the word "obey" is never actually used. Jesus receives and carries out the Father's commandments (12:49; 14:31; 15:10).

Yet this does not imply that the Johannine Jesus has no will; rather, that it is fully in harmony with that of the Father. Few passages in John illuminate as fully the character of the Son's "obedience" as do Jesus' statements regarding his death: "For this reason the Father loves me, because I lay down my life in order to take it up again. No one takes it from me, but I lay it down of my own accord. I have power to lay it down, and I have power to take it up again; I have received this command from my Father" (10:17–18). Here Jesus speaks of his death in terms of a "charge" that he received from his Father, a "charge" that encompasses his resurrection as well (10:18). Yet the passage simultaneously stresses Jesus' sovereignty: he lays down his life freely, not by force (10:18). Indeed, the emphasis on his own initiative sounds a steady drumbeat throughout these two verses: "*I* lay down my life;" "*I* take it up again;" "*I* lay it down of my own accord;" "*I* have power to lay it down;" "*I* have power to take it up again." The climactic statement, "this charge I have received from my Father," stands out almost as a surd element, for now Jesus' command over his own life, death, and resurrection is attributed to the *command* or *charge* of the Father. But the dialectic is resolved in the peculiarity of the Father–Son relationship in John, in which the Father not only gives the Son his life but grants it to him to dispose of as he will— or as the Father wills.

A direct line runs from these statements to the recasting of Jesus' prayer prior to his death. Whereas in the other Gospels Jesus is shown praying, "Father, take this cup from me; nevertheless, not my will but thine be done," in John Jesus prays a rather different prayer prior to his arrest. In a clear echo of the prayer of Jesus in the Synoptic tradition, in John Jesus states, "Now my soul is troubled. And what should I say— 'Father, save me from this hour'? No, it is for this reason that I have come to this hour" (12:27). His prayer becomes entirely a declaration of his intent to do the Father's will. The Son's obedience to the Father does not establish their unity, nor is it an obedience construed in terms of submission to an alien command. Rather, the Son's "obedience" is the expression of the will of the one who sent him. The will of the Father is embodied in him, even as the Father's life is embodied in him.

The connection between Fatherhood and works becomes programmatic particularly in the heated debates of John 8. Beginning especially with 8:31, a bitter controversy is recounted between Jesus and his opponents about their origins and heritage. Jesus grants "the Jews" their claim that they are offspring of Abraham (σπέρμα, 8:37).[28] They are

---

[28]According to 8:30–31, Jesus is addressing "Jews who had believed in him." But like the disciples who are offended and so fall away in 6:60–66, so too these would-be disciples find Jesus' continued teaching impossible to follow (8:59).

physically descended from Abraham, but physical descent is not the ultimate criterion in determining their true relationship either to Abraham or to Jesus' own Father. What is important is conduct: to show themselves to be Abraham's children (τέκνα, 8:39), "the Jews" ought to do what he did.[29] Similarly, Jesus honors God, who is his Father (8:49). But because "the Jews" do not honor the Son, nor hear his words, even though he comes from and speaks of God, then they do not have God as their Father (8:44, 49). They do not do the will of God; hence, God is not their Father.

At first glance, this treatment of the Father–Son imagery seems to tend in a rather different direction from that previously delineated in John. For here Sonship is determined not by kinship or descent but by obedience. But this argument is set in a discourse that begins with the assertion that Jesus is the free Son of the house, the only rightful heir of the Father's inheritance, the one who is not destined for death (8:31–36). As "the Son of the house" (8:35), Jesus is the heir of the Father; he has life from the Father and can bestow it on others; he alone is obedient to the Father. All the elements of genuine Sonship are embodied in him: but his mission is to set others free so that they can enter into the Father's inheritance through him. The exclusivity of Jesus' Sonship actually becomes the means through which others may receive the life and freedom that characterize the true "children of God."

## Summary Reflections: The Life of the World

In the Gospel of John, the father–son relationship becomes the theological grounding for the predications made of the authority and life-giving work of the Father given to and embodied in the Son. This is not to say that the imagery of father-son necessarily generated all aspects of John's Christology; clearly other categories enter into the picture as well. But John has made it central. It plays a dominant role not only in terms of sheer statistics but also in terms of its power to shape the way in which other imagery is taken up and used. The Son comes "in the

---

[29]Ridderbos, *Gospel of John,* 312, denies that this discourse deliberately contrasts offspring (σπέρμα) and children (τέκνα), conceding the first but denying the second to Jesus' disputants. Rather, Ridderbos asserts that the terms are used interchangeably, but that being Abraham's seed is attributed to the Jews "in the natural sense" but denied in the "spiritual sense." In the end, however, the point seems to be much the same.

name of the Father." Because the Son has the Father's life, Father and Son are one, and those who know the Son know the Father. The Son who has the life-giving prerogatives of the Father is "equal to God" (5:18). The Father has placed "all things" into the hands of the Son (3:35; 13:3; cf. 15:15; 16:15); the Father has given "all judgment" to the Son (5:22). As the Son of the Father, the one whose very identity is constituted by the life-giving work of the one designated as Father, Jesus embodies and confers God's creative and sustaining work. Consequently, God's identity as Father expresses itself first in the specific and distinctive relationship to Jesus, the Son. That God is Father is not some "ontological" predication in and of itself but historically and theologically bound to the Father's relationship to the Son and to the embodiment of the Father's life in the Son.

The relationship of father and son assumes at one and the same time an indissoluble unity and a clear separateness: for while a son is not his father, no other human relationship connects people in quite the same way as does the relationship of a parent to a child, for this is a relationship in which the very being of the one comes from the other, and in which neither has an identity as "Father" or "son," "parent" or "child," without the other. Although the language of "intimacy" is often used to speak of the relationship between Jesus and God, this characterization of the relationship between parents and children owes more to Romanticism than to biblical concepts of paternity.[30] The decalogue, after all, commands children to "honor their father and mother," to esteem and obey them. The father always retains authority, merits honor, and remains the progenitor of his offspring.

Put differently, the idea of relationship construed as kinship, rather than as emotional intimacy, grounds the understanding of God as Father and Jesus as Son. When Jesus calls God Father, he points first to the Father as the source or origin of life. But once again there is a distinction between Jesus as the only Son of God and those "born of God." He has life because "the living Father" (6:57) gives it to him; in fact, he has "life in himself" just as the "Father has life in himself" (5:26), a remarkable statement that simultaneously affirms that the Son derives his life from the Father and yet that he has life in a distinct way, as the Father has it. As Father, God is the source of life, the one who lives and gives life to others. That life is embodied in and through the Son. Because the life-giving Word became "flesh," God's life became embodied in Jesus,

---

[30]This point is made by A. E. Harvey in *Jesus and the Constraints of History* (Philadelphia: Westminster, 1982), 158.

was tangibly expressed through his work, and promised as resurrection in the future through faith.

The exclusivity of Jesus' Sonship actually becomes the means through which others may receive the life and freedom that characterizes the true "children of God." Ultimately it will be through Jesus' death and resurrection that others are empowered to enter into the life-giving relationship that characterizes the Father and the Son. The command of the risen Jesus to Mary makes clear the new situation: "Jesus said to her, 'Do not hold on to me, because I have not yet ascended to the Father. But go to my brothers and say to them, I am ascending to my Father and your Father, to my God and your God'" (20:17). This is the first use of "brothers" (ἀδελφούς) to refer to Jesus' disciples and the first and only reference to God as "your Father" (cf. 8:41–42, 44). Still there is no reference in John to God as "our Father" in which Jesus includes the disciples together with himself in such address. Here it is still "my Father and your Father." The differences between the relationship of Jesus to the Father and of the disciples to the Father remain, but through the life-giving work of the Son, the disciples—and others— enter into the relationship of kinship granted to them by the Son. Not surprisingly, after Jesus' resurrection, his followers are referred to with the familiar New Testament designation *adelphoi* ("brothers and sisters"; 21:23), a term that plays an important role in 1 John as the basis for the call to unity and love (1 John 3:13–14, 16). The Father's life is tangibly and concretely embodied not only in the life and work of the Son but also in the life of the community and of the members of it. It is not a life that floats abstractly above the real life of women and men in the world. It is life that is embodied, quite literally, in Jesus and his followers. In this way it can indeed become the life for all the world.

# Concluding Reflections

The word "father" ranges in meaning from the sheerly biological designation of a male person who sires a child to what is typically deemed a metaphorical extension of the term to refer to someone who originates or institutes something ("the father of modern science") or even to something that is the source of another ("the wish was the father of the thought"). In applying the term Father to God, neither the scriptures nor the Christian tradition have in view a biological relationship between God and any other figure, but they clearly have in view some sort of relationship. The question is how we are to construe this relationship. What does it mean to speak of God as Father?

Obviously different answers are given to this question. Some theologians answer the question by taking as their starting point Jesus' address to God as Father. From Jesus' own practice they chart a trajectory through the various Pauline statements in which God is spoken of as "the God and Father of our Lord Jesus Christ," and on through the typically Johannine designation of Jesus as "the only Son of the Father" and of God as "the Father" who sent Jesus. These formulations in the Pauline letters and the Johannine literature solidify Jesus' address to God into theological descriptions of the identity of God as the Father of his Son, Jesus Christ, the Lord of the church. Those who construe the biblical data in terms of this trajectory place the accent almost entirely on the relationship between God and Jesus framed in terms of the relationship of Father and Son. This does not mean that they ignore Jesus' invitation to his followers to address God as Father, even as he does, but the point of beginning and emphasis is always God's relationship as Father to Jesus the Son. From the New Testament, this trajectory moves eventually to the ecclesiastical creeds, which open with the confession of God as Father, then name Jesus as his only Son, explaining that relationship in terms of the Father's begetting of the Son. While this language is not to be construed physically, it is nevertheless literal. Those who read the biblical and theological witness in this way read it along a trajectory which, while it has its roots in scripture, has its culmination *beyond* scripture in the articulation of christological confession in the creeds of the church. For the sake of simplicity, and even at the risk of oversimplification, we may label this the *creedal trajectory,* inasmuch as it is governed by the structure of the first two articles of the creed, in which God is confessed as the Father and Jesus as his only Son.

The point of this book has not been to dismiss this creedal trajectory but to insist that this creedal trajectory must always be fitted into another trajectory, whose culmination also lies beyond the confines of scripture but in a rather different sense than that of the creedal trajectory. For this trajectory aims at an eschatological horizon, when God's promises to all the people of God are ultimately fulfilled and they enjoy that relationship of trust and love signified by calling upon God as Father. For the sake of simplicity, we may label this the *eschatological* trajectory. This trajectory has its starting point in the Old Testament and in the relationship of God to the people of Israel. Here the predication of God's Fatherhood may be called *eschatological,* in that God promises to be the Father of those who are obedient and faithful, wills to redeem the disobedient and unfaithful, and so constitutes that promised relationship. From the Old Testament, the eschatological trajectory moves to the Gospels of the New Testament, to Jesus' own address to God as Father and his instructions to his disciples to likewise call upon God as Father. Since one cannot plot the coordinates of this trajectory without constant reference to God's relationship to his people, first Israel and then also the Israel of the renewed covenant, this trajectory is also inevitably *ecclesiastical.* It focuses not only on God as the Father of the Son but sets this confession within the larger context of the understanding of God as the Father of a people. On this trajectory, the relationship between God and Jesus as Father and Son is spoken of primarily in terms of the *mission* of Jesus in historical context. This trajectory pays close attention to the presentation of Jesus as Son and God as Father with respect to the historical and literary contexts of the texts of scripture.

These two trajectories have different starting points. The creedal trajectory essentially begins with the New Testament and moves on from there. To put it most bluntly, it needs the creeds of the church more than it needs the Old Testament, and it circles back to include the Old and New

Testaments from the point of christological confession. While the eschatological trajectory does not ignore the creeds, it begins with the Old Testament and, because it does so, will always include reference to Israel and the promises made to Israel by God. These two trajectories do not culminate at the same point either. The first trajectory culminates in creedal confessions that speak of the Son, in the elegant words of the Nicene Creed, as "very God of very God." The second trajectory anticipates a distant horizon, when "the creation itself will be set free from its bondage to decay and will obtain the freedom of the glory of the children of God" (Rom. 8:21). This trajectory is thus simultaneously eschatological and ecclesiastical.

On the whole, the recent and vigorous defenses of God as Father have argued their case from the vantage point of the creedal trajectory, and particularly from its culmination point in the confession of God as the Father of the only begotten Son. This approach reads the Bible from the perspective of the church's more fully articulated confession, looking back from it toward its roots in scripture and particularly in the New Testament. But this trajectory needs to be set within the more encompassing framework of the eschatological trajectory, which both presses back to the Old Testament and strains forward to the eschatological fulfillment of God's promises to be a Father to all his people. The robust biblical witness to God as Father is in danger of being eclipsed without this firm anchoring in Israel's story and the hope for the final realization of the promises of God made to Israel and guaranteed in Israel's Messiah, Jesus of Nazareth. Perhaps such renewed attention to the biblical witness may serve to enlarge our diminished capacity to imagine what it might mean to call upon God as Father. For in the present moment it seems that the designation of God as Father has become flat, without contours, depth, or texture. As one commentator put it with reference to the Lord's Prayer:

> Many within the Christian family . . . cannot speak the opening words, "Our Father," without some intense experience of alienation. It is not only women who may have difficulty speaking the words; there are men who have no sense that there is a "Father" behind the dim unknown keeping watch above his own, and there are many who have no sense of the "we" presupposed by the Prayer. Language that earlier generations might have taken for granted may now require attention if the prayer is to serve as a vehicle for conversation with God.[1]

---

[1]Juel, "The Lord's Prayer," 56.

Part of the point, then, of giving closer attention to the witness of the scriptures is to equip ourselves for the catechesis of a generation for whom the language of scripture and confession is too often alien and empty. But a reexamination of the scriptural image of God as Father may also renew our theological capacity to construe the Fatherhood of God in ways that are fruitful for Christian faith and practice. I have tried here to clear away some of the layers of rhetoric that have been laid over the portrait of God as Father in the scriptures. In these concluding reflections, I would like to summarize this study and to suggest that theological discourse would be well served by attending more diligently to the biblical witness to God as Father.

### The Eschatological Trajectory of God's Fatherhood

To chart the eschatological trajectory of God's Fatherhood in scripture, we begin with the promises of the Old Testament that God's steadfast love and faithfulness for Israel will redeem it and restore Israel from exile to live in trust and obedience to God and charity and mercy toward others. These promises are taken up in the Gospels by Jesus, in his invitation to his disciples to call upon God in trust as "our Father" and to treat others with the generous love demonstrated by their heavenly Father. This trajectory also presses relentlessly toward the future and the far horizon of God's saving work with respect to his people. Then God's people shall "inherit the kingdom" or, as Paul would put it, be given their full inheritance in Christ; and as John might phrase it, they shall have eternal life in fellowship with the life-giving Father and his Son, Jesus Christ (cf. 17:3). In other words, the so-called eschatological trajectory acknowledges the specific relationship of God as Father to Jesus, the son and heir, who inherits from God the promises made to his people, who are "heirs of God and joint heirs with Christ" (Rom. 8:17). But the final fulfillment of these promises awaits the full coming of the kingdom, and the "freedom of the glory of the children of God" (Rom. 8:21).

### *God as Father in the Old Testament*

Three aspects of human fatherhood serve to illumine the portrait of God as Father in the Old Testament. First, the father is the source or origin of a family or clan and provides an inheritance to his children; second, a father protects and provides for his children; third, a father is a figure of authority to whom obedience and honor are properly rendered. These characteristics of a human father are used to depict God's relationship to Israel in the Old Testament, to serve as the basis for the promise of God's faithfulness and love, and to call Israel to repentance. Although there are indeed other ways to recount the story of Israel's exile, repentance, and redemption, one way in which the Bible does so is under the heading of God as the Father of Israel. Israel is God's firstborn child and, as such, is also God's heir, who receives from God the promised inheritance, portion, or share of God's blessings specifically intended for Israel. The image of God as Father is thus specifically applied to God's election of Israel and to God's continued blessings and love for Israel. Because the image of God as Father is invoked often to hold out hope to Israel in exile, it has a decidedly forward-looking character, anticipating that day when the relationship of God to Israel can be described as that of a loving Father and a trusting child.

### God as Father in sources of Second Temple Judaism

One notable feature of various Jewish sources is the address to God as "Father" or "my Father." Those familiar with the work of Joachim Jeremias may at first find this surprising, until it is remembered that Jeremias contended that no such address had been found in the literature of *Palestinian Judaism.* But Jeremias had allowed that it was common for Diaspora Judaism to address God as Father because it followed the example of the *Greek world.*[2] It was certainly not unknown to first-century Jews to think or speak of God as Father or "my father," and the Dead Sea Scrolls now also give evidence of the practice in Palestinian Judaism. However, the closer the model of the Greek world is followed, as for example in Josephus and Philo, the less the basic contours of the Old Testament picture are maintained and the more God's Fatherhood is defined in terms of his being the cause, creator, or source of all things. By contrast, in the Old Testament, God's Fatherhood is specifically tied not to the act of creation but to the act of election. God's Fatherhood is

---

[2]Jeremias, *Prayers of Jesus,* 27. Logic would dictate that the Gospels that followed the "example of the Greek world" would show an increase in address to God as Father. But the situation is exactly the opposite. The Gospels typically dubbed "the most Jewish"—Matthew and John—show a significant increase in the use of Father language for God, while Mark and Luke, most generally taken to have either Gentile authors or audiences, use it rarely or more sparingly.

always particular, defined with respect to a particular people, rather than universal, or having all people and creation in view. And on the whole one finds this particular understanding woven regularly throughout various sources of Second Temple Judaism. Together the Old Testament and the sources of Second Temple Judaism provide the framework in which Jesus' address to God as Father must be understood.

### Jesus and the Father

Jesus' references and address to God as Father do not in the first instance articulate some new understanding of God. Rather, Jesus uses the language and imagery of scripture to promise God's faithfulness and love to his own people and to call for renewed trust in God and love for one's neighbor. Jesus' conviction that his mission was to proclaim the kingdom of God cannot be separated from his understanding of God as *abba,* as the one who would be the Father of the renewed community that gathered around him in response to his summons to repent. Thus when Jesus spoke to his disciples, he spoke of "your Father," "your heavenly Father" or "your Father in heaven" and taught them to pray "our Father." Relying on God as on a father, they were directed to trust God's provision and to imitate God's mercy. In speaking of God as Father, Jesus assumes the trustworthiness of God, that God will be faithful to his promises. Jesus does not create a new image of God or offer new propositions about God. He doesn't need to. Instead he calls for trust in God because God is faithful and wills to save his people. Even as Jesus promised the kingdom in the name of the Father, so he received the kingdom as a Son and heir in the name of the people of God. In framing his mission in terms of familial imagery, speaking of himself as the Son and heir, and admonishing his disciples of their obligations as brothers and sisters, Jesus appropriates a prophetic vision of the people of God that entails a call to repent, the promise of restoration, and mutual obligations owed to each other.

### The Synoptic Gospels

On the whole, the Synoptic Gospels portray God as the Father of Jesus and as the Father of the community gathered around Jesus. Mark's portrait of God as Father, however, focuses intently on God's relationship as Father to Jesus as Son, almost to the exclusion of the corporate dimension. Only one reference in Mark looks explicitly to the corporate aspect of God as Father: "And whenever you stand praying, forgive, if you have anything against anyone; so that your Father in heaven may also forgive you your trespasses" (11:25). Mark's Gospel is the only one to include the Aramaic *abba,* in Jesus' prayer to God in the Garden of Gethsemane. In Mark's Gospel Jesus' invocation of God as *abba,* followed as it is by the statement "all things are possible for you," points to the Son's unwavering trust in God; Jesus' subsequent assertion, "nevertheless, not my will but thine be done" indicates his unswerving obedience to the one he calls upon as *abba.* But Mark's exclusive focus on the relationship of God and Jesus as Father–Son suggests that Jesus alone manifests the sort of trust and obedience that God the Father asks of his children. Those who are called to follow him may likewise be called to "take up their cross," but their paths do not simply imitate that of the Son, any more than their relationship to God simply replicates Jesus' relationship to God.

Matthew and Luke continue the particular Markan emphasis on God as the Father of Jesus. But alongside that emphasis runs another, that of God as the Father of the community that Jesus calls together. Matthew and Luke thus simultaneously heighten both aspects of God's Fatherhood. On the one hand, each shows an increase in the *frequency* of the use of Father for God with particular reference to Jesus. On the other hand, each also includes quite a bit of material with a decidedly communal and ethical focus, material that spells out the implications of God as Father for those who would be disciples of the Son.

In Luke the relationship of God as Father to Jesus' disciples comes to expression in particularly poignant imagery. The Father gives Jesus' "little flock" the kingdom and can be expected to give them gifts surpassing the best gifts a human father can offer his children. The Lukan parable of the prodigal son pictures God as a merciful and forgiving Father, who expects that the same sort of mercy be shown to brothers and sisters in the family. But also from the very beginning of the Gospel, Jesus is presented as the unique Son of God whose birth is brought about through God's Holy Spirit. Throughout the Gospel Jesus consistently addresses God as Father. He does so three times from the cross as he gives expression to his trust in God and his forgiveness of his executioners. Jesus not only commends the same form of address to his disciples but models the trust and obedience, as well as the forgiveness and mercy, to which he calls others. In the book of Acts, Luke describes the outpouring of the Spirit as the fulfillment of the promise of the Father, and it is the Spirit that empowers the community's proclamation of salvation and communal life together.

Even more than Luke, Matthew repeatedly shows Jesus as the Son of the one he calls "my Father." Matthew presents Jesus as gathering together a new community which knows God as the only Father (23:9) and honors Jesus as faithful interpreter and authoritative teacher of God's will as it is embodied in the law (23:10). While Jesus, "the son of David, the Son of Abraham" (1:1), and ultimately Son of God, is the only one who can truly claim knowledge of the Father (11:25–26), through his interpretation of the law in terms of the double love commandment Jesus discloses his Father and his Father's will to "the infants" (Matt. 11:25). Through his death for the forgiveness of sins, he seals the renewed covenant promised by the prophet Jeremiah. As Son he also invites others to "inherit the kingdom of my Father" based on their demonstrated love of "the least of these who are members of my family" (25:40).

Paul speaks of what God has done in Christ in many different ways: the justification of the ungodly, the forgiveness of sins, the reconciliation of the world, the liberation of those in captivity to sin, and so on. He also summarizes the Gospel in terms of the adoption of Jew and Gentile as heirs of the promise made to Christ. When he does so, the designation of God that is particularly appropriate is that of Father. The articulation of the Gospel in these terms emphasizes the initiative of God in adopting Jew and Gentile as beloved children, the mercy of God upon both Jew and Gentile, and the faithfulness of God to fulfill the promises made to Abraham which are guaranteed through Jesus, the Son and heir of God. Even as the "mercies of God" are demonstrated through these promises in Christ, so Paul admonishes those in Christ "by the mercies of God" (12:1) to live together in the unity appropriate to a family created by God's gracious act. Living in this way, those in Christ also "wait for adoption" with hope, patience, and yearning (Rom. 8:21–25). Thus Paul's understanding of God's Fatherhood has an orientation to past, present, and future, but all of these are brought together in what God has promised through Jesus Christ.

### The Gospel of John

The Gospel of John accentuates the distinctive relationship of Jesus the Son to God the Father. Jesus frequently refers to himself as Son and to God as "my Father," "the Father," or "the Father who sent me." The Greek word used to speak of Jesus as Son (*huios*) differs from that used to speak of believers as children of God (*tekna*). Only once does Jesus speak to his followers of God as "your Father" (20:17). In all these ways, John heightens the distinctive character of Jesus' Sonship and so also of God's Fatherhood. That relationship is summarized in the assertion that he has "life in himself," which he receives from the Father who gives it to him. Thus the Johannine accent falls on the Father as the source and giver of life, and on the Son, the one who has this divine life, and so mediates it to others, who receive it in faith. Like the Gospel of Mark, John highlights the unique relationship of God as Father to Jesus as Son, but John does so with particular attention to the Father as the source of life for his children. Because the Father gives life to the Son, those who are children of God receive that life, through faith, from the Son.

### *The contribution of Joachim Jeremias*

This review of the data of the Bible and Second Temple Judaism brings us to a brief review of the work of Joachim Jeremias. Here we may simply reiterate that one of his most important observations is one that is most frequently overlooked, namely, that Jesus' address to God as Father belongs in the framework of eschatological conviction and belief in the "nearness of God to save." Jeremias also rightly called attention to the singularly important fact that "Father" is the only mode of *address* for God that the Gospels retain. This fact suggests that the designation of God as Father is contextually determined and that God is referred to as Father when the context calls for or demands it. Some parables feature a father as the central figure. In some sayings Jesus refers to God as Father. But other imagery for God, including master, landowner, king, and judge, also appears. None of these, however, is used in address to God. Address to God as Father presupposes the trustworthiness and goodness of God and points to the confidence that one may have in God. Although Jeremias contributed much to the discussion of the Fatherhood of God, a greater willingness to find continuity between the Old and New Testaments, and between Jesus and the Judaism of his day, would have strengthened rather than damaged his case that for Jesus "the expressions of God's fatherly goodness are *eschatological events.*"

### *Summary: the eschatological trajectory*

Throughout the various documents of the New Testament, two lines run alongside each other. God is the Father of Jesus; and God is the Father of the faithful insofar as this community is the creation of his initiative and love. It is perhaps not surprising that these two strands run alongside each other, for in the Old Testament there are both corporate and individual strands that serve to define God as Father. As Father, God redeems a people. As a particular representative of that people, the king of Israel can also be characterized as the son of the one who is Father to Israel. Hence, the corporate and individual strands already exist in the Old Testament. In various sources of Second Temple Judaism, one finds similar reference to God as Father of Israel or God as Father of the faithful or obedient within Israel. There are also some examples of individuals directly addressing God as Father or "my Father," thus pointing to a relationship between an individual and God as "son" or "child" and "Father." The New Testament not only continues the dual focus of the Old Testament, but also uses the content of the Old Testament picture of God as the basic substance of its portrayal.

What we have termed the "eschatological trajectory" of God's Fatherhood in the scriptures anticipates a time when God will be the "God of all the families of Israel" (Jer. 31:1). This trajectory runs through the New Testament, where the definition of Israel is widened to include the Gentiles, who through Christ are children of Abraham and so children of the promise made to him. In Christ one can rightly speak of that promise as guaranteed for the future when together with all creation the children of God are set free from bondage to decay and adopted to receive their inheritance from God. Thus the eschatological trajectory runs directly through the work of God in Christ and has in view the transformation of all the cosmos. We turn, next, to a discussion of some of the objections raised to this construal of the Fatherhood of God in the scriptures.

## The Particularity of Christian Faith

In her attack on traditional Christianity as inimical to feminist concerns and to the good of women, Daphne Hampson writes that for Christians, "God is bound up with peculiar events, a particular people, above all with the person Jesus of Nazareth. Therefore reference must needs always be made to this history and to this person."[3] The particularity of Christianity and, especially, the centrality that it assigns to Jesus of Nazareth count against its truthfulness. While Hampson rejected Christian faith precisely on the grounds of its particularity, other feminists have undertaken the task of reconstructing the Christian

---

[3]Hampson, *Theology and Feminism,* 8

faith in such a way that mitigates just these claims. For example, Pamela Dickey Young acknowledges that although Christians speak of God's "re-presentation" in Jesus as "decisive revelation," nevertheless, "God chose Jesus as God could choose many other events that are fitting re-presentations of God's grace."[4] And Sallie McFague speaks of the "paradigmatic figure of Jesus of Nazareth":

> To see the story of Jesus as paradigmatic means to see it as illuminative and illustrative of basic characteristics of the Christian understanding of the God-world relationship.[5]

What the paradigmatic figure of Jesus specifically illustrates is, first, that Christian faith *destabilizes* conventional expectations and worldly standards, upsetting usual divisions and dualisms; second, that it is *inclusive* of the weak, the outsider, the stranger, and the outcast; and, third, that it is *antihierarchical* and *antitriumphalist*.[6]

For those who seek to reconstruct rather than reject Christianity, the move to deny the particularity of Christianity apparently has two goals: first, simply to rid the Christian faith of its claims for the distinctive revelatory or saving character of God's particular action in Christ; and, second, to rid the Christian faith of its integral dependence upon a male savior. Such moves have obvious ramifications for thinking of God as Father, for the designation of God as Father always demands a corresponding person or persons of whom God is Father. As long as one speaks of God as the Father of Jesus, or as the Father of a specific set of people, the problem of particularity rears its ugly head. Quite apart from the offense given by the mere attribution of male titles and names to God, if God is the Father of Jesus Christ in a way that is true of no one else, then the offense of God's Fatherhood is merely compounded. One can, of course, jettison the whole complex, thus throwing out the baby and the bathwater. Because the persistent witness of the New Testament is that there exists between God and Jesus a distinctive relationship that is not simply a paradigmatic or parabolic representation of God's grace but the full and unique embodiment of that grace, it is impossible to

---

[4] Pamela Dickey Young, *Feminist Theology/Christian Theology: In Search of Method* (Minneapolis: Fortress, 1990), 99.

[5] Sallie McFague, *Models of God: Theology for an Ecological, Nuclear Age* (Philadelphia: Fortress, 1987), 46.

[6] Ibid., 47–48.

reconstruct the scriptural narrative so as to completely eliminate its particularism. The cost of distancing oneself from this narrative is a radical suspicion of scripture and of the account of God's faithfulness within it. Some may be willing to pay the price, but others will reckon that the cost is too great.

But to speak of God as Father, whether of Israel or of Jesus, is to speak of *how* this relationship came to be and what transpires within it so that the designations "Father" and "child" continue to faithfully represent that relationship. In other words, it is to speak of how God has acted and continues to act with respect to humankind, and to do so concretely in terms, images, and actions appropriate to the relationship of a father and child in the historical contexts in which the scriptures were written. With respect to the world of the scriptures, to speak of God as Father is to evoke a narrative of birth, care, and provision, love and mercy, and of promise and redemption. It is to indicate the account of God's promised love and redemption for Israel, which comes to its fullest expression in the mission of God's Son, Jesus of Nazareth.

But these are not the only words and images with which this narrative can be recounted. For example, when in Isaiah we find the designations "our Redeemer" and "our Father" as parallel terms, we find two terms that designate God's love and initiative toward Israel. In the Gospels of the New Testament, the image of the kingdom and of the family are set alongside each other as equally illuminating of how God's salvation creates a people who will live in accordance with the double command to love God and neighbor. The Apostle Paul employs a rich vocabulary, including justification, reconciliation, redemption, and adoption, in order to articulate the gospel of God's salvation. With the language of adoption and inheritance, Paul sets out the Gospel in familial imagery. On these terms, God's relationship to his people as Father is expressed in the act of their election or adoption. Thus God's gracious saving initiatives to Israel and through Jesus in salvation are constitutive of his Fatherhood in the Bible.[7] Daphne Hampson was correct to say that in Christian theology "reference must needs always be made to this history and to this person."

In her discussion of feminist theology, Blanche Jenson poses the

---

[7]Obviously, this formulation breaks down in speaking of God as the Father of Jesus, for Jesus is never the recipient of God's salvation or the act of adoption. To be sure, this is disputed by those who think that the words uttered at Jesus' baptism reflect an "adoption formula."

question sharply and simply: "Can feminist theology live with the biblical narrative?"[8] Later she reformulates her question in this way:

> When either particularity or history is relativized, can we say the resulting theology is appropriate for the Christian church? . . . The question of this essay—Can feminist theology live with the biblical narrative?—may now be stated more precisely: Can the biblical story in its particularity and history survive feminist reconstruction?[9]

What is at stake in the biblical story is the particularity of God's relationship to Israel, to Jesus Christ, and to the church. Where this particularity is abandoned, the biblical narrative has ceased to provide God's people with its sense of identity, and the sense in which what remains can be called "Christian" is dubious at best.

But it is not only feminist interpreters who in one way or another sidestep the biblical narrative. One can find traditionalist arguments that basically extract the designation of God as Father from the biblical narrative and then defend the abstracted concept as though its meaning were to be explicated quite apart from the historical or literary contexts in which it appears. This is tantamount to a neglect of the biblical narrative in practice. This happens, for example, when the creedal trajectory is taken to extremes, leading to the collapse of the biblical narrative into the christological confessions of the church. Similarly, greater attention to the historical contexts out of which the Bible arose challenges the assertion that Father is presented in the scriptures as the new name of God—a point we will shortly take up in greater detail. And setting these narratives firmly in their historical contexts would have suggested that the role of the father in Israelite culture had rather a larger role to play in shaping the Old Testament picture of God as Father than is sometimes allowed.

### Is Theology Nothing More Than Anthropology?

But the argument that cultural and historical notions of fatherhood have substantially influenced the biblical portrait of God as Father prompted Karl Barth, T. F. Torrance, and others to lodge a theological

---

[8]Blanche Jenson, "The Movement and the Story: Whatever Happened to 'Her'?" in *Speaking the Christian God,* 276.

[9]Ibid., 284.

protest against the assumption that we can know what it means to speak of God as Father on analogy with what it means to speak of our own fathers by that name.[10] As Barth put it, "We do not call God Father because we know what that is; on the contrary, because we know God's Fatherhood we afterwards understand what human fatherhood truly is." Elsewhere Barth writes, "We must not measure by natural human fatherhood what it means that God is our Father (Isa. 63:16). It is from God's fatherhood that our natural human fatherhood acquires any meaning and dignity it has."[11] Barth's vigorous denial that we can know by analogy what it means to call God Father clashes with Jeremias's historical contention that Jesus' use of a first-century familial term of intimacy for God reveals to us Jesus' distinctive filial consciousness.

Nevertheless, for Barth as for Jeremias, Jesus' distinctive Sonship remained central and crucial. Hence Barth argued that the doctrine of the Fatherhood of God derives from the fact that God is the Father of the Son, Jesus Christ. "God is unknown as our Father . . . to the degree that He is not made known by Jesus."[12] Although Barth conceded that the designation of God as Father was not entirely novel to Judaism or Christianity, he refused to allow that the "familiar human name of father" somehow granted to human beings a natural avenue to understanding God apart from God's own revelation.[13] Human beings did not arbitrarily choose the designation of Father for God in keeping with their own experience and because it suited their conceptions of what or who God is. Rather, we call God Father because God is the Father of the Son for all eternity, and it is this reality that is disclosed to us through

---

[10]See Torrance, "Christian Apprehension of God," 130; Karl Barth, *Church Dogmatics* (ed. Thomas F. Torrance; trans. Geoffrey W. Bromiley; 4 vols.; [Edinburgh: T. & T. Clark, 1936–1969], I/1:384–98; Colin Gunton, "Proteus and Procrustes," 72; John W. Miller, *Biblical Faith and Fathering: Why We Call God "Father"* (New York: Paulist, 1989).

[11]Karl Barth, *The Faith of the Church: A Commentary on the Apostles' Creed according to Calvin's Catechism* (New York: Meridian, 1958), 14. Idem, *Church Dogmatics,* I/1:389; cf. 392–93. See above, pp. 36–38.

[12]Barth, *Church Dogmatics,* I/1:390. So also Alvin Kimel contends that only the Son can introduce us to his Father ("The God Who Likes His Name: Holy Trinity, Feminism, and the Language of Faith" in *Speaking the Christian God,* 199). Barth at least wants to underscore the point that since Father means Creator, it is as the Father of Jesus Christ that God is our Creator (*Church Dogmatics,* I/1:389); and hence creation and salvation cannot be radically separated from each other.

[13]Barth, *Church Dogmatics,* I/1:391.

the biblical witness to God as Father of the Son. We might speak of that relationship as the lens through which one focuses more sharply upon, and sees more clearly, the meaning of God's Fatherhood. But having granted Barth's important point, we may wish nevertheless to note that precisely this focus brings into view Israel's filial relationship to God as Father. The proper context for understanding God's Fatherhood is thus the biblical witness beginning first with the witness of the OT to Israel's relationship to God.

Barth further objects to allowing human experience and conceptions to determine our understanding of God, for then God is not the wholly Other, but one who is more like than unlike human beings. Theology has essentially become anthropology. This threat does not particularly trouble certain feminists; in fact, it forms a major plank of their platform. Judith Plaskow and Carol Christ write, "Recognizing that women's perspective had not been included in the Jewish or Christian naming of God, human beings, or the world, feminist theology began with women claiming and naming our own experiences and exploring the ways in which incorporating women's experience might transform traditional religion or lead to the creation of new tradition."[14] In proposing anthropology as the starting point of theology, many feminists do not think that their proposal is particularly novel. Rather, they assert that theology does start with anthropology but that in the past male experience and identity have been projected onto God and then made absolute, without proper acknowledgment that were one to start with women's experience the result might look rather different. Thus Rosemary Radford Ruether writes:

> Feminist theology starts with anthropology. . . . A feminist reconstruction of the images of God thus starts by seeking a just and truthful anthropology. It then constructs images of God that will better manifest and promote the full realization of human potential for women. It assumes that all of our images of God are human projections. . . . The question is: What are worse projections that promote injustice and diminished humanness, and what are better projections that promote fuller humanness?[15]

---

[14]Judith Plaskow and Carol Christ, eds., *Weaving the Visions: New Patterns in Feminist Spirituality* (San Francisco: Harper & Row, 1989), 3.

[15]Rosemary Radford Ruether, "Imago Dei, Christian Tradition and Feminist Hermeneutics," in *Image of God and Gender Models in Judaeo-Christian Tradition* (ed. Kari Elisabeth Børreson; Oslo: Solum Forlag, 1991), 258–81.

That "all of our images of God are human projections" is exactly the presupposition that Barth, Torrance, and others wish to deny, whether the proponents of such views are feminists or not. The options thus stand in stark opposition to each other: either our understanding of God begins with revelation, or it begins with human beings.

What role experience plays in the formulation of theological doctrine or in the reception of revelation is a vastly complex issue and cannot be settled here. But a few comments may be ventured. Feminist scholars want women's experience to play either a more important role than it has in the past or the determinative role for theology, including theology proper, that is, talk of God. However, it is not clear that were women's experience to play such a role that it would necessarily have to eliminate the understanding of God as Father. Quite apart from feminist concerns at this point, it is crucial to note that in the scriptures, the understanding of God as Father does not explicitly serve to legitimate masculine identity or behaviors, nor does scripture draw specific "lessons" from God's Fatherhood for human fathers. The ethical obligations derived from an understanding of God as Father are related directly to relationships with communities rather than within nuclear families. Nor do fathers image God more fully or completely than mothers do simply by virtue of being male or being a father to one's children. Some theologians may have claimed this, but it is not a claim to be found in the Bible.

Not all theologians have been convinced that the only options are theology that is in essence anthropology writ large, or theology that seems to ignore human subjectivity as active in the formulation of theology and in the reception of revelation. In fact, Barth himself admits that scripture uses analogy to talk of God, but he hastens to note that "when Scripture calls God our Father it adopts an analogy only to transcend it at once."[16] William Placher echoes these remarks to some extent when he writes that "God is not one of the things of the world, to be analyzed and compared with categories appropriate to other things in the world."[17] Placher continues with this comment and caveat:

> We cannot simply fit God in as one component of our intellectual systems, or think only of a God who fits our categories and

---

[16]Barth, *Church Dogmatics,* I/1:389.
[17]William Placher, *The Domestication of Transcendence* (Louisville: Westminster John Knox, 1996), 10.

purposes. But we cannot climb to heaven on a pile of negatives and paradoxes either.[18]

According to Placher, the efforts to grasp God via analogy can never entirely succeed, for God is simply not to be found at the very top of any analogy employed, since God *transcends* all analogies. However, this need not imply that our categories are arbitrary.

G. B. Caird defends anthropomorphism in our language about God as indispensable, because it provides the categories for experiencing the reality of relationship to God. But Caird also notes that in adopting an analogy for God, that analogy cannot therefore be rendered absolute:

> Anthropomorphism is something more than the imposing of man's preconceived and limited images on the divine. There is something that answers back in perpetual dialogue and criticism.[19]

To speak of God as Father, then, means that this is an appropriate way to speak of God. But we should be leery of claiming too much for our own construals of God's Fatherhood. For here, too, we see "through a mirror, dimly." To issue such a caveat does not mean that we regard the revelation of the scriptures as untrustworthy. But it does mean that, short of the eschatological disclosure of God, we do not fully understand what it means to apply to God analogically conceptions such as father-hood. A passage from 1 John makes the point as follows:

> See what love the Father has given us, that we should be called children of God; and so we are. . . . Beloved, we are God's chil-dren now; it does not yet appear what we shall be, but we know that when he appears we shall be like him, for we shall see him as he is. (1 John 3:1–2)

Here the full apprehension of God is linked with the full conformity of the children of God to the likeness and image of God. In terms of the

---

[18]Placher, *Domestication of Transcendence,* 17; cf. 182.

[19]G. B. Caird, *The Language and Imagery of the Bible* (Philadelphia: West-minster, 1980), 182. The systematic theologian Louis Berkhof speaks point blank of the anthropomorphic character of God's names: "The names of God are not of human invention, but of divine origin, though they are all borrowed from human language, and derived from human and earthly relations. They are anthropomorphic" (*Systematic Theology* [4th rev. ed.; Grand Rapids: Eerdmans, 1939], 47).

language of family, believers are "God's children now." This is stated by the author as a fact. But, curiously, he goes on to say that "it does not yet appear what we shall be." Some transformation is yet expected. On analogy, God is now known as Father on account of his love for those who are "children of God." And yet there is held out the promise and hope that "we shall see him as he is." Hence this passage clearly suggests an eschatological remaking of the Father–child relationship along lines that we cannot presently grasp or know. In light of such a promise, and especially when we are dealing with the challenging theological and pastoral issues involved in the question of how we should address God, we should adopt a posture of humility with respect to our own claims and toward others, as well as to God.[20]

## Experience and Eschatology

Arguments from experience have figured in another aspect of the interpretation of God as Father in the Bible. As noted earlier, Joachim Jeremias's arguments that in Jesus' use of *abba* we had access to his sense of Sonship has been picked up and made into the tenet of Jesus' so-called *abba* experience. Because Paul asserts that through the Spirit believers call upon God as *abba,* the arguments regarding Jesus' sense of Sonship are then taken to apply to the *experience* and *sense of intimacy* that believers have in relationship to God. In this manner, God's Fatherhood is made primarily the object of human experience. I have argued, by contrast, that to present God as Father along the lines of scripture would be to refer more to how God acts and what God does that makes it possible for human beings to call upon God in this manner than it would to the subsequent human experience of God.

In the case of Jesus' use of *abba,* we simply lack the data to conclude that such address gives us access to Jesus' sense of Sonship or to his experience of God. The relevant texts of the New Testament do not answer the question why Jesus used the term Father for God, however much both biblical scholars and theologians have hastened to fill in the silences with various sorts of historical and dogmatic explanations. One

---

[20]In her review of *Speaking the Christian God,* Catherine La Cugna writes, "No one, on either side of this question, really knows the best answer about how to deal with the profound pastoral and theological problem of how to address God" (in *ProEccl* 3 [1994]: 115).

can assume that Jesus' use of Father reflected something of his understanding of God, but the misplaced reluctance to draw on first-century Judaism for that understanding has opened the doors to inflated speculation about Jesus' filial consciousness and experience. Ironically, the pressure to find the historical Jesus behind the text of the Gospels has led to the need to posit his own experience as the ultimate explanation of his use of Father for God. Ironically, then, often in the name of defending the biblical witness, it is ignored in favor of a putative reconstruction of Jesus' experience to which we have no direct access. The texts of the Gospels do undeniably present the reader with a portrait of God as the Father of Jesus of Nazareth. They do not, however, explain the genesis of such usage nor even precisely what it means in the context of Jesus' own life. The Gospels themselves provide the narrative account of how we are to understand God as the Father of Jesus—and of those who follow him.

Often, the argument about Jesus' "filial consciousness" assumes that either the Bible or Jesus presents God as Father because there is something that is experienced in God's relationship to human beings that is significantly or uniquely disclosed in human fathers—and that what is experienced is a positive good. But there is a dark side to the argument from experience, for clearly not all experiences of human fathers are positive. Curiously, a version of the argument from experience has also been used by traditionalists who recognize the problems raised by a negative experience of one's father in using Father as an image for God. In his defense of maintaining the traditional language of Father, John Cooper acknowledges that for some people the experience of the inadequacies and failures of their own human fathers makes it both difficult and painful to think of God as Father. Nevertheless, he goes on to assert, that in spite of whatever abuse and hurt some people may have experienced at the hands of their own fathers,

> For most people, the need, desire, and ability to relate to a father-figure is still strongly present. . . . In spite of cultural differences or emotional injuries, there is something significant in our experience of human fathers that still resonates deeply with the *Abba Father* of our Lord Jesus. This universal intercultural experience, which binds us to Scripture, is more than enough basis for continuing to love, obey, and pray to our Father who is in heaven.[21]

---

[21]Cooper, *Our Father in Heaven,* 261.

All of Cooper's assertions are just that—assertions. Nowhere does he provide evidence or argument for them or suggest how he knows what "most people" need and desire. But it is particularly the nebulous "something significant" of Cooper's second statement that merits further comment, for it reveals just how difficult it is to build an argument for understanding God as Father from the starting point of experience. What is the "something significant" that resonates with address to God as Father? What is the "intercultural experience" that provides the basis for praying to God as Father? From Cooper's own vantage point, for those who have deep emotional injuries there may actually be *nothing* that resonates deeply with the recognition of God as Father. In this regard, it is striking how rarely passages in the scriptures appeal to one's experience of God as Father. To be sure, Jesus appeals to the provision and care of human fathers and argues that God can be trusted to do more than they, but even these sayings point to the ways in which a father can be expected to act, and so, arguing from the lesser to the greater, the way in which God can be trusted to act. Throughout the Bible, talk of God as Father illumines ways in which God relates and acts toward humankind. In other words, in speaking of God's Fatherhood we are speaking of ways in which God's promises are carried out in this world.

Hence, the real theological issue is not whether God can be experienced in a fatherly way but whether God can be trusted to fulfill the promises and obligations that the Bible ascribes to him as Father. Here, too, the eschatological horizon looms, for whereas much of the theological and pastoral discussion today seems in part an effort to rehabilitate the image of God as Father by making it a benign image of a good deity, the Bible doesn't particularly aim to soften the image of God through appeal to his fatherliness. It assumes that God is merciful, forgiving, and providing, as a good father provides for his children, but the real rub comes in the call to trust such a God. Ultimately, all faith in God as Father must look toward the future and toward the eschatological outworking of the divine purposes and promises. Looking to God as Father is thus always a stance of faith and hope.

The point is not to empty "Father" of all affective content and to speak of it instead as a cipher for a set of divine actions. But when individualistic and experiential elements are overly emphasized, a key aspect of the biblical perspective of God's Fatherhood is lost. For there the language of Father for God says something not about God in the abstract but about how God relates to the community of faith. The imagery of God as Father speaks to one who gives life, provides and cares for his children, and bestows an inheritance upon them. It is language of family and kin and implies relationship, both between father and child and among the children themselves. Because the imagery is first and foremost collective, it raises further questions against undue emphasis on God as *experienced* as Father, unless one carefully considers this in terms of its corporate implications. After all, Jesus taught his disciples to pray "our Father," and Paul argued that the church's capacity to address God as Father indicated the adoption of Jew and Gentile together into God's family through the agency of God's Spirit. "Our Father" assumes a collective reality, the reality of a people who are loved by God and who share together in the redemptive mystery of God. Thus address to God as Father could serve to strengthen the church's corporate sense of what it means to be a people called out by God, which could in turn ground the community's life and worship more deeply in God. Such awareness might renew the sense that prayer is rooted in our relationship with God and in the realities of daily life with other people in our communities.

Finally, an undue emphasis on human *experience* of God as Father can lead to an understanding of that designation abstracted from the narrative context of the scriptures. Individual experience of God as Father need not necessarily come into conflict with the biblical narrative of God's redemptive actions with respect to a people, but it is clear from earlier citations that too many biblical scholars and theologians are willing to sacrifice the broad scriptural content of God's Fatherhood to gain the claim of novelty or distinctiveness for Jesus or the New Testament. This, then, leads them to the conclusion that Christian experience of God will be distinctive or novel, rather than to the conclusion drawn by the New Testament authors themselves, that in Christ God has adopted Jew and Gentile into one family that bears the name of the Father and so receives the promised inheritance from him.

## Is Father a "Name" for God?

Along these lines, one also finds today the frequent assertion that Father is a name for God, perhaps even the new, Christian, or revealed name of God. At this point the bracing caveat of Louis Berkhof is worth noting:

> It is often said that the New Testament introduced a new name of God, namely, *Pater* (Father). But this is hardly correct. The

name Father is used of the Godhead even in heathen religions. It is used repeatedly in the Old Testament to designate the relation of God to Israel.[22]

Such lucid analyses have not settled the point, however, and the debate over whether Father is a name for God or a metaphor rages on. In fact, this seems to be a surprisingly important point for many traditionalists to score, in spite of the fact that on the grounds of the biblical and historical evidence the attempt can scarcely be judged likely to be successful. And it is not likely to be successful because the historical context of Jesus' own day, as well as the New Testament data themselves, mitigate against the claims that the name of God is Father or Father, Son, Holy Spirit.

In Jewish practices of Jesus' own day, God's name was not pronounced aloud, except by the high priest on the day of atonement. But this fact indicates that Jews did know how to pronounce the name, that while it was deemed too holy to utter—Josephus refers to it as that "hair-raising name"—it had not been forgotten. Because the name of God was not to be spoken, numerous circumlocutions were used instead, such as "the Blessed," "the Most High," "Power," "the Place," and so on. God was frequently addressed as "Lord," "God," "King of the Universe," and, according to later rabbinic sources, as "our heavenly Father." Such practices suggest that Jesus' use of Father may well belong in such a category. For while he addresses God as *Father,* he prays that "God's *name* may be sanctified," a likely allusion to the holy name of God, which he does not profane by speaking it. But in making Father the singular mode of address for himself and his disciples, he calls upon the God of Israel as one who is merciful, loving, and forgiving, even as the scriptures of the Old Testament indicate repeatedly.

New Testament authors do not regard Father as the name of God. This is perhaps most clear in the so-called Christ hymn of Philippians, where Jesus is said to be "given the name above every name." In context that name clearly cannot be Father. Most likely that name is Lord, as the confession "Jesus Christ is Lord" indicates. But it should be noted that the "Lord" translates the Greek *kyrios,* which in the Septuagint (the Greek Old Testament) is used frequently to render the Hebrew *Adonai,* which in turn is the reading used so as to avoid pronouncing the divine

---

[22]Berkhof, *Systematic Theology,* 47, 50–51.

name. In other words, there is a direct line between "Lord" (*kyrios*) and the holy name of God in the Old Testament. There is little evidence to justify the assertion that in the New Testament Father or even Father, Son and Holy Spirit, is the new name for God, or a name that precluded address to God in any other form.

In current theological discussion, however, the argument seems to run that because Father is a name, it follows that it cannot be changed since "only God may name himself."[23] Inasmuch as one's name reveals one's identity, and the one who does the naming is regarded as superior to the one who is named, it follows that "no one has the right to name God, for no one stands as God's equal or superior. No one is in a position to give a name and identity to God."[24] In this regard, it is particularly striking that no passage in the Old Testament gives an account in which God names himself as Father. The most explicit Old Testament passage in which God "names himself" is the appearance to Moses in the burning bush, where God answers the question about his identity with the mysterious "I am who I am." Indeed, it is clear that no writer of the Old Testament or New Testament thought that God's name was somehow replaced even by all the other epithets and circumlocutions used for God.

Far too much weight has been placed on designating Father as a name for God. "Father" can render God truly without needing to attain the status of the new or revealed name of God. In Christian theology, God is properly thought of as Father, Son, and Holy Spirit, but in fact few Christians address their prayers to God in this way, and few prayers in most standard denominational prayer books do so. Similarly, many Christians pray to God using a number of different forms of address, without thereby indicating that they regard these appellations as names, even as human beings have many terms of endearment or nicknames which they use for their spouses or children, without somehow suggesting that these replace the given name of that person. Names and nicknames function differently. Names signal what anyone may call a person; a nickname signals what someone with a particular or special relationship may call another. In this regard, "Mom" or "Dad" functions like a nickname, indicating what it is appropriate for the children of a family to call a parent. Although one may choose to call this a name, since the mother or father answers when a child calls "Mom" or "Dad,"

---

[23]So, for example, John W. Cooper, *Our Father in Heaven,* 163. A number of the essays in *Speaking the Christian God* make the same point.

[24]Ibid., 163.

nevertheless, "Mom" and "Dad" are not the "public names" of these individuals but the way in which they are known and the name to which they respond within a particular family unit. The designation Father functions within the Christian family to speak of the one to whom the community owes its life and being and to remind them of their collective identity as the people called out by God.

## God and Gender

Finally, we may offer some comments on one of the most complex issues in this whole debate: how to speak of and to a God without gender. How are we to speak of a God who is neither male nor female, neither "he" nor "she," when the neuter pronoun "it" both misrepresents God and offends piety? No traditionalist theologian argues that God is indeed male, although quite a few suggest that masculine language better or exclusively mediates the biblical understanding of God.[25] And yet more than one theologian has asserted that there is something inherently problematic with the use of female imagery for God which disqualifies it to portray adequately the relationship of God to Israel and the world. Typically, the "problematic" is lodged in the fact that mothers nurture their children in their wombs and give birth to them, so that the child comes forth from the mother's body in a way that differs from the father's role in the whole process of birth. Those who wish to recast the image of God from the prevailing view that God is the transcendent other suggest that were a greater role given to maternal imagery, it would eradicate the dualism inherent in such a view of God's relationship to the world. Rather than picture a God who is radically distinct from his creation, one could think of God as the one from whose being the creation arises or emanates. Appealing to maternal imagery, for example, Rosemary Radford Ruether suggests thinking of God as the "great womb within which all things, gods and humans, sky and earth, human and nonhuman beings are generated."[26]

---

[25]For example, Francis Martin, *The Feminist Question: Feminist Theology in The Light of Christian Tradition* (Grand Rapids: Eerdmans, 1994), esp. 251–52; John Cooper, *Our Father in Heaven.*

[26]Rosemary Radford Ruether, *Sexism and God-Talk: Toward a Feminist Theology* (Boston: Beacon, 1983), 48–49. Similarly, Patricia Wilson-Kastner writes: "One of the most fundamental insights of feminism is that the various divisions of hierarchy—alienation of humanity from the animate and inanimate world about it, dualism of body and spirit—all need to be healed and overcome in us." In *Faith, Feminism and the Christ* (Philadelphia: Fortress, 1983), 114.

Against such construals, traditionalists have objected that maternal imagery conduces to pantheism or at least to an effacement of the radical otherness of God which consequently nullifies the transcendence of God. Obviously Ruether's interpretation renders maternal imagery pantheistically, but it is possible to imagine the use of maternal imagery that does not automatically suggest pantheistic interpretations or pagan fertility goddesses. In fact, the Bible prompts us to imagine just such a use when it speaks of God with the metaphor of a nursing mother and appeals to the faithfulness of a mother to her child. "Can a woman forget her nursing child, or show no compassion for the child of her womb? Even these may forget, yet I will not forget you" (Isa. 49:15). This maternal picture of God's faithfulness is essentially identical with that of God as a faithful, trustworthy, life-giving Father who provides for his children and tends to their needs.

Since various scholars insist that only masculine imagery for God properly allows for God's otherness, we might expect that in the Bible the imagery of God as Father would particularly underscore the separation of God from the created order, or preserve the "otherness" of the Creator with respect to the creature. Yet while some distinction between God and the world is presupposed in the presentation of God as Father in the Bible—after all, a father and child are two distinct individuals—that separateness is never the primary issue in passages that present God as Father. Even more to the point, the image of God as Father is not connected with the act of creation but is linked above all with God's salvation of a people. The portrayal of God as Father does not serve to undergird the separateness of God from the created order; nor, for that matter, does maternal imagery for God collapse the distinction between mother and child. Rather, it preserves it.

Yet arguments to the contrary persist. Francis Martin, for example, contends that in the Hebrew Bible, the use of "masculine forms" for God reflects the unique teaching of Israel concerning God as Creator. He then goes on to state, "It is a transcultural fact that as natural images, *male* mediates transcendence and otherness and *female* mediates immanence and closeness."[27] He cites Mircea Eliade, Gilbert Durand, and Walter Ong in support of his point. Like many other traditionalists, Martin argues that the biblical view of God as Creator cannot be represented in the imagery of a mother, who gives birth to children, but can only be presented by the imagery of a male, or father, whose relationship to his

---

[27]Martin, *The Feminist Question,* 251.

children differs from that of their mother. But in the multifaceted presentation of God as Father in the Bible, no passage underscores the otherness or distinctness of the Father from his children and, contrary to Martin's insistence, the term Father is seldom, if ever, used for God as Creator. Instead, God's Fatherhood typically designates the activity of God as redemptive and nurturing, of God as invested in the welfare of his people. Walter Brueggemann pithily summarizes,

> Biblical faith is quite uninterested in questions of God's sexuality, masculine or feminine, or even in God's asexuality but is singularly and passionately concerned with God's covenanting and the implication of covenanting for human history. In its singular concern, it is free to use various images to articulate that paradigm of covenanting.[28]

Although many traditionalists object to the use of maternal imagery for God, others have sought gingerly to introduce or allow feminine metaphors for God. Consequently, God is sometimes spoken of as having feminine *and* masculine characteristics. The "feminine" characteristics are typically the "soft" virtues, such as caring, nurturing, gentleness, and tenderness. Presumably the male characteristics and virtues would be such things as authority and strength. Gender, however, is no fixed reference point, and characteristics and behavior deemed appropriate to men and women, or fathers and mothers, are not a set of transcultural norms. Rather, notions of gender identity are relative to specific cultures, shaped by social, economic, political, religious, and other forces. Often cultures change their standards of what constitutes "masculinity" and "femininity," or what behaviors ought to characterize or differentiate fathers and mothers. To think of God in terms of "masculine" and "feminine" (or fatherly and motherly) characteristics is but minimally helpful, for to label God "motherly" or "fatherly" means nothing unless we already have some idea of what those terms connote. Thus when John Cooper writes of God that "the one who is like a father is also like a mother," one may appreciate the effort to allow that both fathers and mothers may somehow represent God, but such statements mean little in the abstract.[29]

---

[28]Walter Brueggemann, "Israel's Social Criticism and Yahweh's Sexuality," *JAAR* supplement (Sept. 1977): 739.

[29]Cooper, *Our Father in Heaven,* 146.

Furthermore, the statement sounds suspiciously like the claim that God really is more male than female, more masculine than feminine. The male or masculine side of God is normative, and the feminine side is a sort of afterthought to balance out some trait of the "masculine" deity. As Paul Smith points out, the traditional position that God is without gender is "weakened by a technicality when some say that God is not male but 'he' is masculine. The word 'male' is replaced by 'masculine' and 'sex' is replaced by gender. Therefore, some have arrived at the strange position that God is not male but God is masculine, and God has no sex but God has gender."[30]

Smith's warning was directed to those traditionalists who, while rightly not willing to speak of God as "male," want nevertheless to suggest a determinative role for the predominantly masculine imagery in the Bible. As Smith astutely notes, the attempt is bound to backfire, since it comes close to denying what it seeks to preserve, that God is asexual. Smith's comment also suggests in part what is wrong with the various attempts to "introduce" feminine gender into God, to argue for the "ontologization of gender" in God.[31] Some have sought to introduce a feminine element into the Trinity by speaking of one person of the Trinity, most typically the Holy Spirit, as feminine.[32] Others want to insist on the equivalence of feminine metaphors to masculine metaphors for *all* members of the Trinity.[33] Unfortunately, such approaches end up not with a God who is without gender but with a God of dual gender. The church that has argued that God has no gender must avoid thinking of God as a composite of the male and female gender. However, it must as diligently avoid the error of thinking of and teaching a God who is of *one* gender. Too often the implicit argument seems to be that while it is wrong to think of God as male, it is worse to think

---

[30]Paul R. Smith, *Is It Okay to Call God "Mother": Considering the Feminine Face of God* (Peabody, Mass.: Hendrickson, 1993), 136. He cites as an exemplar of such argumentation Donald G. Bloesch, *The Battle for the Trinity* (Ann Arbor: Servant Publications, 1985), 33.

[31]The phrase "ontologization of gender" is borrowed from Miroslav Volf, *Exclusion and Embrace: A Theological Exploration of Identity, Otherness, and Reconciliation* (Nashville: Abingdon, 1996), 173. His entire discussion of God and gender should be consulted; see chapter IV, "Gender Identity," 167–90 in *Exclusion and Embrace.*

[32]Elisabeth Moltmann-Wendel, *Die Weiblichkeit des Heiligen Geistes: Studien zur Feministischen Theologie* (Gütersloh: Kaiser, 1995).

[33]Elizabeth A. Johnson, *She Who Is: The Mystery of God in a Feminist Theological Discourse* (New York: Crossroad, 1992), 42–57.

of God as female. But the classical Christian notion of God as a God without gender suggests that there ought to be as strong a negative reaction to thinking of God as *male* as there is to thinking of God as *female*. As Paul Smith aptly puts it, "Because Jesus was male we must be exceptionally clear that God is not."[34]

Strikingly, in all the Bible's presentation of God in the "masculine" imagery of Father, God is never held up as the model for "masculinity" for a father or a male over against a mother or a woman. Rather, the way in which God is understood to act obligates human beings in their relationships to each other. The implications of God's Fatherhood are not drawn out for fathers, but for those who wish to live together in the community which God calls into being. At this point the comments of Miroslav Volf are worth quoting at length:

> Since God is beyond sexual difference, there is nothing in God that can correspond to the specifically fatherly relation that a man has toward his progeny. A human father can in no way read off his responsibilities *as a father* from God the Father. What a father can learn from God are his responsibilities as *a human being* who happens to be a father and therefore has a special relationship to his daughters and sons as well as to their mother. One can learn from God the Father no more about what it means to be a human father than one can learn about what it means to be a human mother; inversely, one can learn from God the Mother no more about what it means to be a human mother than one can learn about what it means to be a human father. Whether we use masculine or feminine metaphors for God, God models our common humanity, not our gender specificity. . . . The ontologization of gender would ill serve both the notion of God and the understanding of gender. Nothing in God is specifically feminine; nothing in God is specifically masculine; therefore nothing in our notions of God entails duties or prerogatives specific to one gender; all duties and prerogatives entailed in our notions of God are duties and prerogatives of both genders.[35]

A final complaint that is lodged against the continued use of Father and other male terms for God is that they promote hierarchical notions of God's authority and, by extension, also of human authority, which always threaten to deteriorate into authoritarianism. Many feminists,

---

[34]Smith, *Is It Okay to Call God "Mother,"* 156.
[35]Miroslav Volf, *Exclusion and Embrace,* 171–73.

and other theologians along with them, would like to jettison the view of God as a Father who stands at the top of a hierarchical ordering of the world, since hierarchy is assumed to lead inevitably to oppression and dominance.

While it is true that the biblical portrait of God as Father entails a robust understanding of God's authority, it equally needs to be noted that God's authority as Father is not subsequently transferred to or vested in certain individuals. The appropriate human response is obedience and honor. The fatherly authority of God nowhere legitimates or ensures the authority of human fathers or of other authorities; quite the contrary. For example, in Matthew, all call on God, and only on God, as Father, implying that no other figure, be it emperor or father, may demand the allegiance that rightly belongs to God (23:9). God does not stand at the top of human hierarchies of power and authority but, rather, exists outside them, calling them all into question and subverting human values and standards of honor and power that place those with the greatest claims to status at the top and those with the fewest such claims at the bottom.

### Jesus and God: The Promise of "Our Father"

God's authority as Father does not refer to the power to coerce but to a relationship of trust and to the promise of faithfulness. God's trustworthiness and faithfulness are central to understanding God as Father, but not because these characteristics are either unique to males or distinctive of human fathers. Rather, in the biblical narratives it is the father's role as head of the family in the sense of "founder" of the family line and guardian of its heritage, rather than as controlling or sovereign, that shapes the presentation of God. So, for example, while the Gospel of John portrays God as the Father, arguing that honor and worship are due to him, the primary emphasis of the Gospel's portrayal falls on the Father as the source and giver of life for the world. Paul, too, highlights the life-giving activity of the Father when he envisions God as one who calls a people into being and who remains faithful to the promises made to them.

A few years ago, the Presbyterian Church in the USA (PCUSA) adopted a new confession called "A Brief Statement of Faith." By contrast to the Apostles' Creed or the Nicene Creed, which begin with a confession of belief in "God the Father Almighty, Maker of heaven and earth," the Brief Statement avoids any such claim. Rather, it speaks of God's Fatherhood in the following way: "We trust in God whom Jesus called *Abba,* Father." While the statement stops short of commending this mode of address to others, it does prevent one from *forgetting* Jesus' own practice. It further explicitly acknowledges that trust is the appropriate response to the God whom Jesus called *"Abba,* Father," and that the God who is confessed as trustworthy is properly known as the one designated by Jesus as *abba.* On this point, Robert Jenson comments that " 'Father' in the church's discourse, at whatever juncture, always means 'the one whom Jesus called Father.' "[36] Not only so, but Father in the church's discourse also always means the one whom Israel was to call upon as Father and the one whom the church calls upon as Father. Jesus' address to God as Father cannot be extracted from the trajectory of the biblical narrative, and Christian confession of God as Father must always be plotted along its coordinates. Addressing and thinking of God as Father tie us to the witness of the scriptures and the practice of Jesus.

But in holding on to the designation we should not simply suppose that we know what it means to call God Father. Indeed, such address ought continually to force us again to think clearly and articulate what we do mean. If there were greater emphasis today on the biblical narrative in which the Fatherhood of God takes on texture and shape, and fewer spurious arguments for why God could never be imaged as a mother or with feminine imagery, our theological discourse would be enriched. The ultimate tragedy is that a designation of God that in the Bible evokes a richly textured narrative of mercy, love, and redemption has become an ideological battleground. As Donald Juel notes,

> We do not pray to God as "Male"; we do not speak of God as "Father" because of some natural necessity—e.g., a "natural law" according to which the cosmos is ordered according to gender distinctions. The God to whom we are invited to pray is known only in the particular—as the God whom Jesus addressed as "Father" and who vindicated the crucified Jesus as Christ, Son of God, by raising him from the dead. . . . The words must be heard in their Gospel setting. The particularity of that setting (e.g., that Jesus actually called God "Father" and taught his followers to pray to God as "[our] Father") is the only promise of deliverance from ideologies of any sort that oppress and enslave and finally undermine the possibility of addressing God as one who cares and can be trusted to listen.[37]

---

[36]Jenson, "The Father, He . . . ," 105.
[37]Juel, "The Lord's Prayer," 63.

Put differently, the church's witness is not that it is "meaningful" to speak of God as the Father of Jesus Christ, but that it is true. While God's Fatherhood can be unpacked specifically in terms of his relationship to the Son, it can also be explicated more broadly beginning with God's relationship to Israel and culminating in the fulfillment of God's promises to be a Father to his people. To speak of God as Father is to acknowledge that God has called out a people who know that their life and being depend on the initiative and sustenance of God's grace. To speak of God as Father is to acknowledge that God gives to his people their inheritance in Christ, the heir through whom God's promises are guaranteed and received. These people, when living out the model of God's fatherly compassion, find in their collective lives together a way of living that liberates from the need to dominate or destroy the other. In short, to trust in the one who is known through the scriptures and through the words of Jesus as Father is to trust in God as one who is and will be faithful.

# Index of Ancient Sources

## NEW TESTAMENT

**OLD TESTAMENT APOCRYPHA**

## OLD TESTAMENT PSEUDEPIGRAPHA

## QUMRAN LITERATURE

## PHILO

## JOSEPHUS

## RABBINIC LITERATURE

## TARGUMIM

## GRECO-ROMAN LITERATURE

# Index of Names